Workbook/Study Guide

for use with

Managerial Accounting

Ninth Edition

Ray H. Garrison, D.B.A., CPA
Professor Emeritus
Brigham Young University

Eric W. Noreen, Ph.D., CMA
University of Washington
and
INSEAD

 Irwin
McGraw-Hill

Boston   Burr Ridge, IL   Dubuque, IA   Madison, WI   New York   San Francisco   St. Louis
Bangkok   Bogotá   Caracas   Lisbon   London   Madrid
Mexico City   Milan   New Delhi   Seoul   Singapore   Sydney   Taipei   Toronto

McGraw-Hill Higher Education

A Division of The McGraw·Hill Companies

Workbook/Study Guide for use with
MANAGERIAL ACCOUNTING

4 5 6 7 8 9 0 COU/COU 9 0 9 8 7 6 5 4 3 2 1 0

ISBN 0-07-109246-3

http://www.mhhe.com

Preface

To The Student

This study guide supplements the ninth edition of *Managerial Accounting* by Ray H. Garrison and Eric W. Noreen. Each chapter of the study guide contains three major sections:

1. The *Chapter Study Suggestions* help you study more efficiently.
2. *Chapter Highlights* summarize in outline form the essential points in a chapter.
3. *Review and Self Test* questions and exercises test your knowledge of the material in the chapter. Solutions are provided. *Caution:* If you want to score well on exams, you *must* work out each solution on your own and *then* check to see whether your solution is correct by comparing it to the solution in the study guide. You cannot learn the material by simply reading the solution provided in the study guide. This does not work.

This study guide can be used as an integral part of the process of learning the material in a chapter. When used for this purpose, we recommend that you follow the steps below:

1. Read the *Chapter Study Suggestions* in this study guide.
2. Read the textbook chapter.
3. Read the outline in the *Chapter Highlights* section of the study guide. If you run across anything in the outline you don't understand, refer back to the textbook for a more detailed discussion.
4. Work the questions and exercises in the study guide and then compare your answers to those given in the study guide. If you find something you don't understand, refer to the textbook for help.
5. Work the homework problems assigned by your instructor.

Alternatively, the study guide can also be used as a very effective way to study for exams. Before reading the chapter in your textbook, read the *Chapter Study Suggestions* in this study guide. Then lay the study guide aside until it is time to prepare for an exam. The *Chapter Highlights* section of the study guide can then be used to review the essential material covered in the chapter. The *Review and Self Test* questions and exercises are excellent practice for exams. The questions and exercises in the study guide are particularly effective used in this way since they are likely to be similar to the questions and exercises your instructor will ask on an exam.

Remember, the study guide is not a substitute for the textbook. Rather, its purpose is to *supplement* the textbook by helping you to learn the material.

We welcome your suggestions and comments. You can write to us at the following address:

Prof. Eric Noreen
Box 353200
University of Washington
Seattle, WA 98195-3200

Ray H. Garrison
Eric W. Noreen

Contents

Chapter 1

Managerial Accounting and the Business Environment

Chapter Study Suggestions

This chapter describes the work that managers do and the kinds of information they need in order to do this work effectively. The chapter also describes important aspects of the contemporary business environment. The chapter is unusual in that there are almost no numerical problems to be worked. However, many new terms must be learned.

CHAPTER HIGHLIGHTS

A. An organization is a group of people united for a common purpose. Organizations are run by managers who carry out three major activities: planning, directing and motivating, and controlling. All three of these functions involve decision-making.

1. *Planning* involves identifying alternatives and selecting the alternative that best furthers the organization's objectives.

2. *Directing and motivating* involves mobilizing people to carry out the plans and overseeing day-to-day activities.

3. *Controlling* involves obtaining feedback to ensure that all parts of the organization are following the plans.

B. Financial and managerial accounting differ in a number of ways. In contrast to financial accounting, managerial accounting:

1. Focuses on providing data for internal uses.

2. Places more emphasis on the future.

3. Emphasizes relevance and flexibility rather than precision.

4. Emphasizes the segments of an organization, rather than just looking at the organization as a whole.

5. Is not governed by Generally Acceptable Accounting Practices.

6. Is not mandatory.

C. In many industries today, a company that does not continually improve will find itself quickly overtaken by competitors. The text discusses four major approaches to improvement—Just-In-Time (JIT), Total Quality Management (TQM), Process Reengineering, and the Theory of Constraints (TOC). These approaches can be combined.

D. The Just-In-Time (JIT) approach is based on the insight that reducing inventories—particularly work in process inventories—can be the key to improving operations. Companies maintain work in process inventories to protect against disruptions in the production process and as a con-

sequence of using large batch sizes. However, work in process inventories create a number of problems:

1. Work in process inventories tie up funds and take up space.

2. Work in process inventories increase the *throughput time*, which is the amount of time required to make a product. If there is an average of two weeks of work in process inventories, then it takes two weeks longer to complete a unit than if there were no work in process inventories. Long throughput time makes it difficult to respond quickly to customers and can be a major competitive disadvantage.

3. When work in process inventories are large, partially completed products are stored for long periods of time before being passed to the next workstation. Therefore, defects introduced at a workstation may not be noticed for quite some time. If a machine is out of calibration or incorrect procedures are being followed, many defective units will be produced before the problem is discovered. And when the defects are finally discovered, it may be very difficult to track down the source of the problem.

4. Because of long throughput time, units may be obsolete or out of fashion by the time they are finally completed.

5. Large work in process inventories encourage sloppy procedures and mask inefficiencies and problems in the production process. When inventories are reduced, these problems are uncovered and can be identified and dealt with.

E. *Just-In-Time (JIT)* seeks improvement by reducing inventories to the absolute minimum levels possible.

1. "Just in time" means that raw materials are received just in time to go into production, subassemblies are completed just in time to be assembled into products, and products are completed just in time to be shipped to customers.

2. In JIT, the flow of goods is controlled by a "pull" approach; work is initiated only in response to customer orders.

a.   At the final assembly stage, a signal is sent to preceding workstations as to the exact amounts of parts and materials that will be needed over the next few hours to assemble products ordered by customers.

b.   In contrast, under conventional systems parts and material are "pushed" forward to the next workstation regardless of need. There is also a tendency in conventional systems to seek to "keep everyone busy." The result in both cases is a needless buildup of inventory.

3.   *JIT purchasing* can be used by any company that has inventories, including retailers and wholesalers as well as manufacturers.

a.   In JIT purchasing, the company relies on a few ultra-reliable suppliers who are given long-term contracts. The suppliers must be very dependable since JIT makes the purchaser vulnerable to disruptions in its supplies. For want of a part, the whole assembly process might have to be shut down.

b.   In JIT purchasing, suppliers make frequent deliveries in small lots just before the goods are needed. Rather than deliver a week's or a month's supply of inventory at a time, the supplier may make several deliveries a day of small numbers of items that are needed immediately.

c.   In JIT purchasing, suppliers must deliver defect-free goods. In a JIT system, defects cannot be tolerated. Supplies must be so dependable that incoming goods from suppliers are not inspected for defects.

F.   In addition to JIT purchasing, a successful JIT system involves four key elements.

1.   A JIT company often must improve its product flow lines by creating an individual flow line for each separate product. This may involve setting up a *focused factory* in which all the machines needed to make a particular product or family of products are brought together in one location. This is in contrast to a conventional, "functional plant layout" in which similar machines are grouped together in one location. When a functional plant layout is used, products must be moved long distances between work centers to be completed.

2.   A JIT company must reduce the setup time that is required between batches. A *batch* is consists of a number of units of the same product that are produced together. *Setups* consist of the activities that must be performed whenever production is switched from making one type of unit to another. For example, if a plastic toy is being made in several different colors, each time there is a change in color from one batch to another, the vats containing the colored plastic must be emptied and thoroughly cleaned.

3.   A JIT company should strive for zero defects. If any units in an order are defective, the whole production process would have to be restarted in order to replace the defective units. This would make it impossible to deliver the order on time.

4.   A JIT company must develop a multi-skilled and flexible work force that is capable of operating many different machines and of performing routine maintenance.

G.   Many benefits result from a JIT system. The most important are:

1.   Working capital is increased by recovering funds that were tied up in inventories.

2.   Usable space is increased. Areas previously used to store inventories are made available for other, more productive uses.

3.   Throughput time is reduced, resulting in greater potential output and quicker response to customer needs.

4.   Defect rates are reduced, resulting in less waste and greater customer satisfaction.

H.   *Total Quality Management (TQM)* is an approach to continuous improvement that focuses on the customer and that involves systematic problem-solving using teams of front-line workers. A variety of specific tools are available in TQM including benchmarking and the Plan-Do-Check-Act Cycle.

1.   *Benchmarking* involves studying how a successful "world-class" company runs a particular operation. For example, a company trying to improve its customer service might study how Disney trains its employees.

2.   The *Plan-Do-Check-Act (PDCA) Cycle* is a systematic, fact-based approach to continuous

improvement that resembles the scientific method. Exhibit 1-6 in the text illustrates the PDCA Cycle.

a. In the Plan phase, the current process is studied, data are collected, and possible causes of the problem at hand are identified. A plan is developed to deal with the problem.

b. In the Do phase, the plan is implemented and data are collected. This is done on a small scale if possible since at this point the team is rarely sure that the plan will work.

c. In the Check phase, the data collected in the Do phase are analyzed to verify whether the expected improvement actually occurred.

d. In the Act phase, the plan is implemented on a large scale if it was successful. If the plan was not successful in eliminating the problem, the cycle is started again with the Plan phase.

3. Perhaps the most important characteristics of TQM are that it empowers front-line workers to solve problems and it focuses attention on solving problems rather than on finger-pointing.

I. *Process Reengineering* is a more radical approach to improvement than TQM. It involves completely redesigning business processes and it is often implemented by outside consultants.

1. In Process Reengineering, all of the steps in a business process are displayed as a flowchart. Many of the stops are often unnecessary and are called *non-value-added activities*.

2. The process is then completely redesigned, eliminating non-value-added activities.

3. Process Reengineering should result in a streamlined process that uses fewer resources, takes less time, and generates fewer errors.

4. However, some managers fall into a trap. If Process Reengineering results in laying off workers who are no longer needed, employees will resist further Process Reengineering efforts and morale will suffer.

J. The *Theory of Constraints (TOC)* is based on the idea that every organization has at least one constraint that prevents it from obtaining more of

its objective. For example, a machine that is slower than other machines on an assembly line will prevent the company from increasing its rate of output. To improve (in other words, increase its rate of output), the company must focus its improvement efforts on the constraint. Improvement efforts will be largely wasted if focused on machines that are not constraints.

K. *Organizational Structure.*

1. Almost all organizations are decentralized to some degree. *Decentralization* involves delegating decision-making authority to lower levels in the organization.

2. An *organization chart* shows the levels of responsibility and formal channels of communication in an organization. It shows who reports to whom in the organization. Exhibit 1-8 in the text provides an example of an organization chart.

3. A manager may occupy either a line position or a staff position.

a. *Line positions* are directly related to achieving the basic objectives of the organization.

b. *Staff positions* provide service, assistance, and specialized support to the line positions. They do not have direct authority over line positions. Accounting is a staff position.

4. The *controller* is the manager of the accounting department and often acts as a key adviser to top management.

L. Ethics plays a vital role in an advanced market economy.

1. If people were generally dishonest, it would become more difficult for companies to raise investment funds, the quality of goods and services would decline, fewer goods and services would be available for sale, and prices would be higher.

2. The Institute of Management Accountants has issued Standards of Ethical Conduct for Practitioners of Management Accounting and Financial Management. This is a useful, practical guide for general managers as well as management accountants. The Standards for Ethical Conduct are reproduced in Exhibit 1-10 in the text.

REVIEW AND SELF TEST
Questions and Exercises

True or False

Enter a T or an F in the blank to indicate whether the statement is true or false.

___ 1. Managerial accounting is as concerned with providing information to stockholders as it is with providing information to managers.

___ 2. When carrying out their control function, managers obtain feedback to ensure that each part of the organization is following the plan.

___ 3. When carrying out their planning function, managers mobilize the organization's resources and oversee day-to-day operations.

___ 4. The planning, directing and motivating, and control activities of a manager are kept separate from the manager's decision-making responsibilities.

___ 5. Managerial accounting focuses more on the segments of an organization than on the organization as a whole.

___ 6. Managerial accounting need not follow Generally Accepted Accounting Principles.

___ 7. An objective of a JIT system is to complete products just in time to ship to customers.

___ 8. Under JIT, partially completed units are "pushed" from one workstation to another to ensure all workstations have enough work to keep busy.

___ 9. The maintenance of large work in process inventories helps reduce the number of defective units that are produced.

___ 10. A company will typically have fewer suppliers under JIT than under a conventional system.

___ 11. For JIT to operate successfully, all similar pieces of equipment (such as lathes or drill presses) must be grouped together.

___ 12. JIT requires an increase in funds to finance additional inventories.

___ 13. Total Quality Management involves a focus on serving the customer and systematic problem-solving using teams made up of front-line workers.

___ 14. The Plan-Do-Check-Act Cycle is used in the Theory of Constraints to eliminate constraints.

___ 15. In the plan phase of the Plan-Do-Check-Act Cycle, data are analyzed to identify the possible causes of a problem and a solution is proposed.

___ 16. Process Reengineering is less likely to result in employee resistance than Total Quality Management.

___ 17. Non-value-added activities are the constraints in the system.

___ 18. Efforts that are designed to improve the rate of output of a workstation should generally be focused on the constraint.

___ 19. The Standards of Ethical Conduct promulgated by the Institute of Management Accountants specifically states, among other things, that a management accountant should refuse all gifts and hospitality offered by one of the company's suppliers.

Multiple Choice

Choose the best answer or response by placing the identifying letter in the space provided.

___ 1. Staff positions: a) are not shown on the organization chart; b) are superior in authority to line positions; c) are subordinate in authority to line positions; d) none of these.

___ 2. The controller: a) occupies a staff position; b) occupies a line position; c) has little influence in the decision-making process; d) none of these.

___ 3. Managerial accounting: a) is governed by Generally Accepted Accounting Principles; b) places more emphasis on precision of data than does financial accounting; c) is not mandatory; d) is geared primarily to the past rather than to the future.

___ 4. Financial and managerial accounting are similar in that: a) both emphasize reporting the performance of the entire organization rather than segments of the organization; b) both rely on the same accounting database; c) both focus on providing data for internal uses; d) none of these.

___ 5. In a decentralized organization, decisions are made: a) only by top management; b) only by managers occupying staff positions; c) at the lowest managerial level possible in the organization; d) none of these.

___ 6. In large part, "control" in an organization is achieved through: a) decentralization of decision making authority; b) obtaining feedback on how well the organization is moving toward its objectives; c) preparing an organization chart that shows both line and staff functions; d) none of these.

___ 7. Under JIT: a) the plant floor is laid out in a functional format with similar machines grouped together; b) focused factories are used; c) the plant floor is laid out in a single flow line through which all products pass; d) work in process inventories are maximized in order to ensure that all work stations have enough work to stay busy.

___ 8. Which of the following involves systematic problem-solving by teams consisting of front-line workers? a) The Theory of Constraints; b) Total Quality Management; c) Process Reengineering; d) Automation.

___ 9. The Plan-Do-Check Act Cycle is used to: a) solve problems in Total Quality Management; b) manage constraints in The Theory of Constraints; c) redesign processes in Process Reengineering; d) none of these.

Answers to Questions and Exercises

True or False

1. F The central purpose of managerial accounting is to provide information to managers. The information needs of shareholders are provided through financial accounting.

2. T This is what is meant by control.

3. F Planning involves deciding on the actions to be taken in order to achieve the organization's objectives; it does not involve overseeing day-to-day activities.

4. F Decision making is an integral part of planning, organizing, and controlling.

5. T The primary concern of managerial accounting is with the segments of an organization, rather than with the organization as a whole.

6. T Managerial accounting need not conform to GAAP.

7. T Under JIT, goods are produced and shipped only as needed to satisfy customer orders.

8. F JIT operates under a "pull" approach in which partially completed units are passed to the next workstation only as needed to fill customer orders.

9. F Large work in process inventories increase defect rates. Because of delays in passing units on to the next workstation, problems are not detected until after many units have been affected.

10. T Under JIT, a company uses only a few suppliers who deliver parts and materials on a frequent basis.

11. F Typically under JIT, all of the different pieces of equipment needed to manufacture a product are placed on a single flow line, thus breaking up groupings of similar equipment.

12. F JIT reduces inventories and the need for funds to finance them.

13. T These are common characteristics of TQM.

14. F The Plan-Do-Check-Act Cycle is used in TQM, not TOC.

15. T This statement correctly describes the plan phase of the PDCA Cycle.

16. F The reverse is true. Process Reengineering tends to be imposed from above using outside specialists and it may lead to loss of jobs.

17. F A non-value-added activity is an activity that consumes resources or takes time that adds nothing of value. It may or may not be a constraint.

18. T The rate of output of the constraint determines the output of the entire system. Therefore, improvement efforts should ordinarily be focused on the constraint.

19. F The Standards state that the management accountant should "refuse any gift, favor, or hospitality that would influence or would appear to influence their actions." There is no absolute prohibition. For example, it would be okay to let a supplier pay for one's dinner while on a fact-finding trip to the supplier's plant. This is a common courtesy and it is extremely unlikely that this small favor would influence the management accountant's judgment.

Multiple Choice

1. d   Staff positions such as accounting do appear on the organization chart, but they are neither superior nor equal in authority to line positions. They serve the needs of line positions by providing essential services.

2. a   The controller occupies a staff position that provides support to other positions within the organization.

3. c   Managerial accounting is not required by any external law or regulation.

4. b   Since it would be a waste of money to have two data collecting systems existing side by side, managerial accounting and financial accounting rely on much the same data.

5. c   The purpose of decentralization is to move all decisions to the lowest managerial level possible in an organization.

6. b   By obtaining feedback, management can see how well an organization is moving toward its objectives and thus control is maintained.

7. b   Under JIT, the plant floor is laid out with many product flow lines—one for each family of products.

8. b   Total Quality Management involves systematic problem-solving by teams consisting of front-line workers.

9. a   The Plan-Do-Check-Act Cycle is used to solve problems in TQM.

Chapter 2

Cost Terms, Concepts, and Classifications

Chapter Study Suggestions

This chapter introduces general cost terms that will be used throughout the book. The chapter also gives a broad overview of the flow of costs in a manufacturing company. (Chapter 3 covers cost flows in more depth.) As you read the chapter, note each new term and be sure you under-stand its meaning. It is important to keep in mind that costs are classified in many ways, depending upon how the costs will be used. This is the reason for so many different cost terms. To fit the cost terms into a framework, you should frequently refer to Exhibit 2-8 as you go through the chapter.

Exhibit 2-4 presents the *schedule of cost of goods manufactured.* You should memorize the format of this schedule, as well as the material in Exhibit 2-6. Learning this material will help you in Chapter 3 and will also lay a foundation for many chapters that follow.

CHAPTER HIGHLIGHTS

A. *Manufacturing costs* are the costs involved in making a product. Manufacturing costs can be divided into three basic elements: direct materials, direct labor, and manufacturing overhead.

1. *Direct materials* are those materials that become an integral part of a finished product and can be conveniently traced into it.

 a. An example of direct materials would be the tires on a new Ford.

 b. Small material items, such as glue, are classified as *indirect materials* rather than as direct materials. It is too costly and inconvenient to trace such small costs to individual units.

2. *Direct labor* consists of those labor costs that can be easily traced to individual units of product. Direct labor is sometimes called touch labor.

 a. An example of direct labor would be a worker on a manufacturing assembly line.

 b. Other labor costs, such as supervisors and janitors, are treated as *indirect labor* rather than as direct labor. These costs cannot be traced to individual units of product since these individuals do not directly work on the product.

3. *Manufacturing overhead* consists of all manufacturing costs except direct materials and direct labor.

 a. Manufacturing overhead includes indirect materials, indirect labor, and other manufacturing costs such as factory rent, factory utilities, and depreciation on factory equipment and facilities.

 b. Synonyms for manufacturing overhead include factory overhead and indirect manufacturing costs.

4. The terms prime cost and conversion cost are also used to categorize manufacturing costs.

 a. *Prime cost* consists of direct materials plus direct labor.

 b. *Conversion cost* consists of direct labor plus manufacturing overhead.

B. *Nonmanufacturing costs* are those costs involved with selling and administrative activities.

1. *Selling, or marketing, costs* include all costs associated with marketing finished products such as sales commissions, costs of delivery equipment, costs of finished goods warehouses, and advertising.

2. *Administrative costs* include all costs associated with the general administration of an organization, including secretarial salaries, depreciation of general administrative facilities and equipment, and executive compensation.

C. For purposes of external financial reports, costs can be classified as product costs or period costs.

1. *Period costs* are expensed on the income statement in the period in which they are incurred. (By incurred, we mean the period in which the cost is accrued, not necessarily when it is paid. For example, remember from financial accounting that salaries are counted as costs not when they are paid, but when they are earned by employees. The cost is *incurred* in the period in which it is earned. Just continue to use the rules you learned in financial accounting.)

2. *Product costs* are matched with units of product and are recognized as an expense on the income statement only when the units are sold. Until that time, product costs are considered to be assets and are recognized on the balance sheet as inventory.

3. In a manufacturing company, product costs include direct materials, direct labor, and manufacturing overhead. Thus, in a manufacturing company, product costs and manufacturing costs are synonymous.

4. In a manufacturing company, period costs and nonmanufacturing costs are synonymous terms. Thus, the period costs are selling and administrative costs.

5. In a merchandising company such as Macy's or Walmart, product costs consist solely of the costs of products purchased from suppliers for resale to customers. All other costs are period costs.

D. Income statements and balance sheets prepared by manufacturing firms differ from those prepared by merchandising firms.

1. The balance sheet of a manufacturing firm contains three inventory accounts: Raw Materials, Work in Process, and Finished Goods. By contrast, the balance sheet of a merchandising firm contains only one inventory account—Merchandise Inventory.

a. *Raw Materials* inventory consists of materials on hand in stockrooms that will be used to make products.

b. *Work in Process* consists of unfinished products.

c. *Finished Goods* consists of units of product that are completed and ready for sale.

2. The income statement of a manufacturing firm contains an element termed *cost of goods manufactured*. You should study the schedule of cost of goods manufactured in Exhibit 2-4 in the text very carefully. If you have difficulty understanding this exhibit, look at Exhibit 2-5, which shows the same information in a different format.

E. Manufacturing costs (direct materials, direct labor, and overhead) are also known as *inventoriable costs*.

1. The term inventoriable costs is used since direct materials, direct labor, and overhead costs are assigned to Work in Process and Finished Goods inventory accounts as they are incurred. If goods are either not completed or not sold at the end of a period, these costs will be included as part of these inventory accounts on the balance sheet.

2. You should study Exhibit 2-6 in the text with care. It shows the flow of manufacturing costs through inventory accounts and the way these costs become an expense (cost of goods sold) on the income statement. *This is a key exhibit for Chapter 2.*

3. We can summarize manufacturing and nonmanufacturing cost terms as follows:

Synonymous Cost Terms	Costs Involved
• Manufacturing costs • Product costs • Inventoriable costs	• Direct materials, direct labor, and manufacturing overhead
• Nonmanufacturing costs • Period costs	• Selling and administrative expenses

F. Computation of cost of goods manufactured, cost of goods sold, and preparation of the income statement.

1. Computing the cost of goods sold for a manufacturing company involves a number of steps. These steps rely on the following basic model that describes flows into and out of any inventory account.

Basic inventory flows:
Beginning balance
+ Additions to inventory
= Available
− Ending balance
= Withdrawals from inventory

2. To compute the raw materials used in production, this basic model is written as follows:

Beginning balance raw materials
+ Purchases of raw materials
= Raw materials available for use
− Ending balance raw materials
= Raw materials used in production

The raw materials used in production could include both direct materials and indirect materials. However, unless otherwise stated in a problem, you can assume that there are no indirect materials.

3. The next step is to compute the total manufacturing cost for the period. This is the sum of direct materials, direct labor, and manufacturing overhead costs:

Direct materials
+ Direct labor
+ Manufacturing overhead
= Total manufacturing cost

4. The next step is to compute the *cost of goods manufactured*. This refers to the cost of the

goods that were *finished* during the period. To compute this figure, use the following version of the basic inventory flow model:

>   Beginning balance, work in process
> + Total manufacturing cost
> – Ending balance, work in process
> = Cost of goods manufactured

Note: We don't have any name for the sum of the beginning balance of the work in process inventory and total manufacturing cost, so it has been left out of the calculations.

5. The final step in the computation of cost of goods sold is also based on the inventory flow model:

>   Beginning balance, finished goods
> + Cost of goods manufactured
> = Goods available for sale
> – Ending balance, finished goods
> = Cost of goods sold

6. The income statement in a manufacturing firm may or may not show the computation of the cost of goods sold as above. In the summary income statement below, it is assumed that the details of the cost of goods sold computations are shown separately.

>   Sales
> – Cost of goods sold
> = Gross margin
> – Selling and administrative expenses
> = Net income

G. For purposes of describing how costs behave in response to changes in activity, costs are often classified as variable or fixed. For example, one might be interested in describing how the costs of admitting patients to a hospital behave in response to changes in the number of patients admitted. Or, one might be interested in how much it would cost for paint in a furniture factory if the output of the factory were increased by 10%.

1. *Variable costs* are those costs that vary, in total, in direct proportion to changes in the volume or level of activity within the relevant range. Exhibit 2-9 illustrates variable cost behavior. Examples of variable costs include direct materials, (usually) direct labor, commissions to sales-

persons, and cost of goods sold in a merchandising company such as a shoe store.

2. *Fixed costs* are those costs that remain constant in total amount within the relevant range. They include, for example, depreciation, supervisory salaries, and rent. Exhibit 2-9 illustrates fixed cost behavior.

3. The *relevant range* is the range of activity within which the assumptions about cost behavior can be considered valid. If there is a big enough change in activity (for example, a ten-fold increase in volume), even the "fixed" costs are likely to change. A ten-fold increase in volume would be outside the relevant range.

H. For purposes of assigning costs to objects, costs are classified as direct or indirect.

1. Managers often want to know how much something (e.g., a product, a department, or a customer) costs. The item for which a cost is desired is called a *cost object*.

2. A *direct cost* is a cost that can be easily and conveniently traced to the cost object under consideration. For example, the salaries and commissions of salespersons in a department store's shoe department would be considered direct costs of the shoe department.

3. An *indirect cost* is a cost that cannot be easily and conveniently traced to the cost object. For example, the salary of the manager of a department store would be considered an indirect cost of the shoe department and other departments.

I. For purposes of making decisions, the following cost terms are often used: differential costs, opportunity costs, and sunk costs.

1. Every decision involves choosing from among at least two alternatives. A difference in cost between two alternatives is called a *differential cost*. Only the differential costs are relevant in making a choice between two alternatives. Costs that are the same for the two alternatives do not matter and should be ignored.

2. An *opportunity cost* is the potential benefit given up by selecting one alternative over another. Opportunity costs are not recorded in accounting records. They represent a lost benefit rather than an out-of-pocket cost.

3. A *sunk cost* is a cost that has already been incurred and that cannot be changed by any decision made now or in the future. Sunk costs are never differential costs and should always be ignored when making decisions.

Appendix 2A: Further Classification of Labor Costs

A. Labor costs can be broken down into five main categories: direct labor, indirect labor, idle time, overtime premium, and labor fringe benefits.

1. As mentioned earlier, direct labor consists of those factory labor costs that can be easily traced to products.

2. Indirect labor consists of factory labor costs that are supportive or supervisory in nature. These include the costs of supervisors, superintendents, custodians, maintenance persons, and others whose services are essential to factory operations, but who do not work directly on the product.

3. *Idle time* represents the costs of direct labor workers who are unable to perform their assignments due to material shortages, power failures,

and the like. Idle time is treated as part of manufacturing overhead.

4. *Overtime premium* consists of any amount paid above an employee's base hourly rate.

  a. For example, if the base rate is $6 per hour and an employee is paid time-and-a-half for overtime, then the overtime premium would be $3 per hour. In other words, the total pay would be $9 per hour of overtime.

  b. Overtime premium is ordinarily not charged to specific jobs, but rather is included as part of manufacturing overhead. An exception is when a customer specifically requests a rush job that results in having to work overtime. In such a case, the overtime premium might be charged directly to that job.

5. *Labor fringe benefits* include employment-related costs paid by the employer, such as insurance, retirement plans, etc.

  a. Many firms include all such costs as part of manufacturing overhead.

  b. Other firms include only the labor fringe benefits relating to indirect labor as part of manufacturing overhead and treat the fringe benefits relating to direct labor as added direct labor costs. This is the preferred method.

REVIEW AND SELF TEST
Questions and Exercises

True or False

Enter a T or an F in the blank to indicate whether the statement is true or false.

____ 1. Raw materials consist of basic natural resources, such as iron ore.

____ 2. A supervisor's salary would be considered direct labor if the supervisor works directly in the factory

____ 3. Nonmanufacturing costs consist of selling costs and administrative costs.

____ 4. All selling and administrative costs are period costs.

____ 5. The terms product cost and manufacturing cost are synonymous.

____ 6. The cost of goods manufactured is an expense in a manufacturing firm.

____ 7. Part of a cost such as factory depreciation may be on the balance sheet as an asset if goods are uncompleted or unsold at the end of a period.

____ 8. Inventoriable costs and product costs are synonymous terms in a manufacturing firm.

____ 9. Total variable cost will change in proportion to changes in the level of activity.

____ 10. A fixed cost is constant per unit of product.

____ 11. Manufacturing overhead is an indirect cost with respect to units of product.

____ 12. Sunk costs can be either variable or fixed.

____ 13. Property taxes and insurance on a factory building are examples of manufacturing overhead.

____ 14. (Appendix 2A) Overtime premium is ordinarily charged to the specific jobs worked on during overtime periods.

Multiple Choice

Choose the best answer or response by placing the identifying letter in the space provided.

____ 1. If the activity level increases, one would expect the fixed cost per unit to: a) increase; b) decrease; c) remain unchanged; d) none of these.

____ 2. Which of the following costs would not be a period cost? a) indirect materials; b) advertising; c) administrative salaries; d) shipping costs; e) sales commissions.

____ 3. The term used to describe the cost of goods transferred from work in process inventory to finished goods inventory is: a) cost of goods sold; b) raw materials; c) period cost; d) cost of goods manufactured.

____ 4. Manufacturing cost is synonymous with all of the following terms except: a) product cost; b) inventoriable cost; c) period cost; d) all of the above are synonymous terms.

____ 5. If the activity level drops by 5%, one would expect the variable costs: a) to increase per unit of product; b) to drop in total by 5%; c) to remain constant in total; d) to decrease per unit of product.

____ 6. All of the following are considered to be product costs for financial reporting except: a) indirect materials; b) advertising; c) rent on factory space; d) idle time; e) all of the above would be product costs.

____ 7. Walston Manufacturing Company has provided the following data concerning its raw materials inventories last month:

Beginning raw materials inventory ... $80,000
Purchases of raw materials $420,000
Ending raw materials inventory $50,000

The cost of the raw materials used in production for the month was: a) $500,000; b) $450,000; c) $390,000; d) $470,000.

___ 8. Juniper Company has provided the following data concerning its manufacturing costs and work in process inventories last month:

Raw materials used in production $270,000
Direct labor $140,000
Manufacturing overhead $190,000
Beginning work in process inventory . $50,000
Ending work in process inventory $80,000

The cost of goods manufactured for the month was: a) $730,000; b) $630,000; c) $600,000; d) $570,000.

___ 9. Vonder Inc. has provided the following data concerning its finished goods inventories last month:

Beginning finished goods inventory ... $110,000
Cost of goods manufactured $760,000
Ending finished goods inventory $70,000

The cost of goods sold for the month was: a) $800,000; b) $720,000; c) $950,000; d) $280,000.

___ 10. (Appendix 2A) A machinist earns $10 per hour. During a given week he works 40 hours, of which he is idle 5 hours. For the week: a) $400 cost should be charged to direct labor, b) $50 cost should be charged to overtime premium; c) $50 cost should be charged to overhead; d) $425 cost should be charged to direct labor, and $25 cost should be charged to overhead.

Exercises

2-1.   Classify each of the following costs as either period costs or product costs. Also indicate whether the cost is fixed or variable with respect to changes in the amount of output produced and sold.

		Period Cost	Product Cost	Variable Cost	Fixed Cost
-	Example: Rent on a sales office	X	___	___	X
-	Example: Direct materials	___	X	X	___
a.	Sales commissions	___	___	___	___
b.	Rent on a factory building	___	___	___	___
c.	Headquarters secretarial salaries	___	___	___	___
d.	Assembly line workers	___	___	___	___
e.	Product advertising	___	___	___	___
f.	Cherries in a cannery	___	___	___	___
g.	Top management salaries	___	___	___	___
h.	Lubricants for machines	___	___	___	___
i.	Shipping costs via express service	___	___	___	___
j.	Executive training program	___	___	___	___
k.	Factory supervisory salaries	___	___	___	___

2-2.   Using the following data and the form that appears below, prepare a schedule of cost of goods manufactured.

Lubricants for machines	$ 4,500
Rent, factory building	16,000
Direct labor	90,000
Indirect materials	2,000
Sales commissions	24,600
Factory utilities	5,800
Insurance, factory	2,000
Purchases of raw materials	120,000
Work in process, beginning	16,000
Work in process, ending	11,500
Raw materials, beginning	15,000
Raw materials, ending	5,000
Depreciation of office equipment	4,000

Schedule of Cost of Goods Manufactured

(See Exhibit 2-4 in the text for the proper format)

Direct materials:

_____ .... $_____

_____ ....   _____

_____ ....   _____

_____ ....   _____

_____ ....   _____

Direct labor ....   _____

Manufacturing overhead:

_____ ....   _____

_____ ....   _____

_____ ....   _____

_____ ....   _____

_____ ....   _____

_____ ....   _____

_____ ....   _____

_____ ....   _____

                                                                                     _____

_____ ....   _____

Cost of Goods Manufactured .... $_____

2-3. Harry is considering whether to produce and sell classic wooden surfboards in his spare time. He has a garage that was constructed at a cost of $12,000 several years ago, and which could be used for production purposes. The garage would be depreciated over a 20-year life. Harry has determined that each surfboard will require $30 in wood. He would hire students to do most of the work and pay them $35 for each surfboard completed. He would rent tools at a cost of $400 per month. Harry can draw money out of savings to provide the capital needed to get the operation going. The savings are earning interest at 6% annually. An ad agency would handle advertising at a cost of $500 per month. Harry would hire students to sell the surfboards and pay a commission of $20 per board.

Required:

From the foregoing information, identify all the examples you can of the following types of costs (a single item may be identified as many types of costs). A cost should be classified as variable in this case if it is variable with respect to the number of surfboards produced and sold. A cost should be classified as a differential cost if it differs between the alternatives of producing or not producing the surfboards.

	Variable cost	Fixed cost	Selling & admin. cost	Product cost	Manuf. ovhd. cost	Sunk cost	Opportunity cost	Differential cost
Original cost of garage	___	___	___	___	___	___	___	___
Depreciation on the garage	___	___	___	___	___	___	___	___
Wood for each surfboard	___	___	___	___	___	___	___	___
Student workers	___	___	___	___	___	___	___	___
Tool rental	___	___	___	___	___	___	___	___
Interest on savings	___	___	___	___	___	___	___	___
Advertising costs	___	___	___	___	___	___	___	___
Sales commissions	___	___	___	___	___	___	___	___

2-4. (Appendix 2A) Sally Anderson worked 47 hours last week. She was idle 3 hours and spent the remaining 44 hours working directly on the manufacture of finished products. Sally is paid $8 per hour and time-and-a-half for work in excess of 40 hours per week. Allocate her week's wages between direct labor and manufacturing overhead using the form that appears below.

Direct labor .... $_____

Manufacturing overhead:

Idle time .... $_____

Overtime premium .... _____ _____

Total earnings .... $_____

2-5.   Mary has just been hired by Acme Company to fill a new position. The company is unsure whether to classify her salary as a period cost or as a product cost. From the point of view of the company's annual reported net income, explain why it does or does not matter how her salary cost is classified.

_____

_____

_____

_____

_____

_____

_____

_____

Answers to Questions and Exercises

True or False

1. F Raw materials consist of any materials used to make a product. The finished goods of one company can be the raw materials of another company.

2. F Direct labor can be physically traced to products in a "hands on" sense. Supervisors do not work directly on products and therefore are not direct labor.

3. T Nonmanufacturing cost is synonymous with selling and administrative costs.

4. T Selling and administrative costs are period costs because they are charged against income in the period in which they are incurred, rather than being added to the cost of manufactured or purchased goods.

5. T These two terms are synonymous.

6. F Cost of goods manufactured is not an expense. It is the amount transferred from work in process to finished goods inventory when goods are completed. This is a subtle, but important, point.

7. T Manufacturing costs are assigned to units during production. If these units are not complete or not sold at the end of a period, then the manufacturing costs incurred to date are included as part of Work in Process or Finished Goods inventories which are assets on the balance sheet.

8. T These two terms are synonymous.

9. T Since a variable cost is constant per unit, it will change in total in proportion to changes in the level of activity. If activity increases by 5%, then the total variable cost should also increase by 5%.

10. F A fixed cost is constant in total amount; on a per unit basis, it varies inversely with changes in the level of activity.

11. T Manufacturing overhead cost is an indirect cost; only direct materials and direct labor are direct manufacturing costs.

12. T A sunk cost is a cost that has already been incurred and can be variable or fixed. If obsolete materials have already been purchased, for example, then the cost of the materials is a sunk cost.

13. T Manufacturing overhead consists of all production costs except direct materials and direct labor.

14. F Overtime premium is ordinarily added to manufacturing overhead cost and spread over all jobs worked on during the period.

Multiple Choice

1. b The fixed cost per unit should drop since a constant amount is spread over more units.

2. a Indirect materials would be part of manufacturing overhead, and thus it would be a product cost.

3. d Goods that are completed and ready for sale move out of work in process and into finished goods. The cost of such goods is termed cost of goods manufactured.

4. c A period cost represents a cost charged against the period in which the cost is incurred; it has nothing to do with the manufacture of a product.

5. b By definition, total variable cost changes in proportion to changes in the activity level.

6. b Advertising is a period cost, rather than a product cost.

7. b The computations are as follows:

Beginning raw materials inventory ..... $ 80,000
Add: Purchases of raw materials 420,000
Raw materials available for use 500,000
Deduct: Ending raw materials
          inventory 50,000
Raw materials used in production $450,000

8. d   The computations are as follows:

Raw materials used in production ..	$270,000
Direct labor	140,000
Manufacturing overhead	190,000
Total manufacturing costs	600,000
Add: Beginning work in	
process inventory	50,000
	650,000
Deduct: Ending work in	
process inventory	80,000
Cost of goods manufactured	$570,000

9. a   The cost of goods sold is computed as follows:

Beginning finished goods inventory	$110,000
Add: Cost of goods manufactured	760,000
Goods available for sale	870,000
Deduct: Ending finished	
goods inventory	70,000
Cost of goods sold	$800,000

10. c   All of the cost of idle time is charged to manufacturing overhead. Thus, $10 per hour x 5 hours = $50.

Exercises

2-1.

	Period Cost	*Product Cost*	*Variable Cost*	*Fixed Cost*
a. Sales commissions	X		X	
b. Rent on a factory building		X		X
c. Headquarters secretarial salaries	X			X
d. Assembly line workers		X	X	
e. Product advertising	X			X
f. Cherries in a cannery		X	X	
g. Top management salaries	X			X
h. Lubricants for machines		X	X	
i. Shipping costs via express service	X		X	
j. Executive training program	X			X
k. Factory supervisory salaries		X		X

2-2.   Direct materials:

Raw materials inventory, beginning	$ 15,000	
Add: Purchases of raw materials	120,000	
Raw materials available for use	135,000	
Deduct: Raw materials inventory, ending	5,000	
Raw materials used in production		$130,000
Direct labor		90,000
Manufacturing overhead:		
Lubricants for machines	4,500	
Rent, factory building	16,000	
Indirect materials	2,000	
Factory utilities	5,800	
Insurance, factory	2,000	
Total overhead costs		30,300
Total manufacturing costs		250,300
Add: Work in process, beginning		16,000
		266,300
Deduct: Work in process, ending		11,500
Cost of Goods Manufactured		$254,800

Note: Sales commissions and depreciation on office equipment are not manufacturing costs.

2-3.

	Variable cost	Fixed cost	Selling & admin. cost	Product cost	Manuf. ovhd. cost	Sunk cost	Opportunity cost	Differential cost
Original cost of garage						X		
Depreciation on the garage		X		X	X			(1)
Wood for each surfboard	X			X				X
Student workers	X			X				X
Tool rental		X		X	X			X
Interest on savings							X	(2)
Advertising costs		X	X					X
Sales commissions	X		X					X

(1) This is not a differential cost if the depreciation on the garage is the same regardless of whether it is used to make surfboards or is used conventionally as a residential garage.
(2) This may be considered to be a differential cost, although some would say that it is not since it is a foregone benefit rather than a cost *per se.*.

2-4.	Direct labor (44 hours × $8)		$352
	Manufacturing overhead:		
	Idle time (3 hours × $8)	$24	
	Overtime premium (7 hours × $4)	28	52
	Total earnings		$404

2-5.   From the point of view of the company's annual reported net income, it does matter how Mary's salary cost is classified. If her salary is classified as a period cost, the entire amount of salary will appear as an expense on the company's income statement each year. If her salary is classified as a product cost, then it will go into Work in Process along with other production costs. If any goods are not completed at the end of the year, part of Mary's salary will remain in the Work in Process inventory account as part of the cost of these uncompleted goods. That portion of her salary that is attached to completed goods will go into the Finished Goods inventory account. If any of these goods are not sold at year-end, part of Mary's salary will remain in the Finished Goods inventory account as part of the cost of these unsold goods. Only that portion of Mary's salary that is attached to the goods that are completed and sold during the year would appear as an expense on the income statement (as part of Cost of Goods Sold) if her salary is classified as a product cost.

Chapter 3

Systems Design: Job-Order Costing

Chapter Study Suggestions

This chapter expands on the concepts introduced in Chapter 2 and provides more details concerning how product costs are determined. The costing method illustrated in the chapter is known as *job-order costing*. Exhibit 3-5 provides a overall view of the flow of cost and the documents in a job-order cost system. Pay particular attention to the section in the chapter titled "Application of Manufacturing Overhead." *Overhead application is a key concept in the chapter*.

Exhibits 3-6, 3-7, and 3-8 show how direct materials, direct labor, and overhead costs are assigned to jobs. Study these exhibits with particular care—the concepts they contain will show up often in the homework material. Exhibits 3-10 and 3-11 summarize these concepts. Note particularly the difference between the schedule of cost of goods manufactured in Exhibit 3-11 and the schedule of cost of goods manufactured in Chapter 2. Study and then *restudy* the section titled "Underapplied and Overapplied Overhead," paying particular attention to how under- and overapplied overhead is computed.

CHAPTER HIGHLIGHTS

A. Two basic costing systems are commonly used in manufacturing and in many service organizations: process costing and job-order costing.

1. *Process costing* is used in situations where a single homogeneous product such as bricks are produced for long periods of time.

2. *Job-order costing* is used in situations where many different products or services are produced each period. Examples include special order printing and furniture manufacturing where products are typically produced in small batches. For example, fifty units of a particular type of sofa might be made in one batch. Each batch is called a "job." These concepts also extend to service companies. For example, in a consulting company, a job would be a particular consulting project.

B. We will begin our discussion of job-order costing with raw materials. When materials are purchased, their costs are recorded in the Raw Materials inventory account, which is an asset.

1. Materials are withdrawn from storage using a *materials requisition form* as authorization. The form lists all the materials required to complete a specific job. The journal entry to record withdrawal of raw materials from the storeroom for use in production is:

Work in Process (direct materials) XXX
Manuf. Ovhd. (indirect materials) XXX
    Raw Materials   XXX

Materials that are traced directly to jobs are classified as *direct materials* and are debited to Work in Process. Any materials that are not directly traced to jobs are classified as *indirect materials* and are debited to a special control account called *Manufacturing Overhead.*

2. When materials are placed into production, they are recorded on a *job cost sheet*, which summarizes all production costs assigned to a particular job. Exhibit 3-2 in the text illustrates a job cost sheet.

C. Labor costs are recorded on *time tickets* or *time sheets* that are filled out by employees. These documents list the amount of time each employee works on specific jobs and tasks.

1. Labor time spent working directly on specific jobs is termed *direct labor*. Labor time spent working on supportive tasks (e.g., supervision, maintenance, janitorial) is termed *indirect labor*. The entry to record labor costs is:

Work in Process (direct labor)   XXX
Manuf. Ovhd. (indirect labor)   XXX
    Salaries and Wages Payable   XXX

2. Direct labor costs are added to the individual job cost sheets at the same time they are recorded in the formal accounts.

D. As explained in Chapter 2, manufacturing overhead is an *indirect* cost and therefore must be allocated in order to be assigned to units of product. This allocation is usually done with a *predetermined overhead rate*.

1. The predetermined overhead rate is computed *before* the year begins and is based entirely on estimated data. Ordinarily, the rate is computed for an entire year to eliminate seasonal fluctuations. The formula is:

$$\text{Predetermined overhead rate} = \frac{\text{Estimated total manufacturing overhead cost}}{\text{Estimated total amount of the allocation base}}$$

An *allocation base* is a measure of activity, such as direct labor-hours, direct labor cost, or machine-hours. The allocation base is something that all jobs have in common—for example, all of the jobs may require direct labor-hours. Ideally, the allocation base should actually cause the overhead cost, but in practice this ideal is often ignored.

2. For example, suppose direct labor-hours is used as the allocation base and that the estimated total manufacturing overhead cost for next year is $400,000 and the estimated total number of direct labor-hours is 10,000. Then the predetermined overhead rate would be $40 per direct labor-hour ($400,000 ÷ 10,000 direct labor-hours).

3. To assign overhead costs to a job, the predetermined overhead rate is multiplied by the amount of the allocation base incurred by the job. For example, suppose that a particular job incurs 20 direct labor-hours and the predetermined overhead rate is $40 per direct labor-hour. Then $800 (20 direct labor-hours × $40 per direct labor-

hour) of overhead cost would be *applied* to that job. This $800 is called the *overhead applied*. Note that this is not actual overhead spending on the job. The $800 may have little to do with any overhead that is actually caused by the job. It is simply a way of distributing the overhead costs that were estimated at the beginning of the year among the jobs worked on during the year.

4. The overhead that is applied to a job is entered on its job cost sheet and is recorded in the company's formal accounts with the following journal entry:

Work in Process   XXX
   Manufacturing Overhead   XXX

5. Turn to Exhibit 3-8 in the text to see how overhead costs flow through the accounts and onto the job cost sheets. Notice from the exhibit that applying overhead to jobs and recording actual overhead costs represent two separate and distinct processes. *This is a key concept that you must understand.*

6. Actual overhead costs are *not* charged to Work in Process. Instead, they are charged to the Manufacturing Overhead control account as we saw in the entries for indirect labor and indirect materials above. Note that *actual overhead costs all appear as debits to Manufacturing Overhead.*

E. When jobs are completed, their costs are transferred from Work in Process to Finished Goods. The journal entry is:

Finished Goods   XXX
   Work in Process   XXX

When completed products are sold, their costs are transferred from Finished Goods to Cost of Goods Sold. The journal entry is:

Cost of Goods Sold   XXX
   Finished Goods   XXX

F. Exhibits 3-10, 3-11 and 3-12 are key exhibits that summarize much of the material in the chapter. Study these exhibits with care. Note particularly how the manufacturing overhead costs are handled.

G. Generally there will be a difference between the amount of overhead cost *applied* to Work in Process and the amount of *actual* overhead cost for a period. This difference will be reflected in a debit or credit balance in the Manufacturing Overhead account.

1. If less overhead cost is applied to Work in Process than has actually been incurred, then overhead has been *underapplied* and there is a debit balance in the Manufacturing Overhead account.

2. If more overhead cost is applied to Work in Process than has actually been incurred, then overhead has been *overapplied* and the Manufacturing Overhead account has a credit balance.

3. Under- or overapplied overhead can be computed as follows:

Actual overhead costs .... $XXX
Less: Overhead costs applied
  to Work in Process* XXX
Underapplied (overapplied) overhead . $XXX

* Predetermined overhead rate × Actual amount of the allocation base incurred during the period.

4. At the end of a period, under- or overapplied overhead may be closed out to Cost of Goods Sold or it may be allocated among Work in Process, Finished Goods, and Cost of Goods Sold.

  a. Closing any balance out to Cost of Goods Sold is simpler, since only one account is involved.

If overhead has been underapplied, the entry would be:

Cost of Goods Sold   XXX
   Manufacturing Overhead   XXX

This entry increases Cost of Goods Sold. If overhead has been underapplied, not enough overhead cost was applied to jobs during the period and therefore costs are understated in the accounts. The journal entry above adjusts Cost of Goods Sold so that it is no longer understated.

If overhead has been overapplied, the journal entry would be:

Manufacturing Overhead   XXX
   Cost of Goods Sold   XXX

This entry decreases Cost of Goods Sold. If overhead has been overapplied, too much overhead cost was applied to jobs during the period and therefore costs are overstated in the accounts. The journal entry above adjusts Cost of Goods Sold so that it is no longer overstated.

b. Allocating any under- or overapplied overhead among inventory accounts and Cost of Goods Sold is more complex, but is considered to be more accurate. The allocation is based on the amount of the overhead applied from the current period in the ending balances of the Work in Process, Finished Goods, and Cost of Goods Sold accounts. Assuming that overhead is underapplied, the entry would be:

Work in Process	XXX	
Finished Goods	XXX	
Cost of Goods Sold	XXX	
Manufacturing Overhead		XXX

H. Largely for simplicity, the chapter assumes that a single "plant-wide" overhead rate is used. Many companies use *multiple overhead rates* rather than a single plant wide rate. There may be a different predetermined overhead rate for each processing department or work center and there may be separate overhead rates for activities such as processing purchase orders that are caused by the job. These more complex systems will be investigated in Chapter 5.

Appendix 3A: The Predetermined Overhead Rate and Capacity

A. There is some controversy concerning how the denominator in the predetermined overhead rate should be measured.

$$\text{Predetermined overhead rate} = \frac{\text{Estimated total manufacturing overhead cost}}{\begin{array}{c}\text{Estimated total amount}\\\text{of the allocation base}\end{array}}$$

The denominator is the *estimated* total amount of the allocation base for the next year. This is the traditional method that is most commonly used in practice, but it can lead to some potential problems.

1. If there is a general fall-off in demand due to a recession or other reason, the estimated total amount of the allocation base is likely to fall. For example, if there is a recession, total sales are likely to fall and the company may use less overtime or lay off workers so that the total amount of direct labor-hours declines as well. Since manufacturing overhead cost tends to be relatively fixed, there will tend to be an increase in the predetermined overhead rate as the general level of activity falls. This will result in higher product costs and may lead managers to attempt to increase prices—which would be unwise in a recession.

2. Under the traditional method, products and services are charged for the resources they *don't* use as well as the resources they do use. Suppose, for example, that a particular product uses 10% of the capacity of a machine. If the machine is expected to be idle 50% of the time, the product will be charged for 20% of the cost of the machine. In effect, the product will be charged 10% of the total cost of the machine for the time it uses and 10% of the total cost of the machine for the idle capacity it does not use.

B. An alternative to the traditional method is to base the predetermined overhead rate on the total amount of the allocation base at capacity. For example, the estimated amount of machine-hours for the upcoming year may be 80,000 hours even though the plant has capacity for 100,000 hours. Under this approach:

1. Product costs would be stable and would not increase as the level of activity declines and decrease as the level of activity rises.

2. Products would be charged only for their share of the costs of the resources they actually use.

3. There would usually be underapplied overhead because of idle capacity. Rather than closing out this underapplied overhead to Cost of Goods Sold or allocating it, the underapplied overhead that be treated as a period expense which would be separately disclosed as "Cost of Unused Capacity." This makes the costs of idle capacity much more visible.

REVIEW AND SELF TEST
Questions and Exercises

True or False

Enter a T or an F in the blank to indicate whether the statement is true or false.

___ 1. A company producing many different kinds of furniture would probably use a job-order cost system.

___ 2. Process costing systems are used in situations where output is homogeneous—the company makes a single product for long periods of time.

___ 3. Most factory overhead costs are direct costs and can be easily identified with specific jobs.

___ 4. The predetermined overhead rate is computed using estimates of overhead cost and the amount of the allocation base.

___ 5. The predetermined overhead rate is generally computed on a monthly basis rather than on an annual basis to increase the accuracy of unit costs.

___ 6. The cost of indirect materials used in production is added to the Manufacturing Overhead account rather than added directly to Work in Process.

___ 7. The job cost sheet is used to accumulate the costs charged to a particular job.

___ 8. Actual manufacturing overhead costs are charged directly to the Work in Process account as the costs are incurred.

___ 9. Selling and administrative expenses are charged to the Manufacturing Overhead account.

___ 10. If more overhead is applied to Work in Process than is actually incurred, then overhead cost will be overapplied.

___ 11. A debit balance in the Manufacturing Overhead account at the end of a period would mean that overhead was underapplied for the period.

___ 12. Any balance in the Work in Process account at the end of a period should be closed to Cost of Goods Sold.

___ 13. Under- or overapplied overhead is computed by finding the difference between actual overhead costs and the amount of overhead cost applied to Work in Process.

Multiple Choice

Choose the best answer or response by placing the identifying letter in the space provided.

___ 1. In a job-order costing system, the basic document for accumulating costs for a specific job is: a) the materials requisition form; b) the job cost sheet; c) the Work in Process inventory account; d) the labor time ticket.

___ 2. Suppose $30,000 of raw materials are purchased. What account is debited? a) Work in Process inventory; b) Raw Materials inventory; c) Cost of Goods Sold; d) Manufacturing Overhead.

___ 3. Suppose $20,000 of raw materials are withdrawn from the storeroom to be used in production. Of this amount, $15,000 consists of direct materials and $5,000 consists of indirect materials. What account or accounts will be debited? a) Work in Process $15,000 and Raw Materials $5,000; b) Raw Materials $15,000 and Manufacturing Overhead $5,000; c) Manufacturing Overhead $15,000 and Work in Process $5,000; d) Work in Process $15,000 and Manufacturing Overhead $5,000.

___ 4. Suppose $70,000 of wages and salaries are earned by employees. Of this amount, $20,000 consists of direct labor; $10,000 consists of indirect labor; and $40,000 consists of administrative salaries. What account or accounts will be debited? a) Work in Process $20,000 and Manufacturing Overhead $10,000 and Administrative Salary Expense $40,000; b) Direct Labor $20,000 and Indirect Labor $10,000 and Administrative Salary Expense $40,000; c) Work in Process $20,000 and Manufacturing Overhead $50,000; d) Direct Labor $20,000 and Manufacturing Overhead $50,000.

___ 5. Suppose jobs are completed whose job cost sheets total to $120,000. What account will be debited? a) Manufacturing Overhead $120,000; b) Cost of Goods Sold $120,000; c) Work in Process $120,000; d) Finished Goods $120,000.

___ 6. Suppose a total of $30,000 of overhead is applied to jobs. What account will be debited? a) Manufacturing Overhead $30,000; b) Cost of Goods Sold $30,000; c) Work in Process $30,000; d) Finished Goods $30,000.

___ 7. Last year, a company reported estimated overhead, $100,000; actual overhead, $90,000; and applied overhead, $92,000. The company's overhead cost for the year would be: a) underapplied, $10,000; b) underapplied, $8,000; c) overapplied, $2,000; d) overapplied, $10,000.

___ 8. Jurden Company bases its predetermined overhead rates on machine hours. At the beginning of the year, the company estimated its manufacturing overhead for the year would be $60,000 and there would be a total of 40,000 machine hours. Actual manufacturing overhead for year amounted to $65,100 and the actual machine hours totaled 42,000. Manufacturing overhead for the year would be: a) underapplied by $2,100; b) overapplied by $3,000; c) underapplied by $3,000; d) overapplied by $5,100.

___ 9. On January 1, Hessler Company's Work in Process account had a balance of $18,000. During the year, direct materials costing $35,000 were placed into production. Direct labor cost for the year was $60,000. The predetermined overhead rate for the year was set at 150% of direct labor cost. Actual overhead costs for the year totaled $92,000. Jobs costing $190,000 to manufacture according to their job cost sheets were completed during the year. On December 31, the balance in the Work in Process inventory account would be: a) $13,000; b) $18,000; c) $15,000; d) $8,000.

___ 10. The Cost of Goods Manufactured represents: a) the amount of cost charged to Work in Process during the period; b) the amount transferred from Work in Process to Finished Goods during the period; c) the amount of cost placed into production during the period; d) none of these.

___ 11. If overhead is overapplied for a period, it means that: a) the predetermined overhead rate used to apply overhead cost to Work in Process was too low; b) the company incurred more overhead cost than it charged to Work in Process; c) too much cost has been assigned to jobs; d) none of these.

___ 12. Malt Company's Manufacturing Overhead account showed a $10,000 underapplied overhead balance on December 31. Other accounts showed the following amounts of overhead applied from the current period in their ending balances:

Work in Process	40,000
Finished Goods	60,000
Cost of Goods Sold	100,000

If the company allocates the underapplied overhead among Cost of Goods Sold, Work in Process, and Finished Goods, the amount allocated to Work in Process would be: a) $2,000; b) $4,000; c) $1,600; d) $1,800.

Exercises

3-1.   Bartle Company uses a job-order cost system and applies overhead with a predetermined overhead rate based on direct labor-hours. At the beginning of the year the estimated total manufacturing overhead for the year was $150,000 and the estimated level of activity was 100,000 direct labor-hours. At the end of the year, cost records revealed that actual overhead costs of $160,000 had been incurred and that 105,000 direct labor hours had been worked.

a. The predetermined overhead rate for the year was $_____

b. Manufacturing overhead cost applied to work in process during the year was $_____

c. The amount of underapplied or overapplied overhead cost for the year was $_____

3-2. The following selected account balances are taken from the books of Pardoe Company as of January 1 of the most recent year:

Cash		Work in Process		Accounts Payable		Sales	
12,000		40,000			75,000		

Accounts Receivable		Finished Goods		Salaries and Wages Payable		Cost of Goods Sold	
48,000		100,000			12,000		

Prepaid Insurance		Accumulated Depreciation					
8,000			120,000				

Raw Materials		Manufacturing Overhead					
30,000							

The following data relate to the activities of Pardoe Company during the year:
1. Raw materials purchased on account, $150,000.
2. Raw materials issued to production, $145,000 (all direct materials).
3. Advertising cost incurred for the year, $50,000 (credit accounts payable).
4. Utilities cost incurred for the factory, $35,000 (credit accounts payable).
5. Salaries and wages costs incurred: direct labor, $250,000 (30,000 hours); indirect labor, $75,000; selling and administrative, $140,000.
6. Depreciation recorded for the year, $20,000, of which 75% related to the factory and 25% related to selling and administrative functions.
7. Other factory overhead costs incurred for the year, $30,000 (credit accounts payable).
8. Other selling and administrative expenses incurred for the year, $25,000 (credit accounts payable).
9. Prepaid insurance of $4,000 expired during the year; all of this is related to the factory.
10. The company applies overhead on the basis of direct labor-hours at $5.50 per hour.
11. The cost of goods manufactured for the year totaled $550,000.
12. Goods that cost $540,000 according to their job cost sheets were sold on account for $800,000.
13. Collections on account from customers during the year totaled $790,000.
14. Cash disbursed during the year: on accounts payable, $300,000; for salaries and wages, $460,000.

Required:
a. Post the above entries directly to Pardoe Company's T-accounts on the previous page. Key your entries with the numbers 1-14.
b. Compute the ending balance in each T-account.
c. Is overhead underapplied or overapplied for the year? Close the balance to Cost of Goods Sold. (Key the entry as #15.)
d. Prepare an income statement for the year using the form that appears below.

PARDOE COMPANY
Income Statement

Sales .... $_____

Less cost of goods sold ....   _____

Gross margin ....   _____

Less operating expenses:

_____ .... $_____

_____ ....   _____

_____ ....   _____

_____ ....   _____   _____

Net Income .... $_____

3-3.   The following data were taken from the Precision Milling Machine, Inc., cost records for the current year. Compute the amount of raw materials used in production during the year:

Raw materials inventory, beginning	10,000
Raw materials inventory, ending	15,000
Purchases of raw materials	145,000

_____

_____

_____

_____

_____

_____

_____

_____

3-4.   Suppose all of the raw materials used in production by Precision Milling Machine in the preceding exercise were direct materials. The company has supplied the following additional information:

Direct labor cost...	$240,000
Manufacturing overhead applied	90,000
Work in process inventory, beginning	60,000
Work in process inventory, ending.....................	75,000

Compute the cost of goods manufactured for the year.

_____

_____

_____

_____

_____

_____

_____

_____

3-5.   Precision Milling Machine company has supplied the following additional information. Use this data together with your answer to exercise 3-4 above to compute the (adjusted) Cost of Goods Sold for the company. Close out any balance in Manufacturing Overhead to Cost of Goods Sold.

Actual manufacturing overhead incurred	88,000
Finished goods inventory, beginning	120,000
Finished goods inventory, ending	145,000

_____

_____

_____

_____

_____

_____

_____

3-6.   **Critical thought writing exercise:** Quality Foods, Inc., is a major producer of canned vegetables, fruits, and other goods. This year the company planned a normal year of producing canned goods and set its predetermined overhead rate the same as in other years. However, during the year a major freeze in key growing areas wiped out much of the expected fruit crop and the company was able to do little canning of fruit. A large amount of the manufacturing overhead cost associated with producing canned goods consists of depreciation and other fixed costs. Would you expect Quality Foods, Inc., to have underapplied or overapplied manufacturing overhead cost this year? Explain.

_____

_____

_____

_____

_____

_____

_____

_____

_____

Answers to Questions and Exercises

True or False

1. T Job-order costing is used when many different kinds of products are made.

2. T Process costing is generally used when output is homogeneous.

3. F Only direct materials and direct labor are direct costs; manufacturing overhead cannot be easily identified with specific jobs.

4. T Estimates are used since a rate must be developed before the period begins.

5. F The predetermined overhead rate is usually computed on an annual basis in order to smooth out month-by-month variations in cost and activity.

6. T Indirect costs are charged to the Manufacturing Overhead account.

7. T A separate job cost sheet is prepared for each job entered into production, and is used to accumulate costs as they are charged to the job.

8. F Actual manufacturing overhead costs are charged to the Manufacturing Overhead account—not to Work in Process.

9. F Selling and administrative expenses are period costs, not product costs; thus, they are deducted as expenses on the income statement in the period they are incurred.

10. T This is true by definition.

11. T A debit balance in Manufacturing Overhead would mean that more overhead cost was incurred than was applied to Work in Process. Thus, manufacturing overhead would be underapplied.

12. F Any balance in the Manufacturing Overhead account (not Work in Process) should be closed to Cost of Goods Sold or allocated among ending inventories and Cost of Goods Sold. Work in Process is an inventory account that appears on the balance sheet.

13. T By definition, this is how under- or overapplied overhead cost is computed.

Multiple Choice

1. b The job cost sheet is used to accumulate direct materials, direct labor, and overhead costs.

2. b The journal entry would be:

Raw Materials	30,000	
Cash or Accounts Payable		30,000

3. d The journal entry would be:

Work in Process	15,000	
Manufacturing Overhead	5,000	
Raw Materials		20,000

4. a The journal entry would be:

Work in Process	20,000	
Manufacturing Overhead	10,000	
Administrative Salaries Expense	40,000	
Wages and Salaries Payable		70,000

5. d The journal entry would be:

Finished Goods	120,000	
Work in Process		120,000

6. c The journal entry would be:

Work in Process	30,000	
Manufacturing Overhead		30,000

7. c Under- or overapplied overhead represents the difference between actual overhead cost and applied overhead cost. The computation in this case would be:

Actual overhead cost	$90,000
Applied overhead cost	92,000
Overapplied overhead cost	$(2,000)

8. a   The predetermined overhead rate is $60,000 ÷ 40,000 hours = $1. 50 per hour.

Actual overhead cost	$65,100
Applied overhead cost ($1.50 × 42,000 hours)	63,000
Underapplied overhead cost.	$ 2,100

9. a   The solution would be:

Work in Process

Balance	18,000	190,000	Finished
Direct materials	35,000		
Direct labor	60,000		
Overhead applied*	90,000		
Balance	13,000		

*$60,000 × 150% = $90,000

10. b   The cost of goods manufactured represents the costs of goods completed during a period; thus, it is the amount transferred from Work in Process to Finished Goods.

11. c   If overhead is overapplied, then more overhead cost has been added to jobs than has been incurred. Therefore, too much overhead cost will have been assigned to jobs.

12. a   The computations would be:

Work in Process	$ 40,000	20%
Finished Goods	60,000	30
Cost of Goods Sold	100,000	50
Total cost	$200,000	100%

20% × $10,000 = $2,000.

Exercises

3-1.   a. $\dfrac{\$150,000}{100,000 \text{ DLHs}} = \$1.50 \text{ per DLH}$

b.   105,000 DLHS × $1.50 = $157,500 applied

c.
Actual overhead cost	$160,000
Applied overhead cost	157,500
Underapplied overhead cost	$ 2,500

3-2.   The answers to parts (a) and (b) are on the following page.

c.   Overhead is overapplied by $6,000.

d.

PARDOE COMPANY
Income Statement

Sales		$800,000
Less cost of goods sold ($540,000 – $6,000)		534,000
Gross margin		266,000
Less operating expenses:		
Advertising expense	$ 50,000	
Salaries expense	140,000	
Depreciation expense	5,000	
Other expenses	25,000	220,000
Net Income		$ 46,000

3-2.   a. & b.

Cash	
Bal. 12,000	760,000 (14)
(13) 790,000	
42,000	

Accumulated Depreciation	
	120,000 Bal.
	20,000 (6)
	140,000

Sales	
	800,000 (12a)

Accounts Receivable	
Bal. 48,000	790,000 (13)
(12a) 800,000	
58,000	

Manufacturing Overhead	
(4) 35,000	165,000 (10)
(5) 75,000	
(6) 15,000	
(7) 30,000	
(9) 4,000	
(15) 6,000	6,000

Cost of Goods Sold	
(12b) 540,000	6,000 (15)
534,000	

Prepaid insurance	
Bal. 8,000	4,000 (9)
4,000	

Salaries Expense	
(5) 140,000	

Raw Materials	
Bal. 30,000	145,000 (2)
(1) 150,000	
35,000	

Accounts Payable	
(14) 300,000	75,000 Bal.
	150,000 (1)
	50,000 (3)
	35,000 (4)
	30,000 (7)
	25,000 (8)
	65,000

Advertising Expense	
(3) 50,000	

Work in Process	
Bal. 40,000	550,000 (11)
(2) 145,000	
(5) 250,000	
(10) 165,000	
50,000	

Depreciation Expense	
(6) 5,000	

Finished Goods	
Bal. 100,000	540,000 (12b)
(11) 550,000	
110,000	

Salaries and Wages Payable	
(14) 460,000	12,000 Bal.
	465,000 (5)
	17,000

Other Selling and Administrative Expenses	
(8) 25,000	

3-3.	Raw materials inventory, beginning	$ 10,000
	Add: Purchases of raw materials	145,000
	Total	155,000
	Deduct: Raw materials inventory, ending	15,000
	Raw materials used in production	$140,000

3-4.	Direct materials	$140,000
	Direct labor	240,000
	Manufacturing overhead applied	90,000
	Total manufacturing cost	470,000
	Add: Beginning work in process inventory	60,000
		530,000
	Deduct: Ending work in process inventory	75,000
	Cost of goods manufactured	$455,000

3-5.	Finished goods inventory, beginning	$120,000
	Add: Cost of goods manufactured	455,000
	Goods available for sale	575,000
	Deduct: Finished goods, ending	145,000
	Unadjusted cost of goods sold	430,000
	Deduct: Overapplied overhead (see below)	2,000
	Adjusted cost of goods sold	$428,000
	Actual manufacturing overhead cost incurred.	$88,000
	Applied manufacturing overhead cost	90,000
	Overapplied overhead cost	($ 2,000)

3-6.   Quality Foods, Inc. would probably have underapplied manufacturing overhead cost for the year. Since a large amount of the manufacturing overhead cost associated with producing canned goods is fixed, the company's *actual* manufacturing overhead costs would be about as planned. However, the company's *applied* manufacturing overhead costs would be less than planned since less productive activity would take place in the plant due to the loss of the fruit crop. Thus, with a large amount of *actual* overhead cost and less than planned *applied* overhead cost, the company would end the year with an underapplied balance in its Manufacturing Overhead account.

Chapter 4

Systems Design: Process Costing

Chapter Study Suggestions

The chapter is divided into five main parts. The first part is a comparison of job-order and process costing. Exhibit 4-1, which outlines the differences between the two costing methods, is the key item in this part. The second part gives a perspective of cost flows in a process costing system. Study Exhibit 4-4 carefully, as well as the journal entries that follow. The third part deals with a concept known as equivalent units of production. Pay particular attention to the computations in Exhibits 4-6 and 4-7.

The fourth part illustrates preparing a production report using the weighted-average method. The production report is complex and you will need to devote a large portion of your time to learning how it is constructed. Exhibit 4-10 provides a detailed example of a production report.

Appendix 4A illustrates preparing a production report using the FIFO method. If your instructor assigns this appendix, pay particular attention to Exhibit 4A-3 which shows the format of a FIFO production report, and Exhibit 4A-4 which compares the weighted-average and FIFO methods.

CHAPTER HIGHLIGHTS

A. Process costing is used in industries that produce homogeneous products such as bricks, flour, and cement. It is also used in assembly-type operations, as well as in utilities producing gas, water, and electricity.

B. Process costing is similar to job-order costing in three ways:

1. The same basic purposes exist in both systems, which are to assign material, labor, and overhead costs to products and to provide a mechanism for computing unit costs.

2. Both systems use the same basic manufacturing accounts: Manufacturing Overhead, Raw Materials, Work in Process, and Finished Goods.

3. Costs flow through these accounts in basically the same way in both systems.

C. Process costing differs from job-order costing in four ways:

1. A single product is produced on a continuous basis, and each unit is essentially the same.

2. Costs are accumulated by department, rather than by job.

3. The department production report (rather than the job cost sheet) is the key document showing the accumulation and disposition of cost.

4. Unit costs are computed by department (rather than by job). This computation is made on the department production report.

D. A *processing department* is any work center where work is performed on a product and where materials, labor, or overhead costs are added. Processing departments have two common features. First, the activity carried out in the department is performed uniformly on all units passing through it. And second, the output of the department is basically homogeneous.

E. Less effort is usually required to use a process costing system than a job-order costing system; costs only need to be traced to a few processing departments rather than to many individual jobs.

F. Exhibit 4-4 provides a T-account model of cost flows in a process costing system. A separate work in process account is maintained for each processing department. Materials, labor, and overhead costs are entered directly into each processing department's work in process account.

G. Once costs have been totaled for a department, the department's output must be determined so that unit costs can be computed. Units that have only been partially completed pose a problem. A unit that is only 10% complete should not count as much as a unit that has been completed and transferred on to the next department.

1. *Equivalent units* are the number of whole, complete units one could obtain from the materials and effort contained in completed and partially completed units. Equivalent units are computed using the following formula:

$$\text{Equivalent units} = \begin{array}{c}\text{Number of} \\ \text{partially completed} \\ \text{units}\end{array} \times \begin{array}{c}\text{Percentage} \\ \text{completion}\end{array}$$

2. The *equivalent units of production* is used to compute the cost per equivalent unit. Under the weighted-average method discussed in the chapter, the equivalent units of production are determined as follows:

Units completed and transferred out	XXX
+ Equivalent units of ending inventory	XXX
= Equivalent units of production	XXX

H. A separate cost per equivalent unit figure is computed within each processing department for each cost category. The cost categories may include:

1. Costs of prior departments associated with units transferred into the department.

2. Materials costs added in the department.

3. Direct labor costs added in the department.

4. Manufacturing overhead costs applied to the department.

In process costing, direct labor costs and manufacturing overhead costs are often combined into one cost category called *conversion costs*.

I. Note the following points concerning process costing.

   1. A separate equivalent units of production figure and a separate cost per equivalent unit must be computed for each cost category.

   2. Units transferred out of the department to the next department—or, in the case of the last department, to finished goods—are considered to be 100% complete with respect to the work done by the transferring department.

   3. The first processing department will not have a cost category for the costs of units transferred in, but subsequent departments will have such a cost category. Units in process in a department are considered to be 100% complete with respect to the costs of the prior department.

J. The purpose of the *production report* is to summarize all of the activity that takes place in a department's work in process account for a period. A production report has three parts:

   1. A *quantity schedule*, which shows the flow of units through the department, and the computation of equivalent units for each cost category for the period.

   2. A statement showing computation of the *cost per equivalent unit* for each cost category for the period.

   3. A *reconciliation* of all cost flows into and out of the department during the period.

It would be a good idea to refer to Exhibit 4-10 as you go through the explanation of the production report below.

K. The purpose of the *quantity schedule* on the production report is to show the flow of units through a department. The schedule shows the number of units to be accounted for in a department and it shows how those units have been accounted for.

   1. The format of the quantity schedule under the weighted-average method is:

Units to be accounted for:	
Work in process, beginning	XXX
Started into production	XXX
Total units	XXX

Units accounted for as follows:

Transferred out to the next department or to finished goods	XXX
Work in process, ending	XXX
Total units	XXX

   2. The equivalent units for the units transferred out and for the ending work in process inventory are listed next to the quantity schedule on the production report.

L. The second step in preparing a production report is to compute the *cost per equivalent unit* for each cost category. Under the weighted-average method, this involves summing the costs from the beginning inventory with any costs added during the period to arrive at total cost. This figure is then divided by the equivalent units of production for the cost category to determine the cost per equivalent unit.

M. The final step in a production report is to prepare a *reconciliation* of all costs. Costs are accounted for as either transferred out during the period or assigned to the ending work in process inventory. Costs are determined as follows:

   1. Units transferred out. These units are presumed to be 100% complete. (If they were not complete with respect to the work done in the department, they would not be transferred out.) The costs of units transferred out are computed by multiplying the number of units transferred out by the cost per equivalent unit for each cost category. These costs are then summed.

   2. Units in ending work in process inventory. Within each cost category, the number of equivalent units is multiplied by the cost per equivalent unit for that cost category. These costs are then summed.

N. Study Exhibit 4-10 carefully; it shows how the weighted-average method works. Note that this method combines costs from the beginning inventory with costs from the current period. It is called the weighted-average method because it averages together costs from the prior period with costs of the current period.

O. *Operation costing* is a hybrid system containing elements of both job-order and process costing. It is most commonly used when products use different materials but follow the same basic processing steps. For example, a factory that assembles personal computers might make many different models—all of which go through an assembly department, a testing department, and a packing and shipping department. However, the components (materials) used would depend upon the particular model of personal computer being made.

1. In operation costing, products are handled in batches and each batch is charged with its own specific materials. In this sense, operation costing is similar to job-order costing.

2. Labor and overhead costs are accumulated by department and these costs are assigned to the batches on an average per unit basis as in process costing.

Appendix 4A: FIFO Method

A. The *FIFO method* is more complex than the weighted-average method, but is considered to be more accurate. The FIFO method keeps units and costs from the prior period separate from the units and costs of the current period.

B. The production report under the FIFO method is similar to the production report under the weighted-average method. There are, however, important differences in the reports that are easy to overlook. Refer to Exhibit 4A-3 as you read the explanations that follow below.

C. The format of the quantity schedule under the FIFO method follows:

Units to be accounted for:
  Work in process, beginning   XXX
  Started into production   XXX
    Total units   XXX

Units accounted for as follows:
  Transferred out:
    Units from beginning inventory   XXX
    Units started and completed   XXX
  Work in process, ending   XXX
    Total units   XXX

D. Under the FIFO method, the equivalent units of production are determined as follows:

  Equivalent units to complete the
    beginning inventory   XXX
  + Units started and completed this period XXX
  + Equivalent units in ending inventory   XXX
  = Equivalent units of production   XXX

The difference between the equivalent units of production under the FIFO method and under the weighted-average method is that the weighted-average method includes the equivalent units in beginning inventory whereas the FIFO method does not. This is most easily seen from the following alternative method of computing the equivalent units of production under the FIFO method:

  + Units completed this period   XXX
  − Equivalent units in beginning inventory XXX
  + Equivalent units in ending inventory XXX
  = Equivalent units of production   XXX

E. After preparing the quantity schedule and computing the equivalent units, the costs per equivalent unit are computed. Under the FIFO method, these costs are computed using *only* costs added during the current period.

F. The final step in the production report is to prepare a reconciliation of all costs for the period.

1. Costs are accounted for as either transferred out during the period or assigned to the ending work in process inventory.

2. In computing the cost of units transferred out under the FIFO method, the units in beginning work in process inventory are kept separate from the units started and completed during the current period.

G. In comparing the weighted-average and FIFO methods, four points should be noted:

1. In most situations, the two methods will produce unit costs that are nearly the same.

2. From a standpoint of cost control, the FIFO method is superior to the weighted-average method since it separates the costs of the prior period from the costs of the current period.

3. Although the FIFO method is more complex to apply than the weighted-average method, this complexity is no longer a significant factor because of the power of computers.

4. Any difference in costs reported using the FIFO and weighted-average methods must be due to the existence of beginning work in process inventories. Because work in process inventories are reduced in a JIT program, the differences between the two methods will diminish.

REVIEW AND SELF TEST
Questions and Exercises

True or False

Enter a T or an F in the blank to indicate whether the statement is true or false.

___ 1. A utility such as a water company would typically use a process costing system.

___ 2. Under process costing it is important to identify the materials, labor, and overhead costs associated with a particular customer's order just as under job-order costing.

___ 3. In a process costing system, the production report replaces the job cost sheet.

___ 4. Costing is more difficult in a process costing system than in a job-order costing system.

___ 5. In a process costing system, a work in process account is maintained for each processing department.

___ 6. Operation costing employs aspects of both job-order and process costing systems.

___ 7. Since costs are accumulated by department in a process costing system, there is no need for a finished goods inventory account.

___ 8. In process costing, costs incurred in a department are not transferred to the next department.

___ 9. If beginning work in process inventory contains 500 units that are 60% complete, then the inventory contains 300 equivalent units.

___ 10. (Appendix 4A) Under the FIFO method, costs in the beginning work in process inventory are kept separate from costs of the current period.

___ 11. (Appendix 4A) Under the FIFO method, units in beginning work in process inventory are treated as if they were completed before any new units are completed.

___ 12. (Appendix 4A) Under the FIFO method, units transferred out are treated in separate blocks—one block consisting of the units in the beginning inventory, and the other block consisting of the units started and completed during the period.

___ 13. (Appendix 4A) The weighted-average and FIFO methods will typically produce significantly different unit costs when there are no beginning work in process inventories.

___ 14. (Appendix 4A) From the standpoint of cost control, the weighted-average method is superior to the FIFO method.

Multiple Choice

Choose the best answer or response by placing the identifying letter in the space provided.

___ 1. The mixing department of Deerdon Company started 4,800 units into process during the month. Five hundred units were in the beginning inventory and 300 units were in the ending inventory. How many units were completed and transferred out during the month? a) 5,000; b) 4,600; c) 5,300; d) 5,100.

___ 2. Last month the welding department of Eager Company started 8,000 units into production. The department had 2,000 units in process at the beginning of the month, which were 60% complete with respect to conversion costs, and 3,000 units in process at the end of the month which were 30% complete with respect to conversion costs. A total of 7,000 units were completed and transferred to the next department during the month. Using the weighted-average method, the equivalent units of production for conversion costs for the month would be: a) 7,900; b) 8,500; c) 9,200; d) 9,500.

___ 3. (Appendix 4A) Refer to the data in question 2 above. Using the FIFO method, the equivalent units of production for conversion costs for the month would be: a) 8,300; b) 7,700; c) 6,700; d) 7,300.

___ 4. At the beginning of the month, there were 200 units in process in the stamping department of Farwest Industrials Inc. that were 70% complete with respect to materials. During the month 2,000 units were transferred to the next department. At the end of the month, 100 units were still in process and they were 60% complete

43

with respect to materials. The materials cost in the beginning work in process inventory was $2,721 and $39,200 of materials costs were added during the month. Using the weighted-average method, what is the cost per equivalent unit for materials costs? a) $19.06; b) $20.35; c) $20.42; d) $19.60.

___ 5. The weaving department of Dolly Company had $8,000 of conversion cost in its beginning work in process inventory and added $64,000 of conversion cost during the month. The department completed 37,000 units during the month and had 10,000 units in the ending work in process inventory that were 30% complete as to conversion cost. Using the weighted-average method, the amount of cost assigned to the units in ending inventory would be: a) $12,600; b) $4,800; c) $11,200; d) $5,400.

___ 6. The heat treatment department at Northern Pipe is the third department in a sequential process. The work in process account for the department would consist of: a) costs transferred in from the prior department; b) materials costs added in the heat treatment department; c) conversion costs added in the heat treatment department; d) all of the above.

___ 7. (Appendix 4A) Mercer Corp. uses the FIFO method in its process costing system. The cutting department had $6,000 of materials cost in its beginning work in process inventory and $75,000 in materials cost was added during the period. The equivalent units of production for materials for the period was 20,000. The cost per equivalent unit for materials would be: a) $3.75; b) $4.05; c) $0.30; d) $3.30.

___ 8. (Appendix 4A) Danmount Corp. uses the FIFO method in its processing costing system. The cost per equivalent unit of conversion cost in the first processing department was $4.00 this month. There were 1,000 units in beginning work in process inventory in the department at the beginning of the month. These 1,000 units were 30% complete with respect to conversion cost and had already incurred $1,000 in conversion cost. A total of 10,000 units were transferred to the second processing department during the month. There were 2,000 units in the ending work in process inventory at the end of the month and they were 60% complete with respect to conversion cost. How much conversion cost would have been assigned to the units that were transferred to the second processing department during the month? a) $40,000; b) $39,800; c) $38,800; d) $44,600.

Exercises

4-1.　Diebold Company has a process costing system. Data relating to activities in the Mixing Department for March follow:

	Units	Percent Completed Materials	Percent Completed Conversion
Work in process, March 1	5,000	100%	60%
Units started into production	80,000		
Work in process, March 31	2,000	100%	50%

All materials are added at the start of processing in the Mixing Department.

Using the weighted-average method, fill in the following quantity schedule and a computation of equivalent units for the month:

	Quantity Schedule
Units to be accounted for:	
Work in process, beginning (all materials;	
_____% conversion cost added last month)	_____
Started into production	_____
Total units	_____

		Equivalent Units Materials	Equivalent Units Conversion
Units accounted for as follows:			
Transferred out during the month	_____	_____	_____
Work in process, ending (all materials;			
_____% conversion cost added this month)	_____	_____	_____
Total units	_____	_____	_____

4-2.   Minden Company uses the weighted-average method in its process costing system. Complete the cost reconciliation section of the production report below for the Welding Department, the first processing department in the company.

Production Report, Welding Department

Quantity schedule and equivalent units

Units to be accounted for:	Quantity Schedule
Work in process, beginning (all materials, 20% labor and overhead added last month)	5,000
Started into production	75,000
Total units	80,000

Units accounted for as follows:		Materials	Labor	Overhead
		Equivalent Units		
Transferred out	72,000	72,000	72,000	72,000
Work in process, ending (all materials, 75% labor and overhead added this month)	8,000	8,000	6,000	6,000
Total units and equivalent units of production	80,000	80,000	78,000	78,000

Costs per equivalent unit

	Total Cost	Materials	Labor	Overhead	Whol Unit
Cost to be accounted for:					
Work in process, beginning	$ 9,500	$ 4,500	$ 3,000	$ 2,000	
Cost added by the department	460,500	75,500	231,000	154,000	
Total cost (a)	$470,000	$ 80,000	$234,000	$156,000	
Equivalent units of production(b)		80,000	78,000	78,000	
Cost per equivalent unit (a)÷(b)		$1.00 +	$3.00 +	$2.00 =	$6.0

Cost reconciliation

		Materials	Labor	Overhead
		Equivalent Units		
Cost accounted for as follows:				
Transferred out	$_____	_____	_____	_____
Work in process, ending:				
Materials	_____	_____		
Labor	_____		_____	
Overhead	_____			_____
Total work in process, ending	_____			
Total cost	$ 470,000			

4-3.   (Appendix 4A) Sinclair Company uses the FIFO method in its process costing system. Complete the cost reconciliation section of the production report for the Cooking Department, the first processing department in the company.

Production Report, Cooking Department

Quantity schedule and equivalent units	*Quantity Schedule*			
Units to be accounted for:				
Work in process, begin. (all materials; 25% labor and overhead added last month)	8,000			
Started into production	62,000			
Total units	70,000			

		Equivalent Units		
		Materials	*Labor*	*Overhead*
Units accounted for as follows:				
Transferred out:				
Units from the beginning inventory	8,000	—	6,000	6,000
Units started and completed this month	57,000	57,000	57,000	57,000
Work in process, ending (all materials; 80% labor and overhead added this month)	5,000	5,000	4,000	4,000
Total units and equivalent units of production	70,000	62,000	67,000	67,000

Costs per equivalent unit	*Total Cost*	*Materials*	*Labor*	*Overhead*	*Whole Unit*
Cost to be accounted for:					
Work in process, beginning	$ 16,800				
Added by the department (a)	260,500	$93,000	$134,000	$33,500	
Total cost	$277,300				
Equivalent units of production(b)		62,000	67,000	67,000	
Cost per equivalent unit, (a) ÷ (b)		$ 1.50 +	$ 2.00 +	$ 0.50 =	$ 4.00

Cost reconciliation		*Equivalent Units*		
		Materials	*Labor*	*Overhead*
Cost accounted for as follows:				
Transferred out:				
From the beginning inventory:				
Cost in the beginning inventory	$_____			
Cost to complete these units:				
Materials	_____	_____		
Labor	_____		_____	
Overhead	_____			_____
Total cost	_____			
Units started and completed	_____	_____	_____	_____
Total cost transferred	_____			
Work in process, ending:				
Materials	_____	_____		
Labor	_____		_____	
Overhead	_____			_____
Total work in process, ending	_____			
Total cost	$ 277,300			

Answers to Questions and Exercises

True or False

1. T Process costing is widely used by utilities since their output (water, gas, electricity) is homogeneous.

2. F Since units are indistinguishable from each other, there is no need to identify costs by customer order.

3. T See the discussion in Exhibit 4-1.

4. F Costing is usually easier in a process costing system since material and labor costs do not have to be traced to individual jobs.

5. T In a process costing system a work in process inventory account is maintained for each department. There is also a production report for each department.

6. T In operation costing, materials are often handled as in job-order costing while labor and overhead costs are handled as in process costing.

7. F A finished goods inventory account is needed in a process costing system for unsold finished units, just as in a job-order costing system.

8. F As units move from one department to another, the costs that have been incurred to that point are transferred forward with the units.

9. T 500 units × 60% = 300 equivalent units.

10. T Costs in the beginning work in process inventory are kept separate from costs of the current period so that the cost per equivalent unit of units produced during the current period will reflect only current period costs.

11. T The FIFO method assumes that the units that are first in (i.e., in beginning inventory) are the first out (i.e., completed).

12. T This point is illustrated in Exhibit 4A-3.

13. F When there are no beginning inventories, the weighted-average and FIFO methods will produce identical results.

14. F The reverse is true—from a standpoint of cost control, the FIFO method is superior to the weighted-average method.

Multiple Choice

1. a

Beginning inventory	500
Add: Units started into process	4,800
Total units	5,300
Less ending inventory	300
Completed and transferred	5,000

2. a.

Units completed and transferred	7,000
Work in process, ending:	
3,000 units × 30%	900
Equivalent units of production	7,900

3. c.

Work in process, beginning:	
2,000 units × 40%*	800
Units started and completed**	5,000
Work in process, ending:	
3,000 units × 30%	900
Equivalent units of production	6,700

*100% - 60% = 40%
**7,000 units - 2,000 units = 5,000 units.

4. b

Cost in beginning work in process	$ 2,721
Cost added during the month	39,200
Total cost (a)	$41,921
Units transferred out	2,000
Equivalent units in ending work in process inventory (100 × 60%)	60
Equivalent units (b)	2,060
Cost per EU (a) ÷ (b)	$20.35

5. d Cost in beginning work
     in process $ 8,000
     Cost added during the year   64,000
          Total cost (a) $72,000

     Units transferred out   37,000
     Equivalent units in ending
       work in process inventory
       (10,000 × 30%)   3,000
     Equivalent units (b)   40,000
     Cost per EU (a) ÷ (b) $1.80

        3,000 units × $1.80 = $5,400.

6. d Costs in the department's work in proc-
     ess inventory account include costs
     transferred in from the previous
     department and any costs added in the
     department itself—including materials,

labor, and overhead. Labor and overhead together equal conversion cost.

7. a $75,000 ÷ 20,000 units = $3.75 per unit.

8. b Transferred to the next department:
     From the beginning inventory:
       Cost in the beginning
         inventory $ 1,000
       Cost to complete these
         units (70% × 1,000 × $4)   2,800
     Units started and completed
       this month (9,000* × $4)   36,000
                                   $39,800

     * 10,000 units transferred –
       1,000 units in beginning inventory

Exercises

4-1.

	Quantity Schedule	Equivalent Units	
		Materials	*Conversion*
Units to be accounted for:			
Work in process, beginning (all materials; 60% conversion cost added last month)	5,000		
Started into production	80,000		
Total units	85,000		
Units accounted for as follows:			
Transferred out during the month	83,000	83,000	83,000
Work in process, ending (all materials; 50% conversion cost added this month)	2,000	2,000	1,000
Total units	85,000	85,000	84,000

4-2.

	Total Cost	Equivalent Units		
		Materials	*Labor*	*Overhead*
Cost accounted for as follows:				
Transferred out: (72,000 units × $6)	$432,000	72,000	72,000	72,000
Work in process, ending:				
Materials cost ($ 1 per EU)	8,000	8,000		
Labor cost ($3 per EU)	18,000		6,000	
Overhead cost ($2 per EU)	12,000			6,000
Total work in process, ending	38,000			
Total cost	$470,000			

4-3.

	Total Cost	Equivalent Units		
		Materials	Labor	Overhead
Cost accounted for as follows:				
Transferred out:				
Units from the beginning inventory:				
Cost in the beginning inventory	$ 16,800			
Cost to complete these units:				
Materials ($1.50 per EU)	—	—		
Labor ($2.00 per EU)	12,000		6,000	
Overhead ($0.50 per EU)	3,000			6,000
Total cost	31,800			
Units started and completed during the month: (57,000x $4.00)	228,000	57,000	57,000	57,000
Total cost transferred	259,800			
Work in process, ending:				
Materials cost ($1.50 per EU)	7,500	5,000		
Labor cost ($2.00 per EU)	8,000		4,000	
Overhead cost ($0.50 per EU)	2,000			4,000
Total work in process, ending	17,500			
Total cost	$277,300			

Chapter 5

Cost Behavior: Analysis and Use

Chapter Study Suggestions

Chapter 5 expands on the discussion of fixed and variable costs that was started in Chapter 2. In addition, the chapter introduces a new cost concept—mixed costs—and shows how mixed costs can be broken down into their basic fixed and variable elements. Focus the bulk of your study time on the section titled "The Analysis of Mixed Costs" that is found midway through the chapter. Pay particular attention to how a *cost formula* is derived and how a cost formula is used to predict future costs at various levels.

Memorize the elements of the equation Y = a + bX. You need to understand this equation to complete most of the homework exercises and problems. At the end of the chapter, a new format for the income statement is introduced that emphasizes cost behavior. Exhibit 5-12 illustrates the format of the contribution income statement. *This format should be memorized*—you will be using it throughout the rest of the book.

The appendix at the end of the chapter shows the computations required to analyze mixed costs using the least-squares regression method.

CHAPTER HIGHLIGHTS

A. A *variable cost* is a cost that varies, in total, in proportion to changes in the level of activity. Variable costs are constant on a *per unit* basis.

   1. Activity is usually measured in terms of the volume of goods produced or services provided by the organization. However, for specific purposes other measures of activity may be used such as patients admitted to a hospital, number of machinery setups performed, number of sales calls made, and so on.

   2. A variable cost is shown graphically in Exhibit 5-1. Note that a variable cost is a straight line that goes right through zero (i.e., the origin) on the graph.

B. A *fixed cost* is a cost that remains constant in total within the relevant range. Fixed cost per unit varies inversely with changes in activity. As activity increases, per unit fixed costs fall.

   1. Fixed costs can generally be classified into committed and discretionary fixed costs.

      a. *Committed fixed costs* relate to investments in facilities, equipment, and the basic organization of a firm. These costs are difficult to adjust.

      b. *Discretionary fixed costs* result from annual decisions by management to spend in certain areas, such as advertising, research, and management development programs. These costs are easier to modify than committed fixed costs.

   2. If there is a big enough change in activity, even committed fixed costs may change. Exhibit 5-6 illustrates this idea. However, within the band of activity known as the relevant range, total fixed cost is constant.

C. A *mixed cost* (or semivariable cost) is a cost that contains both variable and fixed cost elements. Exhibit 5-7 illustrates a mixed cost.

   1. Examples of mixed costs include electricity, costs of processing bills, costs of admitting patients to a hospital, and maintenance.

   2. The fixed portion of a mixed cost represents the cost of providing capacity. The variable portion represents the additional cost of using capacity.

   3. Several methods are available for breaking a mixed cost down into its basic variable and fixed cost elements using past records of cost and activity. These methods are the high-low method, the scattergraph method, and the least-squares regression method.

D. The relevant range and curvilinear costs.

   1. For simplicity, a strict linear relation between cost and volume is usually assumed. However, many cost relationships are curvilinear, such as illustrated in Exhibit 5-4.

   2. The manager's straight-line assumption is reasonable since any small portion of a curvilinear cost can be approximated by a straight line. The *relevant range* is the range of activity within which a particular straight line is a valid approximation to the curvilinear cost.

E. Cost formula for a mixed cost.

   1. The fixed and variable cost elements of a mixed cost can be expressed in a *cost formula*, which can be used to predict costs at all levels of activity within the relevant range. This formula is expressed as follows:

   $$Y = a + bX$$
   where:
       Y = *dependent variable* (the total mixed cost)
       a = vertical intercept (the total fixed cost)
       b = slope of the line (the variable rate)
       X = *independent variable* (the activity level)

   2. Each of the methods discussed below can be used to estimate the variable cost per unit (b) and the total fixed cost (a). Then with the use of the cost formula, the expected amount of total cost (Y) can be computed for any expected activity level (X) within the relevant range.

F. The *high-low method* bases its estimates of the variable and fixed elements of a mixed cost on data at the high and low levels of activity.

   1. The high-low method uses a variation of the "rise over run" formula for the slope of a straight line. The difference in cost observed between the two extremes is divided by the change in activity to estimate the amount of variable cost. The formula is:

$$\text{Variable cost per unit of activity} = \frac{\text{Change in cost}}{\text{Change in activity}}$$

2. The estimated variable cost per unit of activity (i.e., variable rate) is then used to estimate the fixed cost as follows:

Total cost at the high activity level .... $XXX
Less variable portion:
   Variable rate × high activity level..... XXX
   Fixed portion of the mixed cost .... $ XXX

3. The high-low method is quick, but is not reliable. It is based on costs and activity for only two periods—the periods with the highest and lowest levels of activity. Other data are ignored and these two periods tend to be unusual and may not be representative of typical cost behavior.

G. In the *scattergraph method*, costs at various levels of activity are plotted on a graph. A *regression line* is then fitted to the plotted points using a ruler. This requires judgment since there are no precise rules concerning how to draw the line.

1. The slope of the regression line is the estimated variable cost per unit of activity. The vertical intercept is the estimated total fixed cost.

2. The scattergraph method is usually better than the high-low method, since all the observed data points can be taken into account when the straight line is drawn. In contrast, the high-low method relies entirely on just two data points.

3. However, the high-low method is subjective and relatively imprecise.

H. The *least-squares regression method* fits a regression line to past cost and activity data by means of a formula.

1. The formula results in straight line that minimizes the sum of the squared errors from the regression line. The computations are covered in the appendix to the chapter.

2. *Multiple regression* analysis should be used when more than one factor causes a cost to vary. Due to the complexity of the formulas, multiple regression analysis is almost always performed using statistical software on a computer.

I. The *contribution approach* to preparation of an income statement emphasizes cost behavior.

1. The *traditional format* for income statements groups expenses into functional categories:

Sales .... $XXX
Less: Cost of Goods Sold XXX
Gross Margin XXX
Less: Admin. and Selling Expense XXX
Net Income .... $XXX

2. The *contribution approach*, in contrast, groups expenses according to their cost behavior.

Sales .... $XXX
Less: Variable Expenses XXX
Contribution Margin XXX
Less: Fixed Expenses XXX
Net Income .... $XXX

3. Note that the *contribution margin* is determined by deducting variable expenses from sales.

4. The contribution approach is very useful to managers for internal reports since it emphasizes the behavior of costs. As you will see in later chapters, this is very important in planning, budgeting, controlling operations, and in performance evaluation. However, in external reports the traditional format that emphasizes cost by function must be used.

Appendix 5A: Least-Squares Regression

A. The formulas for computing the variable cost per unit (b) and total fixed cost(a) using the least-squares regression method are:

$$b = \frac{n(\sum XY) - (\sum X)(\sum Y)}{n(\sum X^2) - (\sum X)^2}$$

$$a = \frac{(\sum Y) - b(\sum X)}{n}$$

where n is the number of observations; X is the activity; and Y is the cost.

1. To use these formulas, you must first compute Y, X, XY, and X^2. The "" indicates that you take a sum. For example, to compute XY, you must multiply X and Y for each observation and then sum the results.

2. The variable cost per unit (b) is computed before you compute the total fixed cost (a) because b is used in the formula for a.

REVIEW AND SELF TEST
Questions and Exercises

True or False

Enter a T or an F in the blank to indicate whether the statement is true or false.

___ 1. Variable costs are costs that change, in total, in proportion to changes in the activity level.

___ 2. In cost analysis work, activity is known as the dependent variable.

___ 3. Within the relevant range, the higher the activity level, the lower the fixed cost per unit.

___ 4. Contribution margin and gross margin are synonymous terms.

___ 5. Contribution margin is the difference between sales and variable expenses.

___ 6. Discretionary fixed costs arise from annual decisions by management to spend in certain areas.

___ 7. Advertising is a committed fixed cost.

___ 8. A mixed cost is a cost that contains both manufacturing and non-manufacturing costs.

___ 9. Within the relevant range, the relation between cost and activity is approximately a straight line.

___ 10. In order for a cost to be variable, it must vary with either units produced or services provided.

___ 11. A cost formula produced by the high-low method and a cost formula produced by the scattergraph method would be the same except for rounding error.

___ 12. The contribution approach to the income statement organizes costs according to behavior, rather than according to function.

Multiple Choice

Choose the best answer or response by placing the identifying letter in the space provided.

___ 1. A company's cost formula for maintenance is $Y = \$4,000 + \$3X$, where X is machine hours. During a period in which 2,000 machine hours are worked, the expected maintenance cost would be: a) $12,000; b) $6,000; c) $10,000; d) $4,000.

___ 2. The costs associated with a company's basic facilities, equipment, and organization are known as: a) committed fixed costs; b) discretionary fixed costs; c) mixed costs; d) variable costs.

___ 3. Last year, Barker Company's sales were $240,000, its fixed costs were $50,000, and its variable costs were $2 per unit. During the year, 80,000 units were sold. The contribution margin was: a) $200,000; b) $240,000; c) $30,000; d) $80,000.

___ 4. An example of a discretionary fixed cost would be: a) depreciation on equipment; b) rent on a factory building; c) salaries of top management; d) items a, b, and c are all discretionary fixed costs; e) none of the above.

___ 5. In March, Espresso Express had electrical costs of $225.00 when the total volume was 4,500 cups of coffee served. In April, electrical costs were $227.50 for 4,750 cups of coffee. Using the high-low method, what is the estimated fixed cost of electricity per month? a) $200; b) $180; c) $225; d) $150.

Exercises

5-1.   Data concerning the electrical costs at Doughboy Company follow:

	Machine hours	Electrical cost
Week 1..............	6,800 hrs.	$1,770
Week 2..............	6,000 hrs.	1,650
Week 3..............	5,400 hrs.	1,560
Week 4..............	7,900 hrs.	1,935

a.   Using the high-low method of cost analysis, what is the variable rate per machine hour?

	Cost	Machine Hours
High activity level	_____	_____
Low activity level	_____	_____
Change	_____	_____

$$\frac{\text{Change in cost}}{\text{Change in activity}} = \frac{\underline{\hspace{3cm}}}{\underline{\hspace{3cm}}} = \$\underline{\hspace{2cm}}\text{per machine hour}$$

b.   Using the high-low method of cost analysis, what is the total fixed cost?

Total cost at the high activity level...   _____
Less variable cost element:

_____.....................   _____

Fixed cost element ....   _____

c.   Express the cost formula for electrical costs in the form Y = a + bX: _____

5-2.   (Appendix 5A) Data on a week's activity in the shipping department of Osan, Inc. are given below:

	Units Shipped	Shipping Cost		
	X	Y	XY	X²
Monday............................	12	$ 580	$ 6,960	144
Tuesday............................	17	655	11,135	289
Wednesday......................	10	550	5,500	100
Thursday.........................	7	505	3,535	49
Friday..............................	9	535	4,815	81
Saturday.	5	475	2,375	25
Totals ()	60	$3,300	$34,320	688

a.   Using the least squares method, estimate the variable cost per unit shipped:

$$b = \frac{n(\sum XY) - (\sum X)(\sum Y)}{n(\sum X^2) - (\sum X)^2}$$

n = _____   X = _____   Y = _____

XY = _____   X² = _____

$$b = \frac{(\underline{\hspace{3cm}}) - (\underline{\hspace{3cm}})(\underline{\hspace{3cm}})}{(\underline{\hspace{2cm}}) - (\underline{\hspace{2cm}})^2}$$

b = _____

b.   Estimate the fixed cost per day:

$$a = \frac{(\sum Y) - b(\sum X)}{n}$$

Substitute the "b" term you solved for in part (a) in the above equation along with Y, X, and n:

$$a = \frac{(\underline{\hspace{3cm}}) - (\underline{\hspace{3cm}})(\underline{\hspace{3cm}})}{(\underline{\hspace{3cm}})}$$

a = _____

c.   Express the cost formula for shipping costs in the form Y = a + bX: _____

5-3.   During July, Cramer's, Inc., a wholesale distributor of a unique software product, sold 500 units. The company's income statement for the month follows:

CRAMER'S, INC.
Income Statement
For the Month Ended July 31

Sales ($100 per unit)		$50,000
Less cost of goods sold ($60 per unit)		30,000
Gross margin		20,000
Less operating expenses:		
Commissions ($6 per unit)	$3,000	
Salaries	8,000	
Advertising	6,000	
Shipping ($2 per unit)	1,000	18,000
Net income		$ 2,000

Redo the company's income statement for the month in the contribution format. Assume that cost of goods sold, commissions, and shipping expenses are variable costs and salaries and advertising expenses are fixed costs.

CRAMER'S, INC.
Income Statement
For the Month Ended July 31

Sales .... $_____

Less _____ :

    _____............ $_____

    _____............   _____

    _____............   _____   _____

Contribution margin ....   _____

Less _____ :

    _____............   _____

    _____............   _____   _____

Net income .... $_____

Answers to Questions and Exercises

True or False

1. T   This is the definition of a variable cost.

2. F   Activity is the independent variable.

3. T   Fixed costs vary inversely with changes in activity when expressed on a per unit basis.

4. F   Contribution margin is sales less variable expenses; gross margin is sales less cost of goods sold.

5. T   This is true by definition.

6. T   Discretionary fixed costs are re-evaluated each year by management.

7. F   Advertising is a discretionary fixed cost since the advertising program is typically re-evaluated on an annual basis.

8. F   Mixed costs contain both variable and fixed cost elements.

9. T   By definition, a straight line is a reasonable approximation to the real cost behavior within a relevant range.

10. F   There can be many measures of activity besides units produced and units sold. Other measures include miles driven, number of occupied beds in a hospital, and number of flight hours.

11. F   The two methods are different and will produce the same results only if the regression line is drawn through the high and low points when the scattergraph method is used.

12. T   The contribution approach groups variable costs together and fixed costs together; thus, the income statement is organized according to cost behavior.

Multiple Choice

1. c
Fixed cost	$ 4,000
Variable cost: $3 × 2,000 hours	6,000
Total cost	$10,000

2. a   Committed fixed costs relate to basic facilities, equipment, and organization.

3. d
Sales	$240,000
Less variable costs:	
$2 × 80,000 units	160,000
Contribution margin	$ 80,000

4. e   All of the listed costs are generally considered to be committed fixed costs.

5. b

	Cost	Cups
High activity level	$227.50	4,750
Low activity level	225.00	4,500
Change	$ 2.50	250

$$\frac{\text{Change in cost}}{\text{Change in activity}} = \frac{\$2.50}{250} = \$0.01 \text{ per cup}$$

Total cost at the high activity	$227.50
Less variable cost element:	
4,750 cups × $0.01 per cup	47.50
Fixed cost element	$180.00

Exercises

5-1.   a.   Variable cost per machine-hour:

	Cost	Machine Hours
High activity level	$1,935	7,900
Low activity level	1,560	5,400
Change	$ 375	2,500

$$\frac{\text{Change in cost}}{\text{Change in activity}} = \frac{\$375}{2,500 \text{ hours}} = \$0.15 \text{ per machine hour}$$

b.   Total fixed cost:

Total cost at the high activity level..........................	$1,935
Less variable cost element:	
7,900 hours × $0.15 per hour	1,185
Fixed cost element	$ 750

c.   Cost formula for electrical costs: $750 per period, plus $0.15 per machine hour, or
Y= $750 + $0.15X

5-2.   a.   Compute the variable cost per unit shipped as follows:

$$b = \frac{n(\sum XY) - (\sum X)(\sum Y)}{n(\sum X^2) - (\sum X)^2}$$

n = 6   X = 60   Y = $3,300   XY = $34,320   X² = 688

$$b = \frac{6(34,320) - (60)(3,300)}{6(688) - (60)^2} = \$15 \text{ per unit shipped}$$

b.   Compute the fixed cost per day as follows:

$$a = \frac{(\sum Y) - b(\sum X)}{n}$$

$$a = \frac{(3,300) - 15(60)}{6} = \$400$$

c.   Y = $400 + $15X

5-3.

CRAMER'S, INC.
Income Statement
For the Month Ended July 31

Sales ($100 per unit)		$50,000
Less variable expenses:		
Cost of goods sold ($60 per unit)	$30,000	
Commissions ($6 per unit)	3,000	
Shipping ($2 per unit)	1,000	34,000
Contribution margin		16,000
Less fixed expenses:		
Salaries	8,000	
Advertising	6,000	14,000
Net income		$ 2,000

Chapter 6

Cost-Volume-Profit Relationships

Chapter Study Suggestions

Chapter 6 is one of the key chapters in the book. Many of the chapters ahead depend on concepts developed here. You should study several sections in the chapter with particular attention. The first of these is the section titled, "Contribution Margin." Note how changes in the contribution margin affect net income. The next section to be studied with particular care is titled "Contribution Margin Ratio." The contribution margin ratio is used in much of the analytical work in the chapter.

Another section to be given particular attention is titled "Some Applications of CVP Concepts." Much of the homework material is drawn from this section. The section titled "Break-Even Analysis" also forms the basis for much of the homework material. *You should memorize the break-even formulas in this section.* Finally, the section titled "The Concept of Sales Mix" shows how to use CVP analysis when there is more than one product.

When studying the material in the chapter, try especially hard to understand the logic behind the solutions.

CHAPTER HIGHLIGHTS

A. The contribution margin is a key concept that will be used throughout the chapter and in subsequent chapters.

1. The contribution margin is defined as the difference between total sales and total variable expenses:

Sales	XXX
Less variable expenses	XXX
Contribution margin	XXX

2. The unit contribution margin is defined as the difference between the unit selling price and the unit variable expenses:

Selling price per unit	XXX
Less variable expenses per unit	XXX
Unit contribution margin	XXX

3. The relation between the contribution margin and the unit contribution margin is simple. The contribution margin is equal to the unit contribution margin multiplied by the number of units sold:

Unit contribution margin	XXX
× Unit sales	XXX
Contribution margin	XXX

The term "total contribution margin" is also commonly used to refer to the contribution margin.

4. Net income is equal to the contribution margin less fixed expenses.

Sales	XXX
Less variable expenses	XXX
Contribution margin	XXX
Less fixed expenses	XXX
Net income	XXX

5. The *break-even point* is the sales at which profits are zero and the total contribution margin just equals fixed expenses.

6. The relation between contribution margin and net income provides a very powerful planning tool. It gives the manager the ability to predict what profits will be at various activity levels without the necessity of preparing detailed income statements.

a. The contribution margin must first cover fixed expenses. If it doesn't, there is a loss. Below the break-even point, every unit sold reduces the loss by the amount of the unit contribution margin.

b. Once the break-even point is reached, net income will increase by the amount of the unit contribution margin for each additional unit sold.

B. The contribution margin ratio (CM ratio), which expresses the contribution margin as a percentage of sales, is another very powerful concept.

1. The contribution margin ratio can be computed in two ways:

$$\text{CM ratio} = \frac{\text{Contribution margin}}{\text{Sales}}$$

$$\text{CM ratio} = \frac{\text{Unit contribution margin}}{\text{Unit selling price}}$$

2. The contribution margin ratio is used to predict the change in total contribution margin that would result from a given change in dollar sales:

Change in dollar sales	XXX
× CM ratio	XXX
Change in contribution margin	XXX

3. If fixed expenses do not change, any increase (or decrease) in contribution margin will be reflected dollar-for-dollar in increased (or decreased) net income.

4. The CM ratio is particularly useful when a company has multiple products since the CM ratio is expressed in terms of total dollar sales, which provides a useful common denominator in which all of the products' volumes can be measured.

C. Cost-volume-profit (CVP) concepts can be used in many day-to-day decisions. Carefully study the examples given under the heading "Some Applications of CVP Concepts" in the early part of the chapter.

1. Notice that each solution makes use of either the unit contribution margin or the CM ratio. This underscores the importance of these two concepts.

2. Also notice that several of the examples employ *incremental analysis*. An incremental analysis is based only on costs and revenues that *differ* between alternatives.

D. Two particular examples of CVP analysis, called *break-even analysis* and *target profit analysis*, are often used by managers. Break-even analysis is a special case of target profit analysis, so target profit analysis will be considered first.

1. Target profit analysis is used when a manager would like to know how much the company would have to sell to attain a specific target profit. The analysis is based on the following equation:

Profits = Sales – Variable expenses – Fixed expenses

In CVP analysis, this equation is often rewritten in the following format:

Sales = Variable expenses + Fixed expenses + Profits

All of the problems can be worked using this basic equation and simple algebra. However, handy formulas are available for answering some of the more common questions. These formulas are discussed below.

2. Target profit analysis is used in two basic variations. In the first variation, the manager would like to know how many *units* would have to be sold to attain the target profit. In the second variation, the manager would like to know how much total dollar sales would have to be to attain the target profit. The formulas are:

$$\frac{\text{Units sold to}}{\text{attain target profit}} = \frac{\text{Fixed expenses} + \text{Target profit}}{\text{Unit contribution margin}}$$

$$\frac{\text{Dollar sales to}}{\text{attain target profit}} = \frac{\text{Fixed expenses} + \text{Target profit}}{\text{CM ratio}}$$

E. Break-even occurs when profit is zero. Thus, break-even analysis is really just a special case of target profit analysis in which the target profit is zero. Therefore, the break-even formulas can be stated as follows:

$$\frac{\text{Breakeven point}}{\text{in units sold}} = \frac{\text{Fixed expenses}}{\text{Unit contribution margin}}$$

$$\frac{\text{Breakeven point}}{\text{in total sales dollars}} = \frac{\text{Fixed expenses}}{\text{CM ratio}}$$

F. CVP and break-even analysis can also be done graphically. Exhibits 6-1 and 6-2 show how a CVP graph is prepared and interpreted. A cost-volume-profit graph shows the relations between sales, costs, and volume throughout wide ranges of activity.

G. The *margin of safety* is the excess of budgeted (or actual) sales over the break-even volume of sales. It is the amount by which sales can drop before losses begin to be incurred. The margin of safety can be stated in terms of either dollars or as a percentage of sales:

Total budgeted (or actual) sales XXX
Less break-even sales XXX
Margin of safety XXX

$$\frac{\text{Margin of safety}}{\text{percentage}} = \frac{\text{Margin of safety}}{\text{Total budgeted (or actual) sales}}$$

H. A company's cost structure—the relative proportion of fixed and variable costs— has an impact on how sensitive the company's profits are to changes in sales. A company with low fixed costs and high variable costs will tend to have a lower CM ratio than a company with a greater proportion of fixed costs. Such a company will tend to have less volatile profits, but at the risk of losing substantial profits if sales trend sharply upward.

I. *Operating leverage* refers to the effect a given percentage increase in sales will have on net income.

1. The "degree of operating leverage" is defined as follows:

$$\frac{\text{Degree of operating}}{\text{leverage}} = \frac{\text{Contribution margin}}{\text{Net income}}$$

2. A given *percentage* in sales is multiplied by the degree of operating leverage to estimate the resulting *percentage* change in net income.

Percentage change in dollar sales ... XXX
× Degree of operating leverage XXX
Percentage change in net income ... XXX

3. *The degree of operating leverage is not constant.* It changes as sales increase or decrease. In general, *the degree of operating leverage decreases the further a company moves away from its break-even point.*

J.   When a company has more than one product, the *sales mix* can be crucial. The sales mix is the relative proportions in which the company's products are sold.

1. When CVP analysis involves more than one product, the analysis is normally based on the *overall contribution margin ratio*. This is computed exactly like the CM ratio is computed in a single product company except that overall figures are used for both the contribution margin and sales:

$$\text{Overall CM ratio} = \frac{\text{Overall contribution margin}}{\text{Overall sales}}$$

2. When there is more than one product, the *overall* CM ratio is used in the target profit and break-even formulas instead of the CM ratio.

3. As the sales mix changes *the overall CM ratio will also change.* If the shift is toward the less profitable products, then the overall CM ratio will fall; if the shift is toward the more profitable products, then the overall CM ratio will rise.

K.   CVP analysis ordinarily relies on the following assumptions:

1. The selling price is constant; it does not change as unit sales change.

2. Costs are linear. Costs can be accurately divided into variable and fixed elements. The variable cost per unit is constant and the total fixed cost is constant.

3. In multi-product situations, the sales mix is constant.

4. In manufacturing companies, inventories do not change.

REVIEW AND SELF TEST
Questions and Exercises

True or False

Enter a T or an F in the blank to indicate whether the statement is true or false.

___ 1. If product A has a higher unit contribution margin than product B, then product A will also have a higher CM ratio than product B.

___ 2. The break-even point occurs where the contribution margin is equal to total variable expenses.

___ 3. The break-even point can be expressed either in terms of units sold or in terms of total sales dollars.

___ 4. If the sales mix changes, the break-even point may change.

___ 5. For a given increase in sales dollars, a high CM ratio will result in a greater increase in profits than will a low CM ratio.

___ 6. If sales increase by 8%, and the degree of operating leverage is 4, then profits can be expected to increase by 12%.

___ 7. The degree of operating leverage remains the same at all levels of sales.

___ 8. Once the break-even point has been reached, net income will increase by the unit contribution margin for each additional unit sold.

___ 9. A shift in sales mix toward less profitable products will cause the overall break-even point to fall.

___ 10. Incremental analysis focuses on the differences in costs and revenues between alternatives.

___ 11. If a company's cost structure shifts toward greater fixed costs and lower variable costs, one would expect the company's CM ratio to fall.

___ 12. One way to compute the break-even point is to divide total sales by the CM ratio.

___ 13. When there is more than one product, a key assumption in break-even analysis is that the sales mix will not change.

Multiple Choice

Choose the best answer or response by placing the identifying letter in the space provided.

___ 1. Lester Company has a single product. The selling price is $50 and the variable cost is $30 per unit. The company's fixed expenses are $200,000 per month. What is the company's unit contribution margin? a) $50; b) $30; c) $20; d) $80.

___ 2. Refer to the data for Lester Company in question 1 above. What is the company's contribution margin ratio? a) 0.60; b) 0.40; c) 1.67; d) 20.00.

___ 3. Refer to the data for Lester Company in question 1 above. What is the company's break-even in sales dollars? a) $500,000; b) $33,333; c) $200,000; d) $400,000.

___ 4. Refer to the data for Lester Company in question 1 above. How many units would the company have to sell to attain target profits of $50,000? a) 10,000; b) 12,500; c) 15,000; d) 13,333.

___ 5. The following figures are taken from Parker Company's income statement: Net income, $30,000; Fixed costs, $90,000; Sales, $200,000; and CM ratio, 60%. The company's margin of safety in dollars is: a) $150,000; b) $30,000; c) $50,000; d) $80,000.

___ 6. Refer to the data in question for Parker Company in 5 above. The margin of safety in percentage form is: a) 60%; b) 75%; c) 40%; d) 25%.

___ 7. Refer to the data for Parker Company in question 5 above. What is the company's total contribution margin? a) $110,000; b) $120,000; c) $170,000; d) $200,000.

___ 8. Refer to the data for Parker Company in question 5 above. What is the company's degree of operating leverage? a) 0.25; b) 0.60; c) 1.25; d) 4.00.

___ 9. If sales increase from $400,000 to $450,000, and if the degree of operating leverage is 6, net income should increase by: a) 12.5%; b) 75%; c) 67%; d) 50%.

___ 10. In multiple product firms, a shift in the sales mix from less profitable products to more profitable products will cause the company's break-even point to: a) increase; b) decrease; c) there will be no change in the break-even point; d) none of these.

___ 11. Herman Corp. has two products, A and B, with the following total sales and total variable costs:

	Product A	Product B
Sales	$10,000	$30,000
Variable expenses	$4,000	$24,000

What is the overall contribution margin ratio? a) 70%; b) 50%; c) 30%; d) 40%.

Exercises

6-1. Hardee Company sells a single product. The selling price is $30 per unit and the variable expenses are $18 per unit. The company's most recent annual contribution format income statement is given below:

Sales	$135,000
Less variable expenses	81,000
Contribution margin	54,000
Less fixed expenses	48,000
Net Income	$ 6,000

a. Compute the contribution margin per unit. $_____

b. Compute the CM ratio. _____%

c. Compute the break-even point in sales dollars. $_____

d. Compute the break-even point in units sold. _____ units

e. How many units must be sold next year to double the company's profits? _____ units

f. Compute the company's degree of operating leverage. _____

g. Sales for next year (in units) are expected to increase by 5%. Using the degree of operating leverage, compute the expected percentage increase in net income. _____%

h. Verify your answer to part g above by preparing a contribution format income statement showing a 5% increase in sales.

Sales	$_____
Less variable expenses	_____
Contribution margin	_____
Less fixed expenses	_____
Net income	$_____

6-2.   Using the data below, construct a cost-volume-profit graph like the one in Exhibit 6-2 in the text:

Sales: 15,000 units at $10 each.
Variable expenses: $6 per unit.
Fixed expenses: $40,000 total.

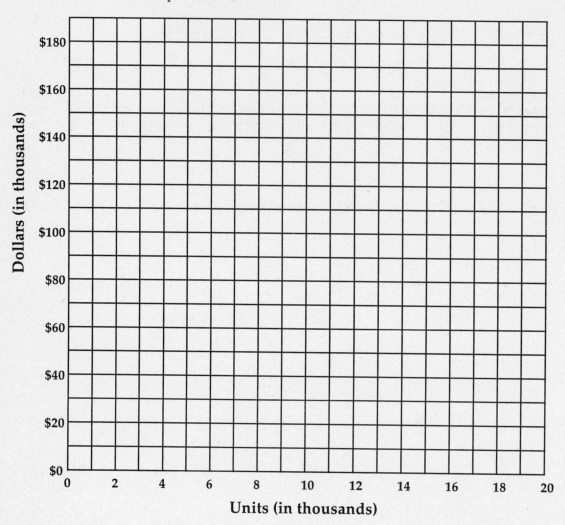

What is the break-even point in units? _____.

What is the break-even point in total sales dollars? _____

6-3. Seaver Company produces and sells two products, X and Y. Data concerning the products follow:

	Product X	Product Y
Selling price per unit	$10	$12
Variable expenses per unit	6	3
Contribution margin per unit	$ 4	$ 9

In the most recent month, the company sold 400 units of Product X and 600 units of Product Y. Fixed expenses are $5,000 per month.

a. Complete the following contribution format income statement for the most recent month (carry percentages to one decimal point):

	Product X		Product Y		Total	
	Amount	%	Amount	%	Amount	%
Sales	$_____	____	$_____	____	$_____	___
Less variable expenses	_____	____	_____	____	_____	___
Contribution margin	$_____	____	$_____	____	_____	==
Less fixed expenses					_____	
Net income (loss)					$_____	

b. Compute the company's overall monthly break-even point in sales dollars. $ _____

c. If the company continues to sell 1,000 units, in total, each month, but the sales mix shifts so that an equal number of units of each product is being sold, would you expect monthly net income to rise or fall? Explain.

_____

_____

_____

_____

_____

_____

d.   Refer to the data in part c above. If the sales mix shifts as explained, would you expect the company's monthly break-even point to rise or fall? Explain.

_____

_____

_____

_____

_____

_____

6-4.   **Critical thought writing exercise:** Able Company and Baker Company are competing firms that sell a product at the same price. Both companies are operating above the break-even point and have similar total profits. Able Company's costs are mostly variable, whereas Baker Company's costs are mostly fixed. In a time of increasing sales which company will tend to realize the most rapid increase in net income? Explain your answer.

_____

_____

_____

_____

_____

_____

_____

_____

_____

_____

_____

Answers to Questions and Exercises

True or False

1. F The CM ratio is the unit contribution margin divided by the unit selling price. One product might have a higher unit contribution than another, but its selling price may be lower.

2. F The break-even point occurs where profit is zero and the contribution margin is equal to fixed expenses.

3. T The break-even point can be computed in terms of units sold or sales dollars.

4. T A change in sales mix usually results in a change in the overall CM ratio. If the overall CM ratio changes, the break-even point will also change.

5. T The CM ratio measures how much of a sales dollar is translated into increased contribution margin and profit.

6. F Profits should increase by 32% = 4 × 8%.

7. F The degree of operating leverage decreases as a firm moves further and further from its break-even point.

8. T At the break-even point all fixed costs have been covered. All contribution margin generated from that point forward increases net income.

9. F The reverse is true—the overall break-even point will rise since the average CM ratio will be lower as a result of selling less profitable products.

10. T By definition, incremental analysis deals only with differences between alternatives.

11. F The reverse is true—one would expect the company's CM ratio to rise. Variable costs would be lower and hence the CM ratio would be higher.

12. F The break-even point is computed by dividing total *fixed costs* by the CM ratio.

13. T This is a key assumption since a change in the sales mix will change the break-even point.

Multiple Choice

1. c

Unit selling price	$50
Less unit variable expenses	30
Unit contribution margin	$20

2. b

Unit contribution margin	$ 20
Unit selling price	÷ $ 50
Contribution margin ratio	0.40

3. a

$$\text{Breakeven point in total sales dollars} = \frac{\text{Fixed expenses}}{\text{CM ratio}}$$

$$= \frac{\$200,000}{0.40} = \$500,000$$

4. b

$$\text{Units sold to attain target profit} = \frac{\text{Fixed expenses} + \text{Target profit}}{\text{Unit contribution margin}}$$

$$= \frac{\$200,000 + \$50,000}{\$20} = 12,500 \text{ units}$$

5. c

$$\frac{\$90,000}{0.60} = \$150,000 \text{ Breakeven sales}$$

Margin of safety = $200,000 − $150,000 = $50,000

6. d $50,000 ÷ $200,000 = 25%

7. b

Sales	$200,000
CM ratio	× 0.60
Contribution margin	$120,000

8. d

Contribution margin	$120,000
Net income	÷ $30,000
Operating leverage	4.0

9. b The computations are:

$$\text{Percentage change in sales} = \frac{\$450,000 - \$400,000}{\$400,000} = 12.5\%$$

Percentage change in dollar sales ...	12.5%
Degree of operating leverage	× 6.0
Percentage change in net income ...	75.0%

10. b A shift to more profitable products would result in an increase in the overall CM ratio. Thus, less sales would be needed to cover the fixed costs and the break-even point would therefore decrease.

11. c

	Product A	Product B	Total
Sales	$10,000	$30,000	$40,000
Variable expenses	4,000	24,000	28,000
Contribution margin	$ 6,000	$ 6,000	$12,000

Overall CM ratio = $12,000 ÷ $40,000 = 30%

Exercises

6-1. a.

	Per Unit	
Selling price	$30	100%
Less variable expenses	18	60
Unit contribution margin	$12	40%

b. CM ratio $= \dfrac{\text{Contribution margin}}{\text{Sales}} = \dfrac{\$54,000}{\$135,000} = 40\%$

c. Sales = Variable expenses + Fixed expenses + Profits
$X = 0.60X + \$48,000 + \$0$
$0.40X = \$48,000$
$X = \$48,000 \div 0.40$
$X = \$120,000$

Alternate solution:

$\dfrac{\text{Breakeven point}}{\text{in total sales dollars}} = \dfrac{\text{Fixed expenses}}{\text{CM ratio}} = \dfrac{\$48,000}{0.40} = \$120,000$

d. Sales = Variable expenses + Fixed expenses + Profits
$\$30Q = \$18Q + \$48,000 + \$0$
$\$12Q = \$48,000$
$Q = \$48,000 \div \$12$
$Q = 4,000 \text{ units}$

Alternate solution:

$\dfrac{\text{Breakeven point}}{\text{in units sold}} = \dfrac{\text{Fixed expenses}}{\text{Unit contribution margin}} = \dfrac{\$48,000}{\$12} = 4,000 \text{ units}$

e. Sales = Variable expenses + Fixed expenses + Profits
$\$30Q = \$18Q + \$48,000 + \$12,000$
$\$12Q = \$60,000$
$Q = \$60,000 \div \$12$
$Q = 5,000 \text{ units}$

Alternate solution:

$\dfrac{\text{Units sold to}}{\text{attain target profit}} = \dfrac{\text{Fixed expenses} + \text{Target profit}}{\text{Unit contribution margin}} = \dfrac{\$48,000 + \$12,000}{\$12} = 5,000 \text{ units}$

f. $\dfrac{\text{Degree of operating}}{\text{leverage}} = \dfrac{\text{Contribution margin}}{\text{Net income}} = \dfrac{\$54,000}{\$6,000} = 9.0$

g.
Percentage change in dollar sales 5%
Degree of operating leverage .... × 9.0
Percentage change in net income 45%

h. New sales volume: 4,500 units × 105% = 4,725 units

Sales (4,725 @ $30)	$141,750
Less variable expenses (4,725 @ $18)	85,050
Contribution margin	56,700
Less fixed expenses	48,000
Net income	$ 8,700
Present net income	$ 6,000
Expected increase: $6,000 × 45%	2,700
Expected net income (as above)	$ 8,700

6-2.   The completed CVP graph:

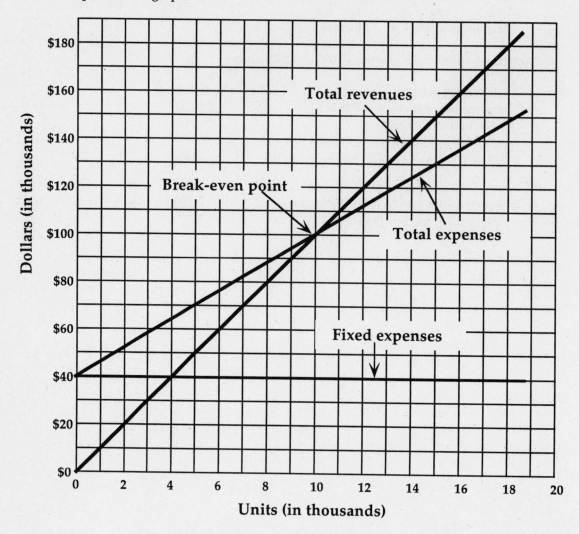

The break-even point in units is 10,000 units and in dollars is $100,000.

6-3.   a.   The completed income statement:

	Product X		Product Y		Total	
	Amount	*%*	*Amount*	*%*	*Amount*	*%*
Sales	$4,000	100	$7,200	100	$11,200	100.0
Less variable expenses	2,400	60	1,800	25	4,200	37.5
Contribution margin	$1,600	40	$5,400	75	7,000	62.5
Less fixed expenses					5,000	
Net income					$ 2,000	

b. $$\text{Breakeven point in total sales dollars} = \frac{\text{Fixed expenses}}{\text{CM ratio}} = \frac{\$5,000}{0.625} = \$8,000$$

c.   Monthly net income will fall. The shift in sales mix will mean that less of Product Y is being sold and more of Product X is being sold. Since Product Y has a higher contribution margin per unit than Product X, this means that less contribution margin in *total* will be available, and profits will therefore fall.

d.   The monthly break-even point will rise. As explained above, the shift in sales mix will be toward the less profitable Product X, which has a CM ratio of only 40% as compared to 75% for Product Y. Thus, the company's *overall* CM ratio will fall, and the break-even point will rise since less contribution margin will be available per unit to cover the fixed costs.

6-4.   Baker Company will realize the most rapid increase in net income. The reason is that Baker Company will have a higher contribution margin ratio (and contribution margin per unit) due to its lower variable costs. Thus, the company's contribution margin (and net income) will increase more rapidly than Able Company's as sales increase. The impact on net income can also be viewed in terms of operating leverage. Baker Company will have a higher degree of operating leverage than Able Company because of its higher contribution margin. Therefore, as sales increase, its net income will rise more rapidly than will Able Company's.

Chapter 7

Variable Costing — A Tool for Management

Chapter Study Suggestions

This chapter introduces a new method of determining unit product costs called variable costing. Throughout the chapter we compare variable costing with absorption costing, which was covered in Chapter 3.

In your study of Chapter 7, note that the difference between the two costing methods centers on the handling of the fixed portion of manufacturing overhead cost. This point is emphasized in Exhibit 7-1. Exhibits 7-2 through 7-6 are the heart of the chapter. These exhibits show how to compute unit product costs under both variable and absorption costing, and they show the impact of the two methods on net income. Be sure you understand the computations in these exhibits. You must thoroughly understand them to complete the homework assignment material.

CHAPTER HIGHLIGHTS

A. Two different methods can be used for determining unit product costs—*absorption costing* and *variable costing*.

1. Under *absorption costing*, all manufacturing costs, both variable and fixed, are included in unit product costs.

Direct materials	$XXX
Direct labor	XXX
Variable manufacturing overhead	XXX
Fixed manufacturing overhead	XXX
Unit product cost	$XXX

2. Under *variable costing*, only variable manufacturing costs—which usually consist of direct materials, direct labor, and variable manufacturing overhead—are included in unit product costs.

Direct materials	$XXX
Direct labor	XXX
Variable manufacturing overhead	XXX
Unit product cost	$XXX

a. Variable costing focuses on cost behavior. One of the strengths of this costing method is that it harmonizes fully with both the contribution approach and the cost-volume-profit concepts discussed in the prior chapter.

b. Under the variable costing method, fixed manufacturing costs are treated as period costs and are charged against revenues in the period in which they are incurred, just like selling and administrative expenses.

B. Under absorption costing, fixed manufacturing costs may be shifted from one period to another.

1. Units of product going into inventory carry a portion of the fixed manufacturing overhead costs of the period with them. If the units are not sold during the period, this results in a *deferral of fixed manufacturing overhead in inventory*. The fixed manufacturing overhead costs assigned to unsold units are not charged against revenues of the current period, but rather are held (or deferred) in inventory until the units are sold in some future period.

2. Exhibit 7-3 is a key exhibit illustrating the differences between variable and absorption costing. *Study this exhibit carefully before going on.*

C. Exhibit 7-4 is also a key exhibit that summarizes the relations between variable and absorption costing. Any difference in net income between the two methods can be traced to changes in the level of inventories.

1. When production and sales (in units) are equal and hence there is no change in inventories, the same net income will be reported under both variable and absorption costing.

2. When production exceeds sales (in units) and hence inventories increase, greater net income will be reported under absorption costing than under variable costing.

a. Some of the current period's fixed manufacturing overhead costs are deferred in the increased inventory

b. The amount of fixed manufacturing overhead cost deferred is equal to the increase in units in inventory multiplied by the fixed manufacturing overhead cost per unit.

3. When production is less than sales (in units) and hence inventories decrease, less net income will be reported under absorption costing than under variable costing.

a. *Fixed manufacturing overhead costs are released from inventory* when the units in inventory are sold.

b. The amount of fixed manufacturing overhead cost released is equal to the decrease in units in inventory multiplied by the fixed manufacturing overhead cost per unit.

4. Over an extended period of time, the net income reported by the two costing methods will tend to be the same. Over the long run sales can't exceed production, nor can production much exceed sales. The shorter the period, the more the net income figures will tend to differ.

D. The following form, which is illustrated in Exhibit 7-5, can be used to reconcile the variable costing and absorption costing net income figures.

Variable costing net income .... $XXX
Add: Fixed manufacturing overhead
    costs deferred in inventory
    under absorption costing XXX
Deduct: Fixed manufacturing overhead
    costs released from inventory
    under absorption costing .... (XXX)
Absorption costing net income .... $XXX

E. Exhibit 7-6 shows the effect of changes in production on net income—holding sales constant— under both variable and absorption.

1. Net income under variable costing *is not* affected by changes in production.

2. Net income under absorption costing *is* affected by changes in production.

a. Net income increases as production increases, and decreases as production decreases. This occurs because of changes in ending inventories. As inventories grow, fixed manufacturing overhead is deferred in inventories. As inventories shrink, fixed manufacturing overhead is released to the income statement.

b. These effects of changes in production on net income are a major drawback of absorption costing, since a company can manipulate its reported net income by simply changing the number of units produced.

F. Several factors should be considered by a manager when choosing between the variable and absorption costing methods.

1. Advantages of variable costing and the contribution approach.

a. The contribution approach works well with cost-volume-profit analysis. The data for the analysis can be taken directly from the contribution format income statement since it categorizes costs by how they behave.

b. Unlike absorption costing, variable costing net income is unaffected by changes in inventories.

c. Under variable costing, unit product costs are variable costs. Under absorption costing, unit product costs are a mixture of variable and fixed costs. This can be confusing to managers who tend to think of unit costs as variable costs.

d. Under variable costing, fixed costs are highlighted rather than buried in cost of goods sold and in inventories.

e. As discussed in later chapters, variable costing data make it easier to estimate the profitability of products.

f. Also as discussed in later chapters, variable costing works well with cost control methods such as standard cost variance analysis and flexible budgets.

g. Variable costing net income is closer to net cash flows than is absorption costing net income. This can be important for organizations that need to closely monitor their cash resources.

2. Nevertheless, absorption costing is the generally accepted method for preparing external financial reports and for preparing income tax returns. Variable costing is usually limited to internal use in a company. And because of the cost and possible confusion of maintaining two separate costing systems, many companies use absorption costing for internal and well as external reports.

G. When companies employ JIT, differences in net income between variable costing and absorption costing are reduced or eliminated.

1. The sometimes erratic movement of net income under absorption costing, and the differences in net income between absorption and variable costing, arise because of changing levels of inventory. Under JIT, goods are produced strictly to customers' orders, so inventories are largely eliminated.

2. Since inventories are largely eliminated, changes in inventories are insignificant. Thus, there is little opportunity for fixed manufacturing overhead costs to be shifted between periods under absorption costing. Thus, net income will be essentially the same whether variable and absorption costing is used, and the sometimes erratic movement of net income under absorption costing will be largely eliminated.

REVIEW AND SELF TEST
Questions and Exercises

True or False

Enter a T or an F in the blank to indicate whether the statement is true or false.

____ 1. Variable costing focuses on cost behavior in computing unit product costs.

____ 2. Under variable costing, variable selling and administrative expenses are treated as product costs.

____ 3. Product costs under the absorption costing method consist of direct materials, direct labor, and both variable and fixed manufacturing overhead.

____ 4. Selling and administrative expenses are treated as period costs under both the variable costing and absorption costing methods.

____ 5. Fixed manufacturing overhead costs are treated the same way under both the variable costing and absorption costing methods.

____ 6. Under absorption costing it is possible to defer some of the fixed manufacturing overhead costs of the current period to future periods.

____ 7. Variable costing will always produce a higher net income figure than will absorption costing.

____ 8. When production and sales are equal, the same net income will be reported regardless of whether variable costing or absorption costing is being used.

____ 9. When production exceeds sales, the net income reported under absorption costing will generally be greater than the net income reported under variable costing.

____ 10. When production is less than sales, the net income reported under absorption costing will generally be less than the net income reported under variable costing.

____ 11. When production exceeds sales, fixed manufacturing overhead costs are released from inventory under absorption costing.

____ 12. Changes in the level of production do not affect net income under the variable costing method.

____ 13. When sales are constant but the level of production fluctuates, the absorption costing method will produce a more stable net income pattern than will the variable costing method.

____ 14. The variable costing method is not generally accepted for external reporting or for income tax purposes.

____ 15. Absorption costing data are generally better suited for cost-volume-profit analysis than variable costing data.

Multiple Choice

Choose the best answer or response by placing the identifying letter in the space provided.

____ 1. White Company manufactures a single product and has the following cost structure:

Variable costs per unit:
Direct materials $3
Direct labor 4
Variable manufacturing overhead ... 1
Variable selling and admin. expense 2
Fixed costs per month:
Fixed manufacturing overhead $100,000
Fixed selling & admin. Expense 60,000

The company produces 20,000 units each month. The unit product cost under absorption costing is: a) $10; b) $13; c) $15; d) $12.

____ 2. Refer to the data in question 1 above. The unit product cost under variable costing would be: a) $8; b) $10; c) $13; d) $11.

____ 3. Refer to the data in question 1 above. Assume there are no beginning inventories and 20,000 units are produced and 19,000 units are sold in a month. If the unit selling price is $20, what is the net income under absorption costing for the month? a) $30,000; b) $38,000; c) $35,000; d) $42,000.

___ 4. Refer to the data in question 1 above. Assume there are no beginning inventories and 20,000 units are produced and 19,000 units are sold in a month. If the unit selling price is $20, what is the net income under variable costing for the month? a) $30,000; b) $38,000; c) $35,000; d) $42,000.

___ 5. Refer to your answers to parts 3 and 4 above. The net income differs between variable and absorption costing in this situation because: a) variable costs are $5,000 higher under variable costing; b) $5,000 in fixed manufacturing overhead has been deferred in inventories under absorption costing; c) $5,000 in fixed manufacturing overhead has been released from inventories under absorption costing; d) none of the above.

___ 6. Which of the following costs are treated as period costs under the variable costing method? a) fixed manufacturing overhead and both variable and fixed selling and administrative expenses; b) both variable and fixed manufacturing overhead; c) only fixed manufacturing overhead and fixed selling and administrative expenses.

___ 7. When production exceeds sales, fixed manufacturing overhead costs: a) are released from inventory under absorption costing; b) are deferred in inventory under absorption costing; c) are released from inventory under variable costing; d) are deferred in inventory under variable costing.

___ 8. When sales are constant but production fluctuates: a) net income will be erratic under variable costing; b) absorption costing will always show a net loss; c) variable costing will always show a positive net income; d) net income will be erratic under absorption costing.

___ 9. Last year, Peck Company produced 10,000 units and sold 9,000 units. Fixed manufacturing overhead costs were $20,000, and variable manufacturing overhead costs were $3 per unit. For the year, one would expect net income under the absorption costing method to be: a) $2,000 more than net income under the variable costing method; b) $5,000 more than net income under the variable costing method; c) $2,000 less than net income under the variable costing method; d) $5,000 less than net income under the variable costing method.

Chapter 7

Exercises

7-1.   Selected data relating to the operations of Dover Company for last year are given below:

Units in beginning inventory	-0-
Units produced	40,000
Units sold	35,000
Units in ending inventory	5,000

Selling price per unit	$27
Variable costs per unit:	
Direct materials	$7
Direct labor	6
Variable manufacturing overhead	3
Variable selling and administration ...	2
Fixed costs:	
Fixed manufacturing overhead	$160,000
Fixed selling and administration	140,000

a.   Assume that the company uses absorption costing.

   Compute the unit product cost. .... $_____

   Determine the value of the ending inventory. .... $_____

   Complete the following absorption costing income statement:

Sales		$_____
Cost of goods sold:		
Beginning inventory	_____	
Add cost of goods manufactured	_____	
Goods available for sale	_____	
Less ending inventory	_____	
Cost of goods sold		_____
Gross margin		_____
Less selling & admin. expenses:		
Variable selling & admin.	_____	
Fixed selling & admin.	_____	_____
Net income		$_____

82

b.   Assume that the company uses variable costing.

Compute the unit product cost. .... $_____

Determine the value of the ending inventory. .... $_____

Complete the following contribution format income statement using variable costing:

Sales   .... $_____
Less variable expenses:
    Variable cost of goods sold:
        Beginning inventory .... $_____
        Add variable manufacturing costs ....   _____
        Goods available for sale ....   _____
        Less ending inventory ....   _____
        Variable cost of goods sold ....   _____
        Variable selling & admin. ....   _____   _____
Contribution margin ....   _____
Less fixed expenses:
    Fixed manufacturing overhead ....   _____
    Fixed selling and administrative ....   _____   _____
Net Income .... $_____

c.   Reconcile the net incomes under the two methods by filling in the following form:

Variable costing net income .... $_____
Add fixed manufacturing overhead cost deferred
    in inventory under absorption costing ....   _____
Deduct fixed manufacturing overhead cost released
    from inventory under absorption costing ....   _____

Absorption costing net income .... $_____

7-2.   The Hodex Company manufactures and sells a unique product that has enjoyed brisk sales. The results of last month's operations are shown below (absorption costing basis):

Sales (10,000 units @ $20)	$200,000
Less cost of goods sold (10,000 units @ $14)	140,000
Gross margin	60,000
Less selling and administrative expenses	45,000
Net Income	$ 15,000

Variable selling and administrative expenses are $2 per unit. Variable manufacturing costs are $10 per unit, and fixed manufacturing overhead costs are $48,000 per month. There was no beginning inventory. The company produced 12,000 units during the month.

a.   Redo the company's income statement in the contribution format, using variable costing.

Sales   .... $_____

Less variable expenses:

　Variable cost of goods sold:

　　Beginning inventory .... $_____

　　Add variable manufacturing costs ....   _____

　　Goods available for sale ....   _____

　　Less ending inventory ....   _____

　　Variable cost of goods sold ....   _____

　　Variable selling & admin. ....   _____   _____

Contribution margin ....   _____

Less fixed expenses:

　Fixed manufacturing overhead ....   _____

　Fixed selling and administrative ....   _____   _____

　Net Income .... $_____

b.   Reconcile the variable costing and absorption costing net income figures:

Variable costing net income .... $_____

_____

_____ ....   _____

Absorption costing net income .... $_____

7-3.　**Critical thought writing exercise:** Lake Company uses absorption costing to prepare its financial statements for the annual report to shareholders. Last year, the company had $10,000,000 in sales and reported a $400,000 loss in its annual report. According to a CVP analysis prepared for management's use (using variable costing), $10,000,000 in sales is the break-even point for the company. Based on these data, was the company's ending inventory greater than, less than, or equal to its beginning inventory? Explain your answer.

_____

_____

_____

_____

_____

_____

_____

_____

_____

_____

_____

_____

Answers to Questions and Exercises

True or False

1. T Variable costing unit product costs include only variable manufacturing costs.

2. F Both variable and fixed selling and administrative expenses are period costs under variable costing, the same as under absorption costing. Apart from differences in the organization of the income statement, the only difference between the two costing methods lies in their treatment of fixed manufacturing overhead.

3. T All manufacturing costs are included as product costs under absorption costing.

4. T Selling and administrative expenses are never treated as product costs under either costing method.

5. F Under variable costing, fixed manufacturing overhead costs are treated as period costs; under absorption costing, fixed manufacturing overhead costs are treated as product costs.

6. T Fixed manufacturing overhead costs will be deferred to the future under absorption costing whenever production exceeds sales.

7. F Variable costing will produce a higher net income figure than absorption costing only when sales exceed production.

8. T When sales and production are equal, fixed manufacturing overhead cost is neither deferred in nor released from inventory under absorption costing.

9. T When production exceeds sales, fixed manufacturing overhead cost is deferred in inventory under absorption costing, thus causing net income to be higher than under variable costing.

10. T When production is less than sales, fixed manufacturing overhead cost is released from inventory under absorption costing, thus causing net income to be lower than under variable costing.

11. F When production exceeds sales, fixed manufacturing overhead costs are deferred in inventory under absorption costing as units of product are added to the inventory account.

12. T Changes in the number of units sold—not produced—affect net income under the variable costing method.

13. F If production fluctuates, the absorption costing method will produce an erratic net income pattern. The reason is that fixed manufacturing overhead cost will be shifted into and out of inventory as production goes up and down.

14. T Variable costing is used internally by managers for planning and decision-making purposes.

15. F The reverse is true—variable costing data are better suited for CVP analysis than absorption costing data.

Multiple Choice

1. b Variable manufacturing costs
       ($3 + $4 + $1) $ 8
       Fixed manufacturing costs
       ($100,000 ÷ 20,000 units)   5
       Unit product cost $13

2. a Only the variable manufacturing costs are treated as product costs under the variable costing method. Thus, the unit product cost is $3 + $4 + $1 = $8.

3. c The absorption costing net income is computed as follows:

Sales	$380,000
Cost of goods sold:	
Beginning inventory	-0-
Add COGM	260,000
Goods available for sale	260,000
Less ending inventory	13,000
Cost of goods sold	247,000
Gross margin	133,000
Less selling & admin. expenses:	
Variable selling & admin.	38,000
Fixed selling & admin.	60,000
Total selling & admin.	98,000
Net income	$ 35,000

4. a The variable costing net income is computed as follows:

Sales	$380,000
Less variable expenses:	
Variable cost of goods sold:	
Beginning inventory	-0-
Add variable manuf. costs	160,000
Goods available for sale	160,000
Less ending inventory	8,000
Variable cost of goods sold	152,000
Variable selling & admin.	38,000
Total variable expenses	190,000
Contribution margin	190,000
Less fixed expenses:	
Fixed manuf. overhead	100,000
Fixed selling & admin.	60,000
Total fixed expenses	160,000
Net income	$ 30,000

5. b Inventories increased by 1,000 units. Under absorption costing, $5 (=$100,000 ÷ 20,000 units) of fixed manufacturing overhead cost is applied to each unit that is produced. Thus, $5,000 in fixed manufacturing overhead costs are deferred in inventories and do not appear on the income statement as part of cost of goods sold.

6. a Fixed manufacturing overhead cost is expensed as incurred under variable costing. Also, both variable and fixed selling and administrative expenses are always treated as period costs under both variable or absorption costing.

7. b When production exceeds sales, units are added to inventory. Thus, fixed manufacturing overhead costs are deferred in inventory under absorption costing.

8. d When production fluctuates, net income will be erratic under absorption costing since fixed manufacturing overhead costs will be shifted into and out of inventory as production goes up and down.

9. a Under the absorption costing method, fixed manufacturing overhead cost per unit will be $2 (= $20,000 ÷ 10,000 units). If only 9,000 units are sold, then 1,000 units will go into inventory. Thus, under absorption costing, $2,000 in fixed manufacturing overhead cost will be deferred in inventory ($2 × 1,000 units = $2,000). Net income will therefore be $2,000 more under absorption costing than under variable costing.

Exercises

7-1. a.

Direct materials		$ 7
Direct labor		6
Variable manufacturing overhead		3
Fixed manufacturing overhead ($160,000 ÷ 40,000 units)		4
Unit product cost		$20
Ending inventory (5,000 units x $20)		$100,000

Absorption costing income statement

Sales (35,000 × $27)		$945,000
Cost of goods sold:		
Beginning inventory	$ -0-	
Add cost of goods manufactured		
(40,000 × $20)	800,000	
Goods available for sale	800,000	
Less ending inventory (5,000 × $20)	100,000	
Cost of goods sold		700,000
Gross margin		245,000
Less selling & admin. expenses:		
Variable selling & admin. (35,000 × $2)	70,000	
Fixed selling & admin.	140,000	210,000
Net income		$ 35,000

b.

Direct materials		$ 7
Direct labor		6
Variable manufacturing overhead		3
Unit product cost		$16
Ending inventory (5,000 units x $16)		$80,000

Variable costing income statement

Sales (35,000 × $27)		$945,000
Less variable expenses:		
Variable cost of goods sold:		
Beginning inventory	$ -0-	
Add variable manufacturing costs		
(40,000 × $16)	640,000	
Goods available for sale	640,000	
Less ending inventory (5,000 × $16)	80,000	
Variable cost of goods sold	560,000	
Variable selling & admin. (35,000 × $2)	70,000	630,000
Contribution margin		315,000
Less fixed expenses:		
Fixed manufacturing overhead	160,000	
Fixed selling and administrative	140,000	300,000
Net Income		$ 15,000

c. Reconciliation of variable costing and absorption costing net incomes:

Variable costing net income	$15,000

Add fixed manufacturing overhead cost deferred
    in inventory under absorption costing
        (5,000 units × $4 per unit) ....
	20,000

Deduct fixed manufacturing overhead cost released from inventory under absorption costing	-0-
Absorption costing net income	$35,000

7-2. a.

Sales (10,000 units × $20)			$200,000
Less variable expenses:			
Variable cost of goods sold:			
Beginning inventory	$ -0-		
Add variable manufacturing costs			
(12,000 units × $10)	120,000		
Goods available for sale	120,000		
Less ending inventory	20,000		
Variable cost of goods sold			
(10,000 units × $10)	100,000		
Variable selling & admin. (10,000 units × $2) ...	20,000	120,000	
Contribution margin		80,000	
Less fixed expenses:			
Fixed manufacturing overhead	48,000		
Fixed selling and administrative	25,000*	73,000	
Net Income		$ 7,000	

*$45,000 - (10,000 units × $2) = $25,000

b.

Variable costing net income	$ 7,000	

Add fixed manufacturing overhead cost deferred
    in inventory under absorption costing
      (2,000 units × $4*) ....
	8,000	

Absorption costing net income	$ 15,000	

*$48,000 ÷ 12,000 units produced = $4 per unit.

7-3.   Since Lake Company reported a loss when its sales were at the break-even level, fixed manufacturing overhead costs must have been released from inventory under the absorption costing approach. (The break-even point is computed assuming either that variable costing is used or that there is no change in inventory.) Therefore, the company's inventory level for the year decreased. When inventory levels decrease, fixed manufacturing overhead costs are released from inventory under absorption costing. Thus, the fixed manufacturing overhead costs released from inventory would have resulted in a loss for the year, even though from a variable costing point of view the company would have broken even.

Chapter 8

Activity-Based Costing:
A Tool to Aid Decision Making

Chapter Study Suggestions

Activity-based costing involves a number of steps. As a consequence, this chapter is one of the more complex chapters in the book. While it is important to learn each of the steps of activity-based costing, it is also important to keep the big picture in mind or you may get lost. As you go through the exhibits in the chapter, you may find it helpful to frequently refer to Exhibit 8-13 at the end of the chapter. This exhibit contains a summary of the steps involved in activity-based costing and shows how the exhibits fit together.

CHAPTER HIGHLIGHTS

A. As discussed in Chapters 2 and 3, traditional costing systems in manufacturing companies are primarily designed to provide product cost data for external financial reports rather than for internal decision making.

1. For external financial reports, all manufacturing costs must be assigned to products— even manufacturing costs that are not actually caused by any particular product. For example, the rent on the factory building is the same regardless(within limits) of which products are produced and how much is produced.

2. For external financial reports, non-manufacturing costs are not assigned to products— even non-manufacturing costs that are caused by specific products. For example, sales commissions are not included in product costs in traditional costing systems.

3. Since all manufacturing costs must be assigned to products for external financial reports, this means that the costs of idle capacity must also be assigned to products. As a consequence, products are charged for the costs of resources they don't use as well as for the costs of resources they do use.

4. In traditional costing systems, overhead costs are usually allocated to products using a single measure of activity such as direct labor-hours. This approach assumes that overhead costs are highly correlated with direct labor-hours. In other words, it is assumed that overhead costs move in tandem with direct labor-hours. If this is not true, product and other costs will be distorted.

B. *Activity-based costing (ABC)* attempts to remedy these deficiencies of traditional costing systems. The key concept in activity-based costing is that products (and customers) cause activities. The activities result in the consumption of resources, which in turn result in costs. Consequently, if we want to do a good job of assigned costs to products and customers, we must identify and measure the activities that link products and customers to costs.

C. The distinction between manufacturing and non-manufacturing costs is critical in traditional costing systems. This distinction is not important at all in activity-based costing. Like variable costing, activity-based costing is concerned with how costs behave. And like variable costing, activity-based costing is used in internal reports and is primarily intended to help managers in making decisions.

D. A significant number of companies have experimented with some form of activity-based costing. Activity-based costing originated in manufacturing companies, but is now being widely applied in service companies as well.

E. Activity-based costing differs from traditional costing in five major ways:

1. Non-manufacturing costs, as well as manufacturing costs, may be assigned to products.

2. Some manufacturing costs may be excluded from products. These are the costs of idle capacity and organization-sustaining costs (explained below).

3. In activity-based costing, there are a number of activity cost pools. Each cost pool is allocated to products and other cost objects using its own unique measure of activity.

   a. An *activity* is an event that causes consumption of overhead resources such as processing a purchase order.

   b. An *activity cost pool* is a "bucket" in which costs are accumulated that relate to a single activity such as processing purchase orders.

4. The allocation bases in activity-based costing (i.e., measures of activity) often differ from those used in traditional costing systems.

5. The overhead rates in activity-based costing (which are called *activity rates* in the chapter), may be based on the level of activity at capacity rather than on the budgeted level of activity.

F. The chapter lists seven steps for implementing an activity-based costing system. You will spend most of your time learning how to do steps 3, 4, 6, and 7. All seven of the steps are listed below.

1. Identify and define activities and activity pools.

2. Wherever possible, trace costs directly to activities and cost objects. For example, direct materials and direct labor costs are often traced directly to products and are not included in the activity-based costing system.

3. Assign costs to activity cost pools.

4. Calculate activity rates. These are like predetermined overhead rates in a traditional costing system.

5. Measure the activities caused by products and other cost objects.

6. Assign costs to cost objects using the activity rates and measures of activity.

7. Prepare management reports.

G. There may be many levels of activities and costs in an activity-based costing system. The text describes five of these levels:

1. *Unit-level activities* are performed each time a unit is produced. An example is testing a completed unit.

2. *Batch-level activities* are performed each time a batch is handled or processed. For example, tasks such as placing purchase orders and setting up equipment are batch-level activities. These activities occur no matter how many units are produced in a batch.

3. *Product-level activities* are required to have a product at all. An example is maintaining an up-to-date parts list and instruction manual for the product. These activities must be performed regardless of how many batches are run or units produced.

4. *Customer-level activities* relate to specific customers and include activities such as sales calls and catalog mailings that are not tied to a specific product.

5. *Organization-sustaining activities* are carried out regardless of which customers are served, which products are produced, how many batches are run, or how many units are produced. Examples include providing a computer network, preparing financial reports, providing legal advice to the board of directors, and so on. Organization-sustaining costs should not be allocated to products or customers for purposes of making decisions.

H. To understand the mechanics of activity-based costing, there is no good substitute for working through the example in the book step-by-step. Nevertheless, the process can be briefly summarized as follows:

1. Prepare the *first-stage allocation* of costs to the activity cost pools.

a. Begin with a listing of the costs that will be included in the activity-based costing system and the results of interviews with employees that indicate how these costs are to be distributed across the activity cost pools. The interview results (which you will always be given) will indicate what percentage of a specific cost such as indirect factory wages should be allocated to the first activity cost pool, the second activity cost pool, and so on.

b. For example, suppose there is an activity cost pool for processing purchase orders. The results of the interviews might indicate that 20% of the resources associated with office staff wages are consumed in processing purchase orders. If the office staff wages are $200,000 per year, then 20% of $200,000, or $40,000, would be allocated to the processing purchase orders cost pool.

2. Calculate the activity rates.

a. An *activity rate* is a cost per unit of activity. For example, the activity rate for machine set-ups might be $14 per machine set-up.

b. Suppose that 2,000 purchase orders are processed per year. If the office staff wages for processing purchase orders are $40,000, then the average cost of office staff wages for processing purchase orders would be $20 per purchase order. ($40,000 ÷ 2,000 = $20.)

c. Activity rates are important in *activity-based management*. Activity rates for similar activities can be compared across organizations or across different locations in the same organization. For example, the average cost of office staff wages for processing purchase orders might be higher than $20 at some locations in a company and lower at others. The high cost locations may learn how to better process purchase orders by studying the techniques used at the lower cost locations.

3. Prepare the *second-stage allocation of costs to products*, customers, and other cost objects.

    a.   To allocate costs to products or other cost objects, multiply the cost object's level of activity by the activity rate.

    b.   For example, if a product requires two purchase orders and the activity rate is $20 per purchase order for office staff wages, it would be allocated $40 (2 purchase orders @ $20 per purchase order). Sum all of the costs of all of the activities associated with the product to determine the total cost of the product.

I.   *Action analysis report*. Before taking any action such as dropping a product or a customer, managers should prepare an action analysis report that shows what costs have been assigned to the product or customer. A simple color scheme can be used to highlight how easy or difficult it would be to adjust a cost if there is a change in activity. (For example, if the product requiring 2 purchase orders were dropped, could the company really save $40 in office staff wages?)

1. *Green costs* are those costs that adjust automatically to changes in activity without any action by managers. For example, the power to run production equipment would automatically decrease if fewer units were made.

2. *Yellow costs* are those costs that could be adjusted in response to changes in activity, but such adjustments require management action. The adjustment is not automatic. Many wages would be classified as yellow costs since managers would have to explicitly lay off workers or redeploy them to more profitable uses so as to actually save any money.

3. Red costs are those costs that could be adjusted to changes in activity only with a great deal of difficulty and the adjustment would require management action. For example, staff salaries are often a red cost.

J.   Product costs computed under activity-based costing and traditional costing systems differ for a number of reasons. There are differences in *what* costs are allocated to products as well as in *how* they are allocated. Focusing just on *how* the costs are allocated, some general patterns emerge.

1. An activity-based costing system will typically shift costs away from high-volume products that are produced in small batches to low-volume products that are produced in small batches. Traditional costing systems apply batch-level and product-level costs uniformly to all products and the high-volume products absorb the bulk of such costs. In an activity-based costing system, such costs are assigned to the products that cause the costs rather than spreading them uniformly over all products on the basis of volume.

2. On a per-unit basis, the effect of the cost increases is usually much larger for low-volume products than for high-volume products. The reason is that if X dollars are shifted from high-volume products to low-volume products, the cost savings for the high-volume products is spread over many units whereas the increase in costs for the low-volume products are spread over relatively few units.

REVIEW AND SELF TEST
Questions and Exercises

True or False

Enter a T or an F in the blank to indicate whether the statement is true or false.

___ 1. If direct labor is used as a base for overhead cost assignment and direct labor is not highly correlated with the overhead cost, the result will be distorted product costs.

___ 2. In activity-based costing, some manufacturing costs may not be assigned to products.

___ 3. In activity-based costing, non-manufacturing costs are not assigned to products.

___ 4. In designing an activity-based costing system, managers should keep in mind that the system must conform to Generally Accepted Accounting Principles (GAAP).

___ 5. In activity-based costing, activity rates should be based on budgeted or estimated activity rather than activity at capacity.

___ 6. In activity-based costing, the first-stage allocations of costs to activity cost pools is often based on the results of interviews with employees.

___ 7. In activity-based costing, the overhead costs of the entire company are distributed to product and other cost objects on the basis of a single well-chosen measure of activity.

___ 8. Direct labor-hours should never be used as an allocation base in activity-based costing.

Multiple Choice

Choose the best answer or response by placing the identifying letter in the space provided.

___ 1. Advertising a product would be considered a: a) unit-level activity; b) batch-level activity; c) product-level activity; d) customer-level activity; e) organization-sustaining activity.

___ 2. Providing legal advice to the president concerning a possible merger with another company would be considered a: a) unit-level activity; b) batch-level activity; c) product-level activity; d) customer-level activity; e) organization-sustaining activity.

___ 3. Writing software for a new computer game at a software company would be considered a: a) unit-level activity; b) batch-level activity; c) product-level activity; d) customer-level activity; e) organization-sustaining activity.

___ 4. A software company orders 100,000 copies of a CD-ROM from a supplier. This CD-ROM will be enclosed in a computer game designed and published by the software company. Ordering the CD-ROMs would be considered a: a) unit-level activity; b) batch-level activity; c) product-level activity; d) customer-level activity; e) organization-sustaining activity.

___ 5. A company that provides photocopying services has an activity-based costing system with three activity cost pools—making photocopies, serving customers, and setting up machines. The activity rates are $0.02 per photocopy, $2.15 per customer, and $0.75 per machine-setup. If a customer requires set-ups on two different machines and makes 200 copies in total, how much cost would be assigned to the job for the customer by the activity-based costing system? a) $4.00; b) $2.15; c) $1.50; d) $7.65.

Chapter 8

Exercises

8-1.   Lambert Fabrication, Inc., is a manufacturing company that uses activity-based costing data for internal decisions. The company has four activity cost pools, which are listed below:

Activity Cost Pool	*Annual Activity*
Producing units	5,000 machine-hours
Processing orders	1,000 orders
Customer support	200 customers
Other	Not applicable

The "Other" activity cost pool consists of the costs of idle capacity and organization-sustaining costs.

The company traces the costs of direct materials and direct labor to jobs (i.e., orders). Overhead costs—both manufacturing and non-manufacturing—are allocated to jobs using the activity-based costing system. The company's overhead costs for the year are listed below:

Annual Overhead Costs

Indirect factory wages	$100,000
Other factory overhead	200,000
Selling and administrative overhead	400,000
Total overhead cost	$700,000

To develop the company's activity-based costing system, employees were asked how they distributed their time and resources across the four activity cost pools. The results of those interviews appear below:

Results of Interviews of Employees

	Distribution of Resource Consumption Across Activities				
	Producing Units	*Processing Orders*	*Customer Support*	*Other*	*Totals*
Indirect factory wages	40%	30%	10%	20%	100%
Other factory overhead	30%	10%	0%	60%	100%
Selling and administrative overhead ...	0%	25%	40%	35%	100%

a. Using the results of the interviews, carry out the first-stage allocation of costs to the activity cost pools.

First-Stage Allocations

	Producing Units	*Processing Orders*	*Customer Support*	*Other*	*Total*
Indirect factory wages					
Other factory overhead					
Selling and administrative overhead ...					
Total overhead cost					

b. Using the results of the first-stage allocation, compute the activity rates for each of the activity cost pools. (Activity rates are not computed for the "Other" activity cost pool. These costs will not be allocated to products or customers.)

Computation of Activity Rates

	Producing Units	Processing Orders	Customer Support
Total activity	5,000 machine-hours	1,000 orders	200 customers
Indirect factory wages			
Other factory overhead			
Selling and administrative overhead ...	_____	_____	_____
Total overhead cost	======	======	======

c. Using the activity rates you derived in part (b) above, compute the total amount of overhead cost that would be allocated to an order that requires 20 machine hours.

The Overhead Cost of An Order Requiring 20 Machine-Hours

	Producing Units	Processing Orders	Customer Support	Total
Total activity	20 machine-hours	1 order	Not applicable	
Indirect factory wages				
Other factory overhead				
Selling and administrative overhead ...	_____	_____	_____	_____
Total overhead cost	======	======	======	======

d. The order in part (c) above required $685 in direct materials and $975 in direct labor costs. The revenue from the job was $2,500. Prepare a report from an activity view that shows the margin from the order.

Margin on the Order from an Activity View

Revenue		$2,500.00
Costs:		
Direct materials	$685.00	
Direct labor	975.00	
Producing units		
Processing orders		
Customer support	_____	_____
Margin		======

e. Using the activity rates, compute the total amount of overhead cost that would be allocated to a customer who had two orders during the year requiring a total of 100 machine hours.

The Overhead Cost of Serving the Customer

	Producing Units	*Processing Orders*	*Customer Support*	*Total*
Total activity	100 machine-hours	2 orders	1 customer	
Indirect factory wages				
Other factory overhead				
Selling and administrative overhead ...	_____	_____	_____	_____
Total overhead cost	========	========	========	========

f. The orders in part (e) above required $3,500 in direct materials and $1,750 in direct labor costs. The revenue from the orders was $8,000. Prepare a report from an activity view that shows the margin on the business with this customer.

Margin on the Customer from an Activity View

Revenue		$8,000.00
Costs:		
Direct materials	$3,500.00	
Direct labor	1,750.00	
Producing units		
Processing orders		
Customer support	_____	_____
Margin		========

8-2. This exercise is a continuation of the previous exercise. Lambert Fabrication's managers would like action analysis reports in addition to the reports you have already completed. For the purpose of this report, management classifies the company's costs as follows:

>**Green:** *Costs that adjust automatically to changes in activity without management action.*
>Direct materials
>
>**Yellow:** *Costs that could, in principle, be adjusted to changes in activity, but management action would be required.*
>Direct labor
>Indirect factory wages
>
>**Red:** *Costs that would be very difficult to adjust to changes in activity and management action would be required.*
>Other factory overhead
>Selling and administrative overhead

a. Prepare an action analysis report for the order in Exercise 8-1, parts (c) and (d) above.

Action Analysis of the Order Requiring 20 Machine-Hours

Revenue		$2,500.00
Green costs:		
Direct materials	$685.00	685.00
Green margin		1,815.00
Yellow costs:		
Direct labor	975.00	
Indirect factory wages	_____	_____
Yellow margin		
Red costs:		
Other factory overhead		
Selling and administrative overhead	_____	_____
Red margin		=======

b. Prepare an action analysis report concerning the customer in Exercise 8-1, part (c), parts (e) and (f) above.

Action Analysis of the Customer

Revenue		$8,000.00
Green costs:		
Direct materials	$3,500.00	3,500.00
Green margin		5,500.00
Yellow costs:		
Direct labor	1,750.00	
Indirect factory wages	_____	_____
Yellow margin		
Red costs:		
Other factory overhead		
Selling and administrative overhead	_____	_____
Red margin		=======

c. Based on your analysis of the margin on this customer's business in Exercises 8-1 and 8-2, what recommendation, if any, would you make to management? Which report would you prefer to rely on for making decisions—the activity view report from Exercise 8-1 or the action analysis report in Exercise 8-2?

_____

_____

_____

_____

_____

_____

_____

_____

_____

_____

_____

Answers to Questions and Exercises

True or False

1. T   It is implicitly assumed that overhead cost is proportional to whatever allocation base is used. If this is not true, overhead costs will be incorrectly assigned to products and other cost objects.

2. T   Activity-based costing does not draw a strong distinction between manufacturing and non-manufacturing costs. Organization-sustaining costs, whether manufacturing or non-manufacturing, should not be assigned to products in activity-based costing.

3. F   In activity-based costing, some non-manufacturing costs may be assigned to products. What matters is whether a cost is caused by the product, not whether it is a manufacturing or non-manufacturing cost.

4. F   An activity-based costing system should be designed to aid decision making, not to conform to GAAP. Under GAAP, manufacturing costs that are not caused by any specific products must be assigned to products anyway and non-manufacturing costs that are caused by products cannot be assigned to them.

5. F   The practice of basing overhead rates on estimated or budgeted activity results in assigning the costs of idle capacity to products that are made during the period.

6. T   Since employee time is a resource, the activity-based costing system requires information about how people spend their time. There is often no better way to get this information than to ask people.

7. F   One of the characteristics of activity-based costing is the use of multiple measures of activity.

8. F   Direct labor-hours can be used as an allocation base if it provides a valid measure of activity for an activity cost pool. Direct labor-hours might, for example, be an appropriate measure of activity for an activity cost pool in which the costs of miscellaneous production supplies are accumulated.

Multiple Choice

1. c   The advertising is incurred on behalf of the product and is not caused by running any particular batch or making any particular unit of that product.

2. e   Providing legal advice, unless it is about a specific product or customer, would be considered an organization-sustaining activity.

3. c   Writing software for a new computer game is a product-level activity. It only has to be done once for the product and does not have to be repeated to make more units of the software.

4. b   This is a batch-level activity since the process of writing an order is the same whether 1 or 1 million copies of the CD-ROM are ordered.

5 d   The costs would be assigned as follows:

Making photocopies (200 copies @ $0.02)	$4.00
Setting up machines (2 set-ups @ $0.75)	1.50
Serving customers (1 customer @ $2.15)	2.15
Total cost	$7.65

101

Chapter 8

Exercises

8-1. a.

	Producing Units	Processing Orders	Customer Support	Other	Totals
Indirect factory wages	$ 40,000	$ 30,000	$ 10,000	$ 20,000	$100,000
Other factory overhead	60,000	20,000	0	120,000	200,000
Selling and administrative overhead ...	0	100,000	160,000	140,000	400,000
Total overhead cost	$100,000	$150,000	$170,000	$280,000	$700,000

Example: 30% of $100,000 = $30,000

Percentage of indirect factory wages attributable to
processing orders according to the interview results.

b.

Computation of Activity Rates

	Producing Units	Processing Orders	Customer Support
Total activity	5,000 machine-hours	1,000 orders	200 customers
Indirect factory wages	$ 8.00	$ 30.00	$ 50.00
Other factory overhead	12.00	20.00	0.00
Selling and administrative overhead ...	0.00	100.00	800.00
Total overhead cost	$20.00	$150.00	$850.00

Example: $30,000 ÷ 1,000 orders = $30.00 per order

Indirect factory wages allocated to the processing orders
activity cost pool in the first-stage allocation above.

c.

The Overhead Cost of An Order Requiring 20 Machine-Hours

	Producing Units	Processing Orders	Customer Support	Total
Total activity	20 machine-hours	1 order	Not applicable	
Indirect factory wages	$160.00	$ 30.00	$0.00	$190.00
Other factory overhead	240.00	20.00	0.00	260.00
Selling and administrative overhead ...	0.00	100.00	0.00	100.00
Total overhead cost	$400.00	$150.00	$0.00	$550.00

Example: $30.00 per order × 1 order = $30.00

Cost per order from part (b) above.

d. The totals at the bottoms of the columns in part (c) above are used to compute the order's margin from the activity view.

Margin on the Order from an Activity View

Revenue		$2,500.00
Costs:		
Direct materials	$685.00	
Direct labor	975.00	
Producing units	400.00	
Processing orders	150.00	
Customer support	0.00	2,210.00
Margin		$ 290.00

e. The overhead cost allocated to a customer can be determined in exactly the same way as for an order. The only difference is that customer support costs are also allocated along with the costs of producing units and processing orders.

The Overhead Cost of Serving the Customer

	Producing Units	Processing Orders	Customer Support	Total
Total activity	100 machine-hours	2 orders	1 customer	
Indirect factory wages	$ 800.00	$ 60.00	$ 50.00	$ 910.00
Other factory overhead	1,200.00	40.00	0.00	1,240.00
Selling and administrative overhead ...	0.00	200.00	800.00	1,000.00
Total overhead cost	$2,000.00	$300.00	$850.00	$3,150.00

f. The totals at the bottoms of the columns in part (e) above are used to compute the margin on the customer's business from the activity view.

Margin on the Customer from an Activity View

Revenue		$8,000.00
Costs:		
Direct materials	$3,500.00	
Direct labor	1,750.00	
Producing units	2,000.00	
Processing orders	300.00	
Customer support	850.00	8,400.00
Margin		($ 400.00)

8-2.   a. The overhead costs for the action analysis can be taken directly from the row totals in the overhead cost analysis in Exercise 8-1, part (c).

Action Analysis of the Order Requiring 20 Machine-Hours

Revenue		$2,500.00
Green costs:		
Direct materials	$685.00	685.00
Green margin		1,815.00
Yellow costs:		
Direct labor	975.00	
Indirect factory wages	190.00	1,165.00
Yellow margin		650.00
Red costs:		
Other factory overhead	260.00	
Selling and administrative overhead	100.00	360.00
Red margin		$ 290.00

b. The overhead costs for the action analysis can be taken directly from the row totals in the overhead cost analysis in Exercise 8-1, part (e).

Action Analysis of the Customer

Revenue		$8,000.00
Green costs:		
Direct materials	$3,500.00	3,500.00
Green margin		4,500.00
Yellow costs:		
Direct labor	1,750.00	
Indirect factory wages	910.00	2,660.00
Yellow margin		1,840.00
Red costs:		
Other factory overhead	1,240.00	
Selling and administrative overhead	1,000.00	2,240.00
Red margin		($ 400.00)

c.   The analysis in Exercise 8-1 (the activity view) indicates that the company is losing $400 on this customer. This suggests that the company might be better off financially if the customer were dropped. However, if this were done, many of the costs that have been allocated to the customer might not go away. This is particularly true since the activity view does not indicate where the costs need to be cut in the organization. For example, the customer support cost of $850 cuts across several departments, but that is not at all clear in the activity view. Since these costs cut across several departments, it would be difficult to pin the responsibility for making cuts on individual managers.

The action analysis provides a much clearer view of the nature of the costs that would have to be cut if the customer were dropped. The manager in charge of the selling and administrative overhead, for example, should be held responsible for cutting $1,000 if this customer were dropped. If the manager would not commit to cutting these costs, there would be no point in dropping the customer. The Green and Yellow margins are positive, so it makes sense to drop this customer only if *at least* $1,840 of the Red costs would be eliminated if the customer were dropped and *all* of the Green and Yellow costs would be eliminated.

Chapter 9

Profit Planning

Chapter Study Suggestions

Before reading the chapter, study the flow of budget data in Exhibit 9-2. This exhibit provides a good overview of the chapter and the budgeting process. Notice particularly how nearly all budgets eventually impact on the cash budget. As suggested by this exhibit, the cash budget is a key budget that serves to tie together much of the budget process. Schedule 8 in the text contains an example of a cash budget.

Schedules 1 and 2, containing the sales and production budgets, are also very important and your homework assignments are very likely to concentrate on these two budgets. As you proceed through the chapter, you will see that all other budgets depend in some way on the sales budget in Schedule 1. Notice that a schedule of expected cash collections accompanies the sales budget. Make sure you understand how the production budget is put together based on the sales budget and desired inventory levels.

CHAPTER HIGHLIGHTS

A. Profit planning is accomplished in most organizations with budgets. A *budget* is a detailed plan for the acquisition and use of financial and other resources over a specified time period.

    1. The master budget is a summary of the company's plans and goals for the future. It sets specific targets for sales, production, and financing activities and indicates the resources that will be supplied to meet those targets. The master budget culminates with a cash budget and a projected income statement and projected balance sheet.

    2. There are two steps in the budgeting process — planning and control.

        a. *Planning* involves developing objectives and formulating steps to achieve these objectives.

        b. *Control* involves the steps taken by management to increase the likelihood that the objectives set down at the planning stage are attained.

    3. Budgeting provides a number of benefits:

        a The budget *communicates* management's plans throughout the entire organization.

        b. The budgeting process forces managers to *think ahead* and to *formalize* their planning efforts.

        c. The budgeting process provides a means of *allocating resources* to those parts of the organization where they can be used most effectively.

        d. Budgeting uncovers potential *bottlenecks* before they occur.

        e. The budget *coordinates* the activities of the entire organization by *integrating* the plans and objectives of the various parts.

        f. The budget provides goals and objectives that serve as *benchmarks* for evaluating subsequent performance.

B. This chapter and the next three chapters are concerned with *responsibility accounting*. The basic idea behind responsibility accounting is that each manager's performance should be judged by how well he or she manages those items—and only those items—under his or her control. Each manager is assigned responsibility for those items of revenues and costs in the budget that the manager is able to control to a significant extent. The manager is then held responsible for deviations between budgeted goals and actual results.

C. Budget preparation is a complex task requiring the cooperative effort of many managers.

    1. Operating budgets (the budgets discussed in this chapter) ordinarily cover a one-year period divided into quarters and months.

    2. Managers should be involved in setting their own budgets rather than having the budgets imposed from above or by the accounting staff. There are two reasons for this. First, managers are likely to have the best information concerning their own operations. Second, a manager is more likely to be committed to attaining the budget if he or she plays a major role in developing his or her own budget.

D. The *master budget* consists of a number of separate but interdependent budgets. Exhibit 9-2 provides an overview of the master budget and shows how the parts of the master budget are linked together. Study this exhibit carefully.

    1. The *sales budget* (Schedule 1 in the text) is the beginning point in the budgeting process. It details the expected sales, in both units and dollars, for the budget period. The sales budget is accompanied by a *Schedule of Expected Cash Collections*, which shows the anticipated cash inflow from sales and collections of accounts receivable for the budget period.

    2. In a manufacturing firm, the sales budget is followed by the *production budget* (Schedule 2 in the text) which shows what must be produced to meet sales forecasts and to provide for desired levels of inventory.

        a. The production budget has the following format:

Budgeted unit sales	XXX
Add desired ending inventory	XXX
Total needs	XXX
Less beginning inventory	XXX
Required production	XXX

b. Study Schedule 2 in the text carefully. Note that the "Year" column is not simply the sum of the figures for the Quarters in Schedule 2. The desired ending inventory for the year is the desired ending inventory for the 4th Quarter. And the beginning inventory for the year is the beginning inventory for the 1st Quarter. Warning: Students often overlook this important detail.

3. In a merchandising firm such as a clothing store, the sales budget is followed by a *merchandise purchases budget* instead of a production budget. This budget details the amount of goods that must be purchased from suppliers to meet customer demand and to maintain adequate stocks of ending inventory.

a. The format for the merchandise purchases budget is (in units or dollars):

Budgeted cost of goods sold XXX
Add desired ending inventory XXX
Total needs XXX
Less beginning inventory XXX
Required purchases XXX

b. Note the similarity between the production budget in a manufacturing company and the merchandise purchases budget in a merchandising company.

4. In a manufacturing firm, the *direct materials budget* follows the production budget. It details the amount of raw materials that must be acquired to support production and to provide for adequate inventories.

a. The format for the direct materials budget is:

Raw materials required for production XXX
Add desired ending inventory XXX
Total raw materials needs XXX
Less beginning inventory XXX
Raw materials to be purchased XXX

b. The direct materials budget should be accompanied by a *Schedule of Expected Cash Disbursements* for raw materials.

c. An example of the direct materials budget appears in Schedule 3 in the text. Note that the "Year" column is not simply the sum of the figures for the Quarters.

5. In a manufacturing firm, a *direct labor budget* (Schedule 4 in the text) also follows the production budget.

6. In a manufacturing firm, a *manufacturing overhead budget* (Schedule 5 in the text) also follows the production budget and details all of the production costs that will be required other than direct materials and direct labor.

7. In a manufacturing firm, the *ending finished goods inventory budget* (Schedule 6 in the text) provides computations of unit product costs and of the carrying value of the ending inventory.

8. In all types of companies, a *selling and administrative expense* budget (Schedule 7 in the text) is prepared that lists expenses falling under the selling and administrative categories.

9. The *cash budget* (Schedule 8 in the text) summarizes all of the cash inflows and cash outflows appearing on the various budgets. In many companies the cash budget is the single most important result of the budgeting process because it can provide critical advance warnings of potential cash problems. The cash budget allows managers to arrange for financing *before* a crisis develops. Potential lenders are more likely to provide financing if managers appear to be in control and looking ahead rather than simply reacting to crises.

a. The cash budget has the following format:

Cash balance, beginning XXX
Add receipts XXX
Total cash available before
    current financing XXX
Less disbursements XXX
Excess (deficiency) of cash available
    over disbursements XXX
Financing XXX
Cash balance, ending XXX

b. Study Schedule 8 with care, noting particularly how the financing section is handled.

c. As with the production budget and the direct materials budget, the "Year" column in Schedule 8 is not simply the sum of the figures for the Quarters. The beginning cash balance for the year is the beginning cash balance for the 1st Quarter. And the ending cash balance for the year is the ending cash balance for the 4th Quarter.

10. The budgeting process culminates with the preparation of a *budgeted income statement* (Schedule 9 in the text) and a *budgeted balance sheet* (Schedule 10 in the text.)

Appendix 9A: Economic Order Quantity and the Reorder Point

A. Managers must decide how low inventories can be allowed to get before reordering and how much should be ordered. These decisions involve balancing the costs of ordering inventory, the costs of carrying inventory, and the costs of not carrying sufficient inventory.

1. The costs of ordering inventory are incurred each time there is an order and are independent of how many units are ordered.

2. The costs of carrying inventory include warehousing costs and the costs of financing the investment in inventories. These costs increase with the number of units held in inventory.

3. The costs of not carrying sufficient inventory occur when a product a customer wants is not in stock or cannot be produced due to an unavailable part.

B. The economic order quantity, or EOQ, is the number of units that should be requested in each order so as to minimize the sum of the costs of ordering inventory and the costs of carrying inventory.

1. If orders are placed more frequently for smaller amounts, the average number of units in inventory will fall. This will have the effect of *increasing* the total ordering costs (since more orders are placed) and *decreasing* the total carrying costs. The EOQ provides the optimal balance.

2. The formula for finding the economic order quantity is:

$$E = \sqrt{\frac{2QP}{C}}$$

where: E = the economic order quantity; Q = the annual quantity used; P = the cost of placing one order; and C = the annual cost of carrying one unit in stock.

3. The EOQ formula can also be used to find the optimal production lot size. The problem with running small production lots is that each time a new lot is processed, setup costs are incurred to change over from one product to another. The economic production lot size is found by using the set-up costs in place of the "cost of placing one order" in the above formula.

C. Once the EOQ has been determined, the next step is to decide when to place orders. If the level of inventory is allowed to get too low, the inventory may run out before a new shipment is received from suppliers. To prevent this, a *reorder point* is set that indicates the level of inventory at which an order should be initiated.

1. The reorder point depends on the lead time and the rate of usage. *Lead time* is the amount of time between when an order is placed and when it is finally received from the supplier. The larger the lead time, the more protective inventory the company requires and hence the higher the reorder point. The *rate of usage* of the item also affects the reorder point. The higher the rate of usage, the more protective inventory the company will require.

2. If the rate of usage during the lead time is known with certainty, the reorder point is determined by the following formula:

Reorder point = Lead time × Average usage

3. If usage during the lead time is erratic, then an additional safety stock must be carried. The safety stock protects the company from stock-outs in the worst case scenario—when the rate of usage is at its maximum.

a. The safety stock is computed as follows when the lead time is measured in days:

Maximum expected usage .	XX units per day
Less average usage	XX units per day
Excess	XX units per day
× Lead time	XX days
Safety stock	XX units

b. With safety stocks, the formula for the reorder point becomes:

$$\text{Reorder point} = \left(\text{Lead time} \times \text{Average usage} \right) + \text{Safety stock}$$

or, more simply,

Reorder point = Lead time × Maximum usage

REVIEW AND SELF TEST
Questions and Exercises

True or False

Enter a T or an F in the blank to indicate whether the statement is true or false.

___ 1. The usual starting point in budgeting is to make a forecast of sales.

___ 2. A self-imposed budget is one prepared by top management and imposed on other management levels as it is passed downward through an organization.

___ 3. Budgets are planning devices rather than control devices.

___ 4. The basic idea behind responsibility accounting is that each manager's performance should be judged by how well he or she manages those items directly under his or her control.

___ 5. Ending inventories occur because an organization is unable to sell all that it had planned to sell during a period.

___ 6. The required production in units for a budget period is equal to the expected unit sales for the period.

___ 7. Because of the technical nature of budgeting, it is best to leave budgeting entirely in the capable hands of the accounting staff.

___ 8. (Appendix 9A) The economic order quantity formula minimizes the sum of ordering costs and the costs of carrying inventory.

___ 9. (Appendix 9A) The lead time is a critical factor in computing the reorder point.

Multiple Choice

Choose the best answer or response by placing the identifying letter in the space provided.

___ 1. Actual sales in Ward Company were $30,000 in June, $50,000 in July, and $70,000 in August. Sales in September are expected to be $60,000. Thirty percent of a month's sales are collected in the month of sale, 50% in the first month after sale, 15% in the second month after sale, and the remaining 5% is uncollectible.

Budgeted cash receipts for September should be: a) $60,500; b) $62,000; c) $57,000; d) $70,000.

___ 2. Beecher Inc. is planning to purchase inventory for resale costing $90,000 in October, $70,000 in November, and $40,000 in December. The company pays for 40% of its purchases in the month of purchase and 60% in the month following purchase. What would be the budgeted cash disbursements for purchases of inventory in December? a) $40,000; b) $70,000; c) $58,000; d) $200,000.

___ 3. Archer Company has budgeted sales of 30,000 units in April, 40,000 units in May, and 60,000 units in June. The company has 6,000 units on hand on April 1. If the company requires an ending inventory equal to 20% of the following month's sales, production during May should be: a) 32,000 units; b) 44,000 units; c) 36,000 units; d) 40,000 units.

___ 4. Refer to the data for Archer Company in question 3. Each unit requires 3 pounds of a material. A total of 24,000 pounds of the material were on hand on April 1, and the company requires materials on hand at the end of each month equal to 25% of the following month's production needs. The company plans to produce 32,000 units of finished goods in April. How many pounds of the material should the company plan to purchase in April? a) 105,000; b) 19,000; c) 87,000; d) 6,000.

___ 5. If the beginning cash balance is $15,000, the required ending cash balance is $12,000, cash disbursements are $125,000, and cash collections from customers are $90,000, the company must borrow: a) $32,000; b) $20,000; c) $8,000; d) $38,000.

___ 6. (Appendix 9A) An item that costs $40 to purchase has an annual carrying cost of $2 per unit. The ordering cost is $16 per order and the annual usage of the item is 10,000 units. What is the economic order quantity for the item? a) 10,000 units; b) 250 units; c) 400 units; d) 500 units.

109

___ 7. (Appendix 9A) The average daily usage of an item is 10 units, the maximum daily usage is 15 units, and the lead time is 5 days for an order. What is the reorder point with safety stock for the item? a) 50 units; b) 75 units; c) 150 units; d) 100 units.

Exercises

9-1. Billings Company produces and sells a single product. Expected sales for the next four months are given below:

	April	May	June	July
Sales in units	10,000	12,000	15,000	9,000

The company needs a production budget for the second quarter. Experience indicates that end-of-month inventories should equal 10% of the following month's sales in units. At the end of March, 1,000 units were on hand. Complete the following production budget for the quarter:

	April	May	June	Quarter
Budgeted sales				
Add desired ending inventory				
Total needs				
Less beginning inventory				
Required production				

9-2. Dodero Company's production budget for the next four months is given below:

	July	August	September	October
Required production	15,000	18,000	20,000	16,000

Each unit of product uses five ounces of raw materials. At the end of June, 11,250 ounces of material were on hand. The company wants to maintain an inventory of materials equal to 15% of the following month's production needs.

Complete the following materials purchases budget for the third quarter:

	July	August	September	Quarter
Required production (units)				
Raw material needed per unit (ounces)				
Production needs (ounces)				
Add desired ending inventory (ounces)				
Total needs (ounces)				
Less beginning inventory (ounces)				
Raw materials to be purchased (ounces)				

9-3.   Whitefish Company budgets its cash two months at a time. Budgeted cash disbursements for March and April, respectively, are: for inventory purchases, $90,000 and $82,000; for selling and administrative expenses (includes $5,000 depreciation each month), $75,000 and $70,000; for equipment purchases, $15,000 and $6,000; and for dividend payments, $5,000 and $-0-. Budgeted cash collections from customers are $150,000 and $185,000 for March and April, respectively. The company will begin March with a $10,000 cash balance on hand. There should be a minimum cash balance of $5,000 at the end of each month. If needed, the company can borrow money at 12% per year. All borrowings are at the beginning of a month, and all repayments are at the end of a month. Interest is paid only when principal is being repaid.

Complete the following cash budget for March and April:

	March	*April*	*Two Months*
Cash balance, beginning	_____	_____	_____
Add collections from customers	_____	_____	_____
Total cash available	_____	_____	_____
Less disbursements:			
_____.....................	_____	_____	_____
_____.....................	_____	_____	_____
_____.....................	_____	_____	_____
_____.....................	_____	_____	_____
Total disbursements	_____	_____	_____
Excess (deficiency) of cash available over			
disbursements	_____	_____	_____
Financing:			
Borrowings (at beginning)	_____	_____	_____
Repayments (at ending)	_____	_____	_____
Interest (12% per year)	_____	_____	_____
Total financing	_____	_____	_____
Cash balance, ending	=======	=======	=======

9-4.   (Appendix 9A) Glidden Products produces a number of consumer items, including a microwave oven. A component part for the ovens is purchased from an outside supplier. In total, the company purchases 2,700 of the parts each year. It costs approximately $15 to place an order, and it costs $0.40 to carry one part in inventory for a year. The company works 50 weeks per year.

a.   Compute the economic order quantity for the part, using the following formula:

$$E = \sqrt{\frac{2QP}{C}}$$

$$E = \sqrt{\rule{4cm}{0pt}}$$

$$E =$$

b.   It takes about three weeks to receive an order of parts from the supplier. The company normally uses 54 parts each week in production; however, usage can be as much as 75 parts per week.

Compute the safety stock:

Maximum expected usage per week	_____	parts
Average usage per week	_____	parts
Excess	_____	parts
Lead time	× _____	
Safety stock	_____	parts

c.   Compute the reorder point:

Average weekly usage	_____	parts
Lead time	× _____	
Normal usage	_____	parts
Safety stock	_____	parts
Reorder point	_____	parts

d.   Referring to your answers above, explain when and in what quantity orders should be made:

_____

_____

_____

_____

_____

_____

9-5. **Critical thought writing exercise:** "The most important reason a company prepares a cash budget is to see how much cash it will have in the bank at the end of the year." Explain why you do or do not agree with this statement.

_____

_____

_____

_____

_____

_____

_____

_____

_____

_____

_____

Answers to Questions and Exercises

True or False

1. T   A forecast of sales forms the basis for the company's sales budget. The sales budget, in turn, is the basis for most of the other parts of the master budget.

2. F   A self-imposed budget is one in which a manager prepares his or her own budget estimates.

3. F   Budgeting involves both planning and control. Once a budget is set, it then becomes a control device. It is the benchmark for assessing actual results.

4. T   This is a clear, straightforward statement of the purpose of responsibility accounting.

5. F   Ending inventories are carefully planned if a company is following good budget procedures.

6. F   Production requirements are determined by the level of beginning inventory and the desired level of ending inventory as well as by the expected unit sales.

7. F   The accounting staff may provide help in preparing budgets, but the underlying estimates and data must come from operating managers. There are two reasons for this. First, the operating managers generally have better information about their own operations than the accounting staff. Second, the operating managers must be involved in preparing their own budgets or they will not be committed to them.

8. T   This point is illustrated in Exhibit 9A-2.

9. T   The lead time is critical since there must be inventories on hand during the lead time to support production or sales. Exhibit 9A-3 illustrates this point.

Multiple Choice

1. a   The computations are:

September sales, ($60,000 × 30%)	$18,000
August sales, ($70,000 × 50%)	35,000
July sales, ($50,000 × 15%)	7,500
Total cash receipts	$60,500

2. c   The computations are:

November purchases ($70,000 × 60%) ..	$42,000
December purchases ($40,000 ×40%)	16,000
Total cash disbursements	$58,000

3. b   The computations are:

Budgeted sales	40,000
Desired ending inventory (20% × 60,000)	12,000
Total needs	52,000
Less beginning inventory (20% × 40,000)	8,000
Required production	44,000

4. a   The computations are:

Required production	32,000
Material per unit	× 3 lbs
Production needs	96,000
Desired ending inventory (25% × 44,000 × 3 lbs)	33,000
Total needs	129,000
Less beginning inventory (25% × 96,000 lbs)	24,000
Required purchases	105,000

5. a   The computations are:

Beginning cash balance	$ 15,000
Cash receipts	90,000
Cash available	105,000
Cash disbursements	125,000
Deficiency of cash	$(20,000)

Since the company desires an ending cash balance of $12,000, the company must borrow $32,000 to make up for the cash deficiency of $20,000.

6. c   The computations are:

$$E = \sqrt{\frac{2QP}{C}} = \sqrt{\frac{2(10,000)(\$16)}{\$2}} = 400 \text{ units}$$

7. b   The computations are:

Average usage per day	10 units
Lead time in days	× 5
Reorder point without safety stock	50 units
Maximum usage per day	15 units
Average usage per day	10 units
Excess	5 units
Lead time in days	× 5
Safety stock	25 units

Reorder point with safety stock = 50 + 25
                                                   = 75 units

Chapter 9

Exercises

9-1.

	April	May	June	Quarter
Budgeted sales	10,000	12,000	15,000	37,000
Add desired ending inventory	1,200	1,500	900	900
Total needs	11,200	13,500	15,900	37,900
Less beginning inventory	1,000	1,200	1,500	1,000
Required production	10,200	12,300	14,400	36,900

9-2.

	July	August	September	Quarter
Required production (units)	15,000	18,000	20,000	53,000
Raw material needs per unit (ounces)	× 5 oz	× 5 oz	× 5 oz	× 5 oz
Production needs (ounces)	75,000	90,000	100,000	265,000
Add desired ending inventory (ounces)	13,500	15,000	12,000*	12,000
Total needs (ounces)	88,500	105,000	112,000	277,000
Less beginning inventory (ounces)	11,250	13,500	15,000	11,250
Raw materials to be purchased (ounces)	77,250	91,500	97,000	265,750

*16,000 units for October × 5 oz = 80,000 oz; 80,000 oz × 15%= 12,000 oz

9-3.

	March	April	Two Months
Cash balance, beginning	$ 10,000	$ 5,000	$ 10,000
Add collections from customers	150,000	185,000	335,000
Total cash available	160,000	190,000	345,000
Less disbursements:			
Inventory purchases	90,000	82,000	172,000
Selling and admin. expenses (net of depreciation)	70,000	65,000	135,000
Equipment purchases	15,000	6,000	21,000
Dividends	5,000	—	5,000
Total disbursements	180,000	153,000	333,000
Excess (deficiency) of cash available over cash disbursements	(20,000)	37,000	12,000
Financing:			
Borrowings (at beginning)	25,000	—	25,000
Repayments (at ending)	—	(25,000)	(25,000)
Interest (12% per year)	—	(500)*	(500)
Total financing	25,000	(25,500)	(500)
Cash balance, ending	$ 5,000	$ 11,500	$11,500

* $25,000 × 12% × 2/12 = $500

9-4.   a. $E = \sqrt{\dfrac{2QP}{C}} = \sqrt{\dfrac{2(2,700)(\$15)}{\$0.40}} = \sqrt{202,500} = 450 \text{ parts}$

      b.   The safety stock is computed as follows:

Maximum expected usage per week	75	parts
Average usage per week	54	parts
Excess	21	parts
Lead time	× 3	weeks
Safety stock	63	parts

      c.   The reorder point is computed as follow:

Average weekly usage	54	parts
Lead time	× 3	weeks
Normal usage	162	parts
Safety stock	63	parts
Reorder point	225	parts

      d.   An order for 450 parts should be placed when the stock on hand drops to 225 parts.

9-5.   This is not the most important reason a company prepares a cash budget, although it is one reason. The most important reason is to see the inflows and outflows of cash and additional cash needs *during* the year. By knowing cash needs during the year, a company will be able to foresee periods in which borrowing will be required, periods in which borrowing can be repaid, and any problems that may be developing regarding the company's uses of cash. Thus, bank loans and other sources of financing can be anticipated and arranged well in advance of the actual time of need, and cash flow problems can be anticipated and perhaps avoided.

Chapter 10

Standard Costs and the Balanced Scorecard

Chapter Study Suggestions

The first part of the chapter covers setting standard costs. Exhibit 10-1 presents a standard cost card, which is the final product of the standard setting process. You will be using a standard cost card in the homework assignments in both this chapter and in Chapter 11, so be sure you understand what a standard cost card contains and how it is constructed.

The second part of the chapter covers standard cost variance analysis. Exhibit 10-2 provides an overall perspective of variance analysis, and Exhibits 10-3 through 10-6 give detailed examples of the analysis of materials, labor, and variable overhead. Notice that the data from the standard cost card in Exhibit 10-1 are used in Exhibits 10-3, 10-4, and 10-5. As you study, follow the data from Exhibit 10-l into the following exhibits. This will help you tie the various parts of the chapter together into one integrated whole.

The third part of the chapter discusses the balanced scorecard. Most of this material is conceptual, but make sure you understand the computations of delivery cycle time, throughput, and manufacturing cycle efficiency.

CHAPTER HIGHLIGHTS

A. A *standard* is a benchmark or norm for evaluating performance. Manufacturing firms commonly set exacting standards for materials, labor, and overhead for each product. Some service companies, such as auto repair shops and fast food outlets also set standards.

    1. Standards are set for both the quantity and the price (cost) of inputs.

    2. Actual quantities and prices of inputs are compared to the standards. Differences are called variances. Only the significant variances are brought to the attention of management. This is called *management by exception*.

B. Setting accurate quantity and price standards is a vital step in the control process.

    1. Many persons should be involved in setting standards: accountants, purchasing agents, industrial engineers, production supervisors, and line managers.

    2. Standards tend to fall into two categories— either ideal or practical.

        a. Ideal standards are those that can be attained only by working at top efficiency 100% of the time. They allow for no machine breakdowns or lost time.

        b. Practical standards, by contrast, allow for breakdowns and normal lost time (such as for rest breaks). Practical standards are standards that are "tight, but attainable."

        c. Most managers feel that practical standards provide better motivation than ideal standards. The use of ideal standards can easily lead to frustration.

    3. Direct material standards are set for both the price and quantity of inputs that go into units of product.

        a. Price standards should reflect the final, delivered cost of materials. This price should include freight, handling, and other costs necessary to get the material into a condition ready to use. It should also reflect any cash discounts allowed.

        b. Quantity standards should reflect the amount of material that is required to make one unit of product, including allowances for unavoidable waste, spoilage, and other normal inefficiencies.

    4. Direct labor price and quantity standards are usually expressed in terms of labor rate and labor hours.

        a. The standard direct labor rate per hour should include not only wages earned but also fringe benefits, employment taxes, and other labor related costs.

        b. The standard labor hours per unit should include allowances for rest breaks, personal needs of employees, clean-up, and machine down time.

    5. As with direct labor, the price and quantity standards for variable overhead are generally expressed in terms of a rate and hours. The rate represents the variable portion of the predetermined overhead rate. The quantity is usually expressed in terms of direct labor-hours.

    6. The price and quantity standards for materials, labor, and overhead are summarized on the *standard cost card*.

        a. Study the standard cost card in Exhibit 10-1 and trace the figures in it back through the examples on the preceding pages in the text.

        b. Essentially, the standard cost per unit represents the budgeted variable production cost for a single unit of product.

C. The General Variance Model. A *variance* is a difference between standard prices and quantities on the one hand and actual prices and quantities on the other hand. The general model in Exhibit 10-2 is very helpful in variance analysis. Study this model with care.

    1. A price variance and a quantity variance can be computed for each of the three variable cost categories—materials, labor, and overhead.

    2. Variance analysis is a form of input/ output analysis. The inputs are materials, labor, and overhead; the output is the units produced during the period.

3. The *standard quantity allowed for the output* represents the amount of inputs that *should have been used* in completing the output of the period. This is a key concept in the chapter!

D. Direct Materials Variances. Exhibit 10-3 illustrates the variance analysis of direct materials. As you study the exhibit, notice that the center column (Actual Quantity of Inputs, at Standard Price) plays a part in the computation of both the price and quantity variances.

1. The *materials price variance* can be expressed in formula form as:

Price variance = (AQ × AP) — (AQ × SP)
or
Price variance = AQ (AP — SP)

where:
  AQ = Actual quantity of inputs purchased
  AP = Actual price of inputs purchased
  SP = Standard price of inputs

There are many possible causes of an unfavorable materials price variance including excessive freight costs, loss of quantity discounts, improper grade of materials purchased, rush orders, and inaccurate standards.

2. The *materials quantity variance* can be expressed in formula form as:

Quantity variance = (AQ × SP) — (SQ × SP)
or
Quantity variance = SP (AQ — SQ)

where:
  AQ = Actual quantity of inputs used
  SQ = Standard quantity of input allowed
        for the actual output
  SP = Standard price of inputs

Possible causes of an unfavorable materials quantity variance include untrained workers, faulty machines, low quality materials, and inaccurate standards.

3. The materials price variance is usually computed when materials are purchased, whereas the materials quantity variance is computed when materials are used in production. Consequently, the price variance is computed based on the amount of material purchased whereas the quantity variance is computed based on the amount of material used in production.

E. Direct Labor Variances. Exhibit 10-5 shows the variance analysis of direct labor. Notice that the format is the same as for direct materials, but the terms "rate" and "hours" are used in place of the terms "price" and "quantity".

1. The price variance for labor is called the *labor rate variance*. The formula is:

Rate variance = (AH × AR) — (AH × SR)
or
Rate variance = AH (AR - SR)

where:
  AH = Actual labor hours
  AR = Actual labor wage rate
  SR = Standard labor wage rate

Possible causes of an unfavorable labor rate variance include poor assignment of workers to jobs, unplanned overtime, pay increases, and inaccurate standards.

2. The quantity variance for labor is called the *labor efficiency variance*. The formula is:

Efficiency variance = (AH × SR) — (SH × SR)
or
Efficiency variance = SR (AH - SH)

where:
  AH = Actual labor hours
  SH = Standard labor hours allowed
        for the actual output
  SR = Standard labor wage rate

Possible causes of an unfavorable labor efficiency variance include poorly trained workers, low quality materials, faulty equipment, poor supervision, insufficient work to keep the everyone busy, and inaccurate standards.

F. Variable Manufacturing Overhead Variances. Exhibit 10-6 illustrates the variance analysis of variable manufacturing overhead. Notice that the format is the same as for direct labor.

1. The price or rate variance for variable manufacturing overhead is called the *variable overhead spending variance*. The formula for this variance is:

Spending variance = (AH × AR) — (AH × SR)
or
Spending variance = AH (AR - SR)

where:

AH = Actual hours (usually labor hours)

AR = Actual variable manufacturing overhead rate

SR = Standard variable manufacturing overhead rate

2. The quantity, or efficiency, variance for variable manufacturing overhead is called the *variable overhead efficiency variance*. The formula for this variance is:

$$\text{Efficiency variance} = (AH \times SR) - (SH \times SR)$$

or

$$\text{Efficiency variance} = SR(AH - SH)$$

where:

AH = Actual hours (usually labor hours)

SH = Standard hours allowed for the actual output

SR = Standard variable manufacturing overhead rate

G. Performance in a standard cost system is communicated to management through a pyramiding system of reports.

1. Performance reports build upward, with each manager receiving information on his or her own performance, as well as on the performance of subordinates.

2. Each manager is responsible *only* for those costs over which he or she has control. Exhibit 10-7 shows how reports are structured in a standard costing system.

H. Not all differences between standard costs and quantities and actual costs and quantities warrant management attention. The manager should be interested only in the differences that are significant. Statistical control charts, such as is illustrated in Exhibit 10-8, can be used to identify the variances that are worth investigating.

I. There are some potential problems with the use of standard costs. Most of these problems result from improper use of standard costs and the management by exception principle or from using standard costs in situations in which they are not appropriate.

1. Standard cost variance reports are usually prepared on a monthly basis and may be released too late to be really useful. Some companies are now reporting variances and other key operating data daily or even more frequently.

2. Managers must avoid using variance reports as a way to find someone to blame. Management by exception, by its nature, tends to focus on the negative. Managers should remember to reward workers for a job well done.

3. If labor is fixed, the only way to avoid an unfavorable labor efficiency variance is to keep labor busy all the time producing output—even if there is no demand. This can lead to excess work in process and finished goods inventories.

4. A favorable variance may not be good. For example, Pizza Haven has a standard for the amount of mozzarella cheese on a 9- inch pizza. If there is a favorable variance, it means that less cheese was used than the standard specifies. The result is a substandard pizza.

5. There can be a tendency with standard cost reporting systems to emphasize meeting the standards to the exclusion of other important objectives such as maintaining and improving quality, on-time delivery, and customer satisfaction.

6. Just meeting standards may not be sufficient; continual improvement may be necessary.

J. The Balanced Scorecard. A *balanced scorecard* is an integrated set of performance measures that are derived from the company's strategy and that support the company's strategy throughout the organization. The important things to remember about the balanced scorecard are the following:

1. Each company's balanced scorecard should be different because each company's strategy is different.

2. The balanced scorecard emphasizes continual improvement and trends rather than meeting preset targets or standards.

3. The performance measures on a balanced scorecard should be linked together on a cause-and-effect basis. The cause-and-effect links are essentially hypotheses of the form "If there is an improvement in this performance measure, then there will be improvement in that performance measure."

a. For example, managers of a fast food restaurant might reason that if the amount of time hamburgers sit on the warming rack before being served is reduced, then customers will like the hamburgers better. And if customers like the hamburgers better, then more hamburgers will be sold. The performance measures on the balanced scorecard would be "time on the warming rack", "customer satisfaction with hamburgers," and "sales of hamburgers."

b.   Most performance measures fall into four categories: financial, customer, internal business processes, and learning and growth. "Time on the warming rack" is a measure of internal business process performance. "Customer satisfaction" is a customer-oriented performance measure. And "sales of hamburgers" is a financial measure of performance.

c.   The performance measures and the hypotheses underlying them should tell a story about how improvements in internal business processes will ultimately lead to improvements in meeting the company's objectives.

d.   If real, sustained improvement in one performance measure does not lead to the expected improvement in another performance measure, then the company's strategy should be reconsidered. The assumptions underlying the strategy may be false.

4.   The entire company should have a comprehensive balanced scorecard. In addition, individuals should have scorecards that contain only those performance measures they can actually influence.

K.   Measures of Internal Business Process Performance. There are many measures of internal business process performance, such as the percentage of orders that are delivered on time. Most of these measures are self-explanatory, but some are not.

1.   Study Exhibit 10-10 carefully in order to understand the definitions of *Wait Time*, *Process Time*, *Inspection Time*, *Move Time*, and *Queue Time*.

2.   *Throughput time* measures the amount of time required to turn raw materials into completed products. It is also known as the manufacturing cycle time.

Throughput Time = Process Time + Inspection Time + Move Time + Queue Time

3.   The *delivery cycle time* represents the amount of time required from receipt of an order from a customer to shipment of the completed goods. It is computed as follows:

Delivery Cycle Time = Wait Time + Throughput Time

4.   The *manufacturing cycle efficiency (MCE)* is a measure of the efficiency of the production process. It is computed with the following formula:

$$MCE = \frac{Value - Added\ (Process)\ Time}{Throughput\ (Manufacturing\ Cycle)\ Time}$$

If the MCE is less than 1, non-value-added time is present in the production process. An MCE of 0.25 for example, would mean that 75% of the total production time consisted of Inspection Time, Move Time, and Queue Time—all non-value-added activities.

Appendix 10A: General Ledger Entries to Record Variances

A.   Many companies carry inventories at standard cost and record standard cost variances in the general ledger. This simplifies bookkeeping.

B.   Favorable variances are recorded as credits, and unfavorable variances are recorded as debits.

1.   The entry to record an unfavorable material price variance upon purchase of materials on account would be:

Raw Materials	XXX	
Materials Price Variance (U)	XXX	
Accounts Payable		XXX

2.   The entry to record a favorable material quantity variance would be:

Work in Process	XXX	
Materials Quantity Variance (F)		XXX
Raw Materials		XXX

3.   The entry to record an unfavorable labor efficiency variance and a favorable labor rate variance would be:

Work in Process	XXX	
Labor Efficiency Variance (U)	XXX	
Labor Rate Variance (F)		XXX
Wages Payable		XXX

REVIEW AND SELF TEST
Questions and Exercises

True or False

Enter a T or an F in the blank to indicate whether the statement is true or false.

___ 1. Practical standards are generally viewed as better than ideal standards for motivating employees.

___ 2. Ideal standards allow for machine breakdown time and other normal inefficiencies.

___ 3. In determining a material price standard, any freight or handling costs should be excluded.

___ 4. The standard rate for variable overhead consists of the variable portion of the predetermined overhead rate.

___ 5. Raw materials price variances should be computed and reported only when materials are placed into production.

___ 6. Variances similar to price and quantity variances can be computed for materials, labor, and overhead.

___ 7. Waste on the production line will result in a materials price variance.

___ 8. If the actual price or quantity exceeds the standard price or quantity, the variance is unfavorable.

___ 9. Labor rate variances are largely out of the control of management.

___ 10. Managers should thoroughly investigate all differences (variances) between standard cost and actual cost.

___ 11. In a company with fixed labor, an undue focus on labor efficiency variances may result in the production of needless inventories.

___ 12. The balanced scorecard approach focuses more on trends over time than on meeting any specific standards.

___ 13. Any two companies should have basically the same balanced scorecard.

___ 14. If the MCE is less than 1, there is non-value-added time in the production process.

___ 15. (Appendix 10A) The use of standard costs simplifies bookkeeping.

___ 16. (Appendix 10A) An unfavorable variance would be recorded as a debit in the general ledger.

Multiple Choice

Choose the best answer or response by placing the identifying letter in the space provided.

___ 1. The labor rate variance is determined by multiplying the difference between the actual labor rate and the standard labor rate by: a) the standard hours allowed; b) the actual hours worked; c) the budgeted hours allowed; d) none of these.

___ 2. If inferior-grade materials are purchased, the result may be: a) an unfavorable materials price variance; b) a favorable materials price variance; c) an unfavorable labor efficiency variance; d) a favorable labor efficiency variance; e) responses b and c are both correct; f) responses a and d are both correct.

___ 3. During June, Bradley Company produced 4,000 units of product. The standard cost card indicates the following labor standards per unit of output: 3.5 hours @ $6 per hour = $21. During the month, the company worked 15,000 hours. The standard hours allowed for the month were: a) 14,000 hours; b) 15,000 hours; c) 24,000 hours; d) 18,000 hours.

___ 4. Refer to the data in question 3 above. What is the labor efficiency variance for June? (F indicates a Favorable variance and U indicates an Unfavorable variance.) a) $1,000 F; b) $1,000 U; c) $6,000 F; d) $6,000 U.

___ 5. Refer to the data in question 3 above. The total labor cost during June was $88,000 for the 15,000 hours that were worked. What is the labor rate variance for June? a) $6,000 F; b) $6,000 U; c) $2,000 F; d) $2,000 U.

___ 6. During July, Bradley Company produced 3,000 units of product. The standard cost card indicates the following materials standards per unit of output: 2 pounds @ $0.50 = $1. During July, 8,000 pounds of material were purchased at a cost of $3,900. The materials price variance for July is: a) $100 F; b) $100 U; c) $4,100 F; d) $4,100 U.

___ 7. Refer to the data in question 6 above. 6,100 pounds of material were used in July to produce the output of 3,000 units. The materials quantity variance for July is: a) $1,550 F; b) $1,550 U; c) $50 F; d) $50 U.

___ 8. During August, Bradley Company produced 3,500 units of product using 12,750 labor hours. The standard cost card indicates the following variable manufacturing overhead standards per unit of output: 3.5 labor hours @ $2 per labor hour = $7. During the month, the actual variable manufacturing overhead cost incurred was $25,000. The variable overhead spending variance was: a) $500 U; b) $500 F; c) $24,500 U; d) $24,500 F.

___ 9. Refer to the data in question 8 above. The variable overhead efficiency variance was: a) $7,000 F; b) $7,000 U; c) $1,000 F; d) $1,000 U.

___ 10. The "price" variance for variable overhead is called a: a) rate variance; b) spending variance; c) budget variance; d) none of these.

___ 11. The delivery cycle time consists of: a) the time required to get a product to a customer after production is complete; b) the time required to get delivery of raw materials; c) the velocity of production plus the throughput time; d) the time required from receipt of an order from a customer to shipment of the completed goods.

___ 12. The following data are average times per order over the last month.

Wait time to start production	15.0 days
Inspection time	0.6 days
Process time	3.0 days
Move time	1.4 days
Queue time	7.0 days

The throughput time would be: a) 12.0 days; b) 7.0 days; c) 5.0 days; d) 20.0 days.

___ 13. Refer to the data in question 12 above. The MCE would be: a) 75%; b) 30%; c) 25%; d) 42%.

___ 14. Refer again to the data in question 12 above. What percentage of the throughput time is spent in non-value-added activities: a) 25%; b) 70%; c) 75%; d) 58%.

Exercises

10-1. Selected data relating to Miller Company's operations for April are given below:

Number of units produced .... 500 units
Number of actual direct labor hours worked .... 1,400 hours
Total actual direct labor cost $10,850

The standard cost card indicates that 2.5 hours of direct labor time is allowed per unit, at a rate of $8 per hour.

a. Complete the following analysis of direct labor cost for the month:

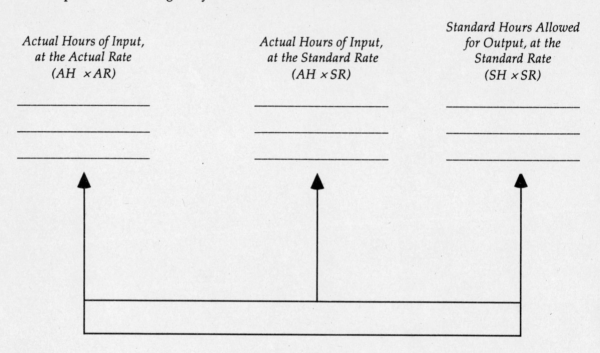

| Actual Hours of Input, at the Actual Rate (AH × AR) | Actual Hours of Input, at the Standard Rate (AH × SR) | Standard Hours Allowed for Output, at the Standard Rate (SH × SR) |

b. Redo the above analysis of direct labor cost for the month, using the following formulas:

Labor Rate Variance = AH (AR— SR)

Labor Efficiency Variance = SR (AH— SH)

10-2. The following activity took place in Solo Company during May:

Number of units produced .... 450 units
Material purchased .... 1,500 feet
Material used in production .... 720 feet
Cost per foot for material purchased $3

The standard cost card indicates that 1.5 feet of materials are allowed for each unit of product. The standard cost of the materials is $4 per foot.

a. Complete the following analysis of direct materials cost for the month:

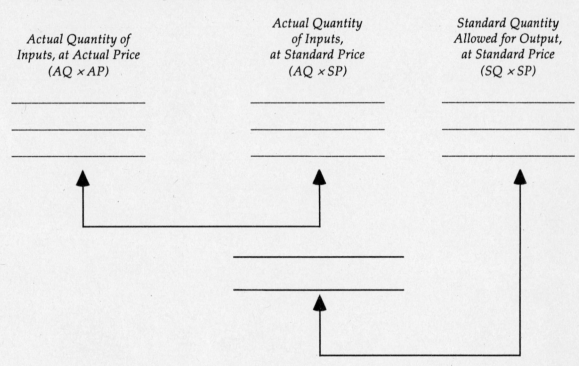

| *Actual Quantity of Inputs, at Actual Price (AQ × AP)* | *Actual Quantity of Inputs, at Standard Price (AQ × SP)* | *Standard Quantity Allowed for Output, at Standard Price (SQ × SP)* |

(A total variance can't be computed in this situation, since the amount of materials purchased differs from the amount of materials used in production.)

b. Redo the above analysis of direct materials cost for the month, using the following formulas:

Materials Price Variance = AQ (AP— SP)

Materials Quantity Variance = SP (AQ— SQ)

127

10-3.   (Appendix 10A) Refer to the data for Solo Company in exercise 10-2 on the previous page. Prepare journal entries to record all activity relating to direct materials for the month:

	Debit	Credit

10-4.   During the last quarter, Scott Company recorded the following average times per order received and processed:

Wait time to start production	9.0 days
Inspection time	0.8 days
Process time	3.0 days
Move time	0.2 days
Queue time	6.0 days

a.   Compute the throughput time.

Throughput time =

b.   Compute the manufacturing cycle efficiency (MCE).

MCE =

c.   What percentage of the production time is spent in non-value-added activities?

d.   Compute the delivery cycle time.

Delivery Cycle Time =

10-5. **Critical thought writing exercise:** What information, if any, does the variable overhead efficiency variance convey concerning the efficiency with which variable overhead resources were used?

_____

_____

_____

_____

_____

_____

_____

_____

_____

_____

_____

Answers to Questions and Exercises

True or False

1. T   Practical standards provide better motivation because they are attainable by workers.

2. F   Ideal standards do not allow for either machine breakdowns or other normal inefficiencies.

3. F   Freight and handling costs should be included in the material price standard since the purchasing manager should be responsible for the total cost of acquiring materials.

4. T   This statement is true by definition.

5. F   The purchasing manager is responsible for the materials price variance. This variance should be computed when the purchasing manager does his or her work—not when the materials are put into production.

6. T   This point is illustrated in Exhibit 10-2.

7. F   Waste will result in a materials quantity variance.

8. T   This statement is true by definition.

9. F   Labor rate variances can arise from how labor is used, and the use of labor is within the control of management.

10. F   Managers should not waste time investigating insignificant variances.

11. T   When labor is fixed, the only way to generate a more favorable labor efficiency variance is to keep everyone busy producing output—even if there is no demand.

12. T   The balanced scorecard approach emphasizes continual improvement.

13. F   Since companies have different strategies, their balanced scorecards should be different.

14. T   Since the MCE is measured by value-added time divided by throughput time, an MCE of less than 1 means that the throughput time contains some amount of non-value-added time.

15. T   The use of standard costs simplifies the bookkeeping process since standards permit all units to be carried at the same cost.

16. T   Unfavorable variances have the effect of decreasing income. Therefore, they are debit entries just as an expense is a debit entry.

Multiple Choice

1. b   This point is illustrated in Exhibit 10-5.

2. e   The materials price variance will probably be favorable, since the inferior grade materials probably will cost less. The labor efficiency variance will probably be unfavorable, since the inferior grade materials will probably require more work.

3. a   The computation is: 4,000 units × 3.5 hours per unit = 14,000 standard hours.

4. d   Efficiency variance = SR (AH - SH)
    = $6 (15,000 - 14,000)
    = $6,000 U

5. c   Rate variance = (AH × AR) - (AH × SR)
    = ($88,000) - (15,000 × $6)
    = $2,000 F

6. a   Price variance = (AQ × AP) - (AQ × SP)
    = ($3,900) - (8,000 × $0.50)
    = $100 F

7. d   Quantity variance = SP (AQ - SQ)
    = $0.50 (6,100 - 2x3,000)
    = $50 U

8. b   Spending
    variance = (AH × AR) - (AH × SR)
    = ($25,000) - (12,750 × $2)
    = $500 F

9. d   Efficiency
$$\text{variance} = SR (AH - SH)$$
$$= \$2\ (12{,}750 - 3.5 \times 3{,}500)$$
$$= \$1{,}000\ U$$

10. b   This point is illustrated in Exhibit 10-2.

11. d   This point is illustrated in Exhibit 10-10.

12. a   Throughput time
= Process time + Inspection time
+ Move time + Queue time
= 3.0 days + 0.6 days + 1.4 days + 7.0 days
= 12.0 days

13. c   MCE = $\dfrac{\text{Value-added time}}{\text{Throughput time}}$
$$= \frac{3.0\ \text{days}}{12.0\ \text{days}} = 25\%$$

14. c   If the MCE is less than one, non-value-added time is present in the production process. In this case, since the MCE is 25%, 75% of the time is spent in non-value-added activities (1.00- 0.25 = 0.75 or 75%)

Exercises

10-1.   a.

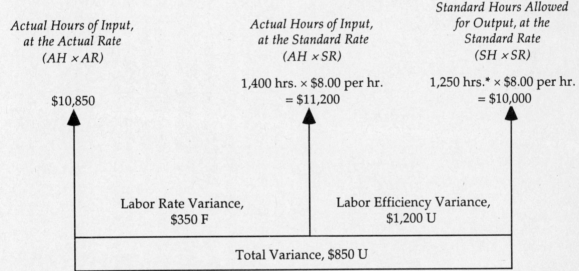

Actual Hours of Input, at the Actual Rate (AH × AR)	*Actual Hours of Input, at the Standard Rate (AH × SR)*	*Standard Hours Allowed for Output, at the Standard Rate (SH × SR)*
	1,400 hrs. × \$8.00 per hr. = \$11,200	1,250 hrs.* × \$8.00 per hr. = \$10,000
\$10,850		
	Labor Rate Variance, \$350 F	Labor Efficiency Variance, \$1,200 U
	Total Variance, \$850 U	

*500 units × 2.5 hrs. = 1,250 hrs.

b. AR = \$10,850 ÷ 1,400 hrs. = \$7.75 per hr.
Labor Rate Variance = AH (AR - SR)
= 1,400 hrs. (\$7.75 per hr. - \$8.00 per hr.) = \$350 F

Labor Efficiency Variance = SR (AH - SH)
= \$8.00 per hr. (1,400 hrs. - 1,250 hrs.) = \$1,200 U

10-2.   a.

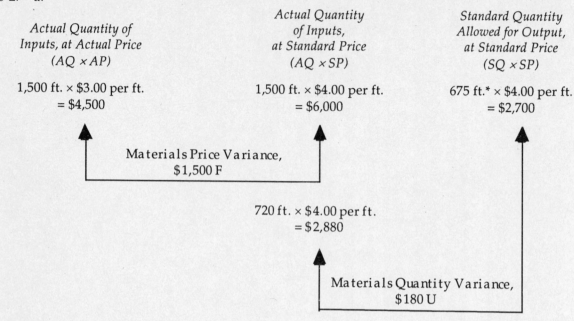

Actual Quantity of
Inputs, at Actual Price
(AQ × AP)

Actual Quantity
of Inputs,
at Standard Price
(AQ × SP)

Standard Quantity
Allowed for Output,
at Standard Price
(SQ × SP)

1,500 ft. × \$3.00 per ft.
= \$4,500

1,500 ft. × \$4.00 per ft.
= \$6,000

675 ft.* × \$4.00 per ft.
= \$2,700

Materials Price Variance,
\$1,500 F

720 ft. × \$4.00 per ft.
= \$2,880

Materials Quantity Variance,
\$180 U

*450 units × 1.5 ft. = 675 ft.

b.   Materials Price Variance = AQ (AP - SP)
$$= 1,500 \text{ ft. } (\$3.00 \text{ per ft. } - \$4.00 \text{ per ft.}) = \$1,500 \text{ F}$$
Materials Quantity Variance = SP (AQ - SQ)
$$= \$4.00 \text{ per ft. } (720 \text{ ft. } - 675 \text{ ft.}) = \$180 \text{ U}$$

Note that a different quantity of materials was purchased (1,500 ft.) than was used in production (720 ft.). When computing the price variance, use the quantity of materials purchased. When computing the quantity variance, use the quantity of materials used in production.

10-3.

Raw Materials	6,000	
Materials Price Variance		1,500
Accounts Payable		4,500
Work in Process	2,700	
Materials Quantity Variance	180	
Raw Materials		2,880

10-4.   a.   Throughput time = Process time + Inspection time + Move time + Queue time
= 3.0 days + 0.8 days + 0.2 days + 6.0 days
= 10.0 days

b.   MCE = $\dfrac{\text{Value-added-time, 3.0 days}}{\text{Throughput time, 10.0 days}}$ = 30%

c.   Since the MCE is 30,% the complement of this figure, or 70% of the total production time, is spent in non-value-added activities.

d.   Delivery cycle time = Wait time + Throughput time
= 9.0 days + 10.0 days
= 19.0 days

10-5.	The variable overhead efficiency variance is computed as follows: SR (AH - SH). The variance is unfavorable if the actual hours exceeds the standard hours allowed for the actual output and is favorable otherwise. The hours refers to the basis on which variable manufacturing overhead is applied to products, which is usually direct labor-hours. Consequently, the variable overhead efficiency variance is unfavorable if "too many" direct labor-hours were used to make the actual output of the period. While this may tell us something about the efficiency of direct labor, it is not clear that it tells us anything about the efficiency with which variable manufacturing overhead resources were used. In other words, too many direct labor hours may have been used during a period, but managers and workers may have done a good job of using only as much of the variable overhead resources such as miscellaneous supplies as was absolutely necessary.

Chapter 11

Flexible Budgets and Overhead Analysis

Chapter Study Suggestions

The chapter is divided into three parts. The first part covers flexible budgets, with Exhibit 11-3 providing a comprehensive example of how a flexible budget is prepared. Pay close attention to the differences between a flexible budget and a static budget.

The middle part of the chapter expands on the variance analysis of variable overhead that was introduced in Chapter 10. Exhibits 11-and 11-7 are the key exhibits here.

The last part of the chapter covers fixed overhead analysis. Three things in this part deserve special attention. First, be sure you understand fully what the "denominator activity" is, and how it is used. Second, be sure you understand the difference between a "normal-cost system" and a "standard-cost system," as illustrated in Exhibit 11-9. Third, be sure you understand the variance analysis of fixed overhead illustrated in Exhibit 11-10.

The chapter concludes with a detailed example of flexible budgets and fixed overhead analysis. Follow the example through step by step before attempting the homework material.

CHAPTER HIGHLIGHTS

A. The sales budgets, production budgets, and cash budgets in Chapter 8 are *static budgets*. They are static in the sense that they are geared toward a single level of activity. The static budget can't be used to assess how well individuals were able to control costs, since actual activity will rarely coincide with the original activity level assumed in the static budget. If, for example, activity is higher than was assumed in the original budget, variable costs should be higher than originally budgeted.

B. A *flexible budget* is geared to a range of activity, rather than to a single level. This can be seen from the flexible budget presented in Exhibit 11-3. Notice especially how a "cost formula" is used in the flexible budget for the variable costs.

1. The flexible budget is a dynamic tool. It can be used to quickly develop a budget for any level of activity within the relevant range. The variable costs are adjusted by multiplying the cost per unit by the activity level. Fixed costs remain unchanged within the relevant range.

2. The activity base underlying the flexible budget must be carefully chosen. Three general criteria are used in selecting an activity base:

a. The flexible budget assumes that the variable costs change in proportion to changes in the activity base, so the activity base should actually drive the variable costs.

b. The activity base should not be expressed in dollars. For example, direct labor cost should not be used as an activity base. A change in the labor wage rate would change the measure of activity, but may have little real effect on the costs in the flexible budget.

c. The activity base should be simple and easy to understand.

C. A *flexible budget performance report* can be easily constructed to evaluate how well costs were controlled.

1. Compute the amount for each variable cost in the flexible budget by multiplying its cost per unit for the cost by the actual level of activity for the period.

2. If the actual activity is within the relevant range, the fixed cost amounts are constant and can be copied from the static budget.

3. Variances are computed for each of the costs. If the actual cost exceeds the flexible budget cost for the actual level of activity, the variance is unfavorable. If the actual cost is less than the flexible budget cost for the actual level of activity, the variance is favorable.

4. Fixed costs can have variances. There can be a difference between budgeted fixed costs and actual fixed costs.

a. A cost is fixed if it does not depend on the level of activity. However, that does not mean a fixed cost cannot change for other reasons or that it cannot be controlled.

b. For example, the cost of heating and lighting an administrative office is fixed—it does not depend upon how many goods or services the company sells. Nevertheless, this cost can change from period to period due to seasonal factors, how conscientious people are in turning off lights, the thermostat setting they use, and so on.

c. It is often easier to control fixed costs than variable costs. Many fixed costs involve discretionary activities such as travel costs, entertainment, and executive seminars.

D. The middle portion of the chapter focuses on variable manufacturing overhead. Two types of *variable overhead performance reports* are illustrated for variable manufacturing overhead. One type of report shows just a spending variance. The other type of report shows both a spending and an efficiency variance. This is a review of material from Chapter 10.

1. If the flexible budget allowances in the performance report are based on the actual number of hours worked during the period, then there will be just a spending variance.

a. In preparing a performance report under this approach, the cost formulas in the flexible budget are applied to the actual number of hours worked for the period.

b. The budget allowances computed in "a" above are then compared to actual costs of the period and a spending variance results. Exhibit 11-6 illustrates this procedure.

c. The overhead spending variance combines both price and quantity variances. An unfavorable variance could occur because the standard is in error, prices paid for overhead items were too high, or too many overhead resources were used.

2. If the flexible budget allowances in the performance report are based on both the actual number of hours worked and the standard hours allowed for the output of the period, there will be both a spending and an efficiency variance.

a. Exhibit 11-7 contains a performance report using this approach. Study the column headings in this exhibit carefully.

b. The term "variable overhead efficiency variance" is a misnomer. This variance has nothing to do with how efficiently or inefficiently variable overhead resources were used. The inefficiency is really in the base underlying the application of overhead. For example, if direct labor-hours are used as the activity base, there will be an unfavorable variable overhead efficiency variance if the actual direct labor-hours exceed the standard number of direct labor-hours allowed for the actual output. The assumption is that the excessive use of direct labor will have the indirect effect of increasing the spending on variable overhead.

E. The flexible budget often serves as the basis for computing predetermined overhead rates for product costing purposes. The formula is:

$$\text{Predetermined overhead rate} = \frac{\text{Overhead from the flexible budget for the denominator level of activity}}{\text{Denominator level of activity}}$$

1. The denominator level of activity is whatever level of activity (usually in direct labor-hours or machine-hours) that is assumed when the predetermined overhead rate is computed. The numerator in the rate is the amount of manufacturing overhead for that level of activity.

2. The predetermined overhead rate can be divided into two parts, one for the variable overhead costs and the other for the fixed overhead costs.

a. The fixed portion of the predetermined overhead rate depends upon the level of the denominator activity that is chosen. The larger the denominator activity, the lower the rate will be.

b. Most managers want stable unit costs, so the denominator activity is usually changed no more frequently than once a year.

F. Exhibit 11-9 is an extremely important exhibit. It shows that overhead is applied to work in process differently under a *standard cost system* than it is under a *normal cost system*.

1. We studied normal cost systems in Chapter 3. There we learned that overhead is applied by multiplying the predetermined overhead rate by the actual hours of activity for a period.

2. In contrast, under a standard cost system overhead is applied to work in process by multiplying the predetermined overhead rate by the *standard hours allowed for the output of the period*. As in Chapter 10, the standard hours allowed for the output is computed by multiplying the standard hours per unit of output by the actual output of the period.

G. The last part of the chapter is concerned with fixed manufacturing overhead variances. Two variances are computed for fixed overhead—a budget variance and a volume variance.

1. The *fixed overhead budget variance*, or simply "budget variance," is the difference between actual fixed overhead costs and budgeted fixed overhead costs. The formula for the variance is:

$$\text{Budget variance} = \text{Actual fixed overhead cost} - \text{Flexible budget fixed overhead cost}$$

The "flexible budget fixed overhead cost" refers to how much the fixed overhead cost should be for the actual level of activity during the period, according to the flexible budget.

2. The formula for the *fixed overhead volume variance*, is:

$$\text{Volume variance} = \text{Fixed overhead rate} \times \left(\text{Denominator hours} - \text{Standard hours allowed} \right)$$

The "fixed overhead rate" is the fixed portion of the predetermined overhead rate. The volume variance does not measure how well spending was controlled. It is completely determined by the relation between the denominator hours and the standard hours allowed for the actual output.

    a. If the denominator activity is greater than the standard hours allowed for the output of the period, then there is an unfavorable volume variance.

    b. If the denominator activity is less than the standard hours allowed for the output of the period, then the volume variance is favorable.

I. In a standard cost system, the amount of overhead applied to products is determined by the standard hours allowed for the actual output.

    1. As in Chapter 3, if the actual overhead cost exceeds the amount of overhead cost applied to units of product, then the overhead is under-applied. If the actual overhead cost incurred is less than the amount of overhead cost applied to units, then the overhead is overapplied.

    2. In a standard cost system, the sum of the overhead variances equals the amount of under- or overapplied overhead.

Overhead under- or overapplied =
    Variable overhead spending variance
+ Variable overhead efficiency variance
+ Fixed overhead budget variance
+ Fixed overhead volume variance

If the sum of the variances is unfavorable, the overhead is underapplied. If the sum of the variances is favorable, the overhead is overapplied.

REVIEW AND SELF TEST
Questions and Exercises

True or False

Enter a T or an F in the blank to indicate whether the statement is true or false.

___ 1. A budget prepared for a single level of activity is called a static budget.

___ 2. Fixed costs are not controllable and therefore should be omitted from performance reports.

___ 3. A manger should be judged on the basis of how well he or she is able to keep costs to their originally budgeted levels.

___ 4. Direct labor cost would generally be a better base to use in preparing a flexible budget than direct labor hours.

___ 5. A variable overhead spending variance is affected by waste and excessive usage as well as price differentials.

___ 6. The term "overhead efficiency variance" is really a misnomer since this variance has nothing to do with efficiency in the use of overhead.

___ 7. If overhead is applied to production on the basis of direct labor hours, the labor efficiency variance and the overhead efficiency variance will always be favorable or unfavorable together.

___ 8. The fixed overhead volume variance measures how well fixed overhead spending was controlled.

___ 9. If the denominator activity level exceeds the standard hours allowed for the output, the volume variance will be favorable.

___ 10. In a standard cost system, if overhead is overapplied, then the sum of the four manufacturing overhead variances will be favorable.

Multiple Choice

Choose the best answer or response by placing the identifying letter in the space provided.

___ 1. In a standard cost system, overhead is applied to production on the basis of: a) the actual hours required to complete the output of the period; b) the standard hours allowed to complete the output of the period; c) the denominator hours chosen for the period; d) none of these.

___ 2. If the standard hours allowed for the output of a period exceed the denominator hours used in setting overhead rates, there will be: a) a favorable budget variance; b) an unfavorable budget variance; c) a favorable volume variance; d) an unfavorable volume variance.

___ 3. Baxter Company uses a standard cost system in which manufacturing overhead is applied to units of product on the basis of direct labor hours. The variable portion of the company's predetermined overhead rate is $3 per direct labor hour. The standards call for 2 direct labor hours per unit of output. In March, the company produced 2,000 units using 4,100 direct labor hours and the actual variable overhead cost incurred was $12,050. What was the variable overhead spending variance? a) $250 U; b) $250 F; c) $6,050 U; d) $6,050 F.

___ 4. Refer to the data in part (3) above concerning Baxter Company. What was the variable overhead efficiency variance for March? a) $6,300 F; b) $6,300 U; c) $300 F; d) $300 U.

___ 5. Baxter Company's flexible budget for manufacturing overhead indicates that the fixed overhead should be $30,000 at the denominator level of 3,000 standard direct labor hours. In March, the actual fixed overhead cost incurred was $33,000. Recall from the above data concerning Baxter Company that the standards call for 2 direct labor hours per unit of output and that in March, the company produced 2,000 units using 4,100 direct labor hours (DLHs). What is the fixed portion of the predetermined overhead rate? a) $10 per DLH; b) $11 per DLH; c) $30 per DLH; d) $2 per DLH.

___ 6. Refer to the data in parts (3) and (5) above concerning Baxter Company. How much overhead (both variable and fixed) was applied to units of product during March? a) $12,000; b) $30,000; c) $52,000; d) $42,000.

___ 7. Refer to the data in part (5) above concerning Baxter Company. What was the fixed overhead budget variance for March? a) $10,000 F; b) $10,000 U; c) $3,000 U; d) $3,000 F.

___ 8. Refer to the data in part (5) above concerning Baxter Company. What was the fixed overhead volume variance for March? a) $10,000 F; b) $10,000 U; c) $3,000 U; d) $3,000 F.

Exercises

11-1. Herbold Corporation uses the following cost formulas in its flexible budget for manufacturing overhead:

Item	Cost Formula
Utilities	$ 6,000 per year, plus $0.30 per machine hour (MH)
Supplies	$10,000 per year, plus $0.80 per machine hour
Depreciation	$25,000 per year
Indirect labor	$21,000 per year, plus $0.40 per machine hour

Using these cost formulas, complete the following flexible budget:

Overhead Costs	Cost Formula (per MH)	8,000	Machine Hours 10,000	12,000
Variable overhead costs:				
_____	_____	_____	_____	_____
_____	_____	_____	_____	_____
_____	_____	_____	_____	_____
Total variable costs	_____	_____	_____	_____
Fixed overhead costs:				
_____		_____	_____	_____
_____		_____	_____	_____
_____		_____	_____	_____
_____		_____	_____	_____
Total fixed costs		_____	_____	_____
Total overhead costs		_____	_____	_____

11-2. Refer to the flexible budget data in Exercise 11-1. The standard time to complete one unit of product is 1.6 machine hours. Last year the company budgeted to operate at the 10,000 machine-hour level of activity. During the year the following actual activity took place:

Number of units produced .... 5,000 units
Actual machine hours worked .... 8,500 hours

Actual overhead costs:

	Variable	Fixed
Utilities	$2,600	$ 5,900
Supplies	6,700	10,300
Indirect labor	3,300	21,700
Depreciation		25,000

Prepare a performance report for the year using the format that appears below. Do not compute efficiency variances for variable overhead items.

Performance Report
Herbold Corporation

Budgeted machine hours .... _____

Actual machine hours .... _____

Standard machine hours .... _____

	Cost Formula (per MH)	Actual Costs 8,500 MHs	Budget Based on ____ MHs	Spending or Budget Variance
Variable overhead costs:				
_____	_____	_____	_____	_____
_____	_____	_____	_____	_____
_____	_____	_____	_____	_____
Total variable costs	======	_____	_____	_____
Fixed overhead costs:				
_____		_____	_____	_____
_____		_____	_____	_____
_____		_____	_____	_____
_____		_____	_____	_____
Total fixed costs		_____	_____	_____
Total overhead costs		======	======	======

11-3. The flexible budget for manufacturing overhead for Marina Company is given below:

MARINA COMPANY
Flexible Budget

Overhead Costs	Cost Formula (per DLH)	Direct Labor Hours 10,000	12,000	14,000
Variable costs:				
Electricity	$0.15	$ 1,500	$ 1,800	$ 2,100
Indirect materials	0.50	5,000	6,000	7,000
Indirect labor	0.25	2,500	3,000	3,500
Total variable costs	$0.90	9,000	10,800	12,600
Fixed costs:				
Depreciation		11,500	11,500	11,500
Property taxes		8,500	8,500	8,500
Insurance		4,000	4,000	4,000
Total fixed costs		24,000	24,000	24,000
Total overhead costs		$33,000	$34,800	$36,600

Marina Company uses a standard cost system in which manufacturing overhead is applied to units of product on the basis of direct labor hours (DLHs). A denominator activity level of 12,000 direct labor hours is used in setting predetermined overhead rates. The standard time to complete one unit of product is 1.5 direct labor hours.

For the company's most recent year, the following actual operating data are available:

Units produced	9,000 units
Actual direct labor hours worked	14,000 hours
Actual variable overhead cost	$12,880
Actual fixed overhead cost	$23,750

a. Compute the predetermined overhead rate that would be used by the company, and break it down into variable and fixed cost elements:

Predetermined overhead rate .... _____

Variable cost element .... _____

Fixed cost element .... _____

b. How much overhead would have been applied to work in process during the year? _____

c. Complete the following variance analysis of variable overhead cost for the company's most recent year (see Chapter 10):

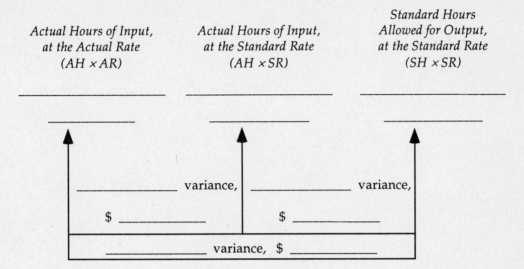

Actual Hours of Input,
at the Actual Rate
(AH × AR)

Actual Hours of Input,
at the Standard Rate
(AH × SR)

Standard Hours
Allowed for Output,
at the Standard Rate
(SH × SR)

_____ variance,   _____ variance,

$ _____ $ _____

_____ variance, $ _____

d. Complete the following variance analysis of fixed overhead cost for the company's most recent year:

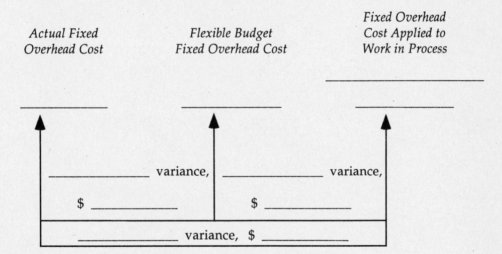

Actual Fixed
Overhead Cost

Flexible Budget
Fixed Overhead Cost

Fixed Overhead
Cost Applied to
Work in Process

_____ variance,   _____ variance,

$ _____ $ _____

_____ variance, $ _____

Answers to Questions and Exercises

True or False

1. T   A static budget is prepared for only one level of activity.

2. F   Many fixed costs are controllable and must be on someone's performance report or no one will control them.

3. F   This may be true in government, but is not true in commercial enterprises. Costs will be higher or lower than budgeted simply due to changes in activity. It is unreasonable to expect , for example, that a production manager will be able to make 10% more units than budgeted (if requested by marketing) without spending more than was originally budgeted.

4. F   It is generally best to avoid using dollars in the activity base.

5. T   The overhead spending variance contains elements of both price and quantity variances.

6. T   The overhead efficiency variance really reflects efficiency in the base underlying the application of overhead.

7. T   The reason for the close relationship is that both variances are based on the difference between the actual direct labor hours and the standard direct labor hours allowed for the actual output.

8. F   The fixed overhead volume variance results from a difference between the denominator level of activity and the standard hours allowed for the actual output of the period. It has nothing to do with spending.

9. F   The reverse is true—the volume variance would be unfavorable.

10. T   Overapplied overhead is equivalent to favorable variances and underapplied overhead is equivalent to unfavorable variances.

Multiple Choice

1. b   This point is illustrated in Exhibit 11-9.

2. c   The volume variance is favorable any time the standard hours allowed for the actual output of the period exceeds the denominator level of activity.

3. b
$$\text{Spending var.} = (AH \times AR) - (AH \times SR)$$
$$= (\$12,050) - (4,100 \times \$3)$$
$$= \$250 \text{ F}$$

4. d
$$\text{Efficiency var.} = (AH \times SR) - (SH \times SR)$$
$$= (4,100 \times \$3) - (4,000^* \times \$3)$$
$$= \$300 \text{ U}$$
$$* 2,000 \text{ units} \times 2 \text{ DLHs/unit} = 4,000 \text{ DLHs}$$

5. a
$$\begin{array}{l}\text{Fixed portion of} \\ \text{the predetermined} \\ \text{overhead rate}\end{array} = \frac{\$30,000}{3,000 \text{ DLHs}}$$
$$= \$10 \text{ per DLH}$$

6. c
$$\begin{array}{l}\text{Predetermined} \\ \text{overhead rate}\end{array} = \$3 + \$10$$
$$= \$13 \text{ per DLH}$$
$$\begin{array}{l}\text{Standard hours} \\ \text{allowed for} \\ \text{the output}\end{array} = \frac{2,000}{\text{units}} \times \frac{2 \text{ DLH}}{\text{per unit}}$$
$$= 4,000 \text{ DLHs}$$
$$\text{Overhead applied} = \$13 \times 4,000$$
$$= \$52,000$$

7. c
$$\begin{array}{l}\text{Budget} \\ \text{variance}\end{array} = \begin{array}{l}\text{Actual fixed} \\ \text{overhead} \\ \text{cost}\end{array} - \begin{array}{l}\text{Flexible budget} \\ \text{fixed overhead} \\ \text{cost}\end{array}$$
$$= \$33,000 - \$30,000$$
$$= \$3,000 \text{ U}$$

8. a
$$\begin{array}{l}\text{Volume} \\ \text{variance}\end{array} = \begin{array}{l}\text{Fixed} \\ \text{overhead} \\ \text{rate}\end{array} \times \left(\begin{array}{l}\text{Denominator} \\ \text{hours}\end{array} - \begin{array}{l}\text{Standard} \\ \text{hours} \\ \text{allowed}\end{array} \right)$$
$$= \$10 \times (3,000 - 4,000) = \$10,000 \text{ F}$$

Exercises

11-1.

Overhead Costs	Cost Formula (per MH)	Machine Hours 8,000	10,000	12,000
Variable overhead costs:				
Utilities	$0.30	$ 2,400	$ 3,000	$ 3,600
Supplies	0.80	6,400	8,000	9,600
Indirect labor	0.40	3,200	4,000	4,800
Total variable costs............	$1.50	12,000	15,000	18,000
Fixed overhead costs:				
Utilities.		6,000	6,000	6,000
Supplies		10,000	10,000	10,000
Depreciation..........................		25,000	25,000	25,000
Indirect labor		21,000	21,000	21,000
Total fixed costs.................		62,000	62,000	62,000
Total overhead costs		$74,000	$77,000	$80,000

11-2.

Performance Report
Herbold Corporation

Budgeted machine hours	10,000
Actual machine hours	8,500
Standard machine hours	8,000

	Cost Formula (per MH)	Actual Costs 8,500 MHs	Budget Based on 8,500 MHs	Spending or Budget Variance
Variable overhead costs:				
Utilities	$0.30	$ 2,600	$ 2,550	$ 50 U
Supplies	0.80	6,700	6,800	100 F
Indirect labor	0.40	3,300	3,400	100 F
Total variable costs	$1.50	12,600	12,750	150 F
Fixed overhead costs:				
Utilities		5,900	6,000	100 F
Supplies		10,300	10,000	300 U
Depreciation		25,000	25,000	--
Indirect labor		21,700	21,000	700 U
Total fixed costs		62,900	62,000	900 U
Total overhead costs		$75,500	$74,750	$750 U

11-3. a. Predetermined overhead rate ($34,800 ÷ 12,000 DLH) $2.90 per DLH
           Variable element ($10,800 ÷ 12,000 DLH) $0.90 per DLH
           Fixed element ($24,000 ÷ 12,000 DLH) $2.00 per DLH

       b. Overhead applied:
               9,000 units × 1.5 DLHs per unit = 13,500 DLHs allowed
               13,500 DLHs × $2.90 per DLH = $39,150 overhead applied

       c. Variable overhead variance analysis:

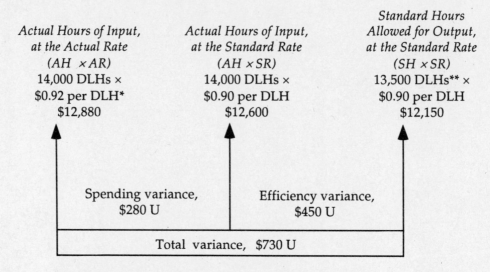

Actual Hours of Input, at the Actual Rate (AH ×AR)	Actual Hours of Input, at the Standard Rate (AH ×SR)	Standard Hours Allowed for Output, at the Standard Rate (SH ×SR)
14,000 DLHs × $0.92 per DLH*	14,000 DLHs × $0.90 per DLH	13,500 DLHs** × $0.90 per DLH
$12,880	$12,600	$12,150

Spending variance, $280 U   Efficiency variance, $450 U

Total variance, $730 U

           * $12,880 ÷ 14,000 DLHs = $0.92 per DLH
           ** 9,000 units × 1.5 DLHs per unit = 13,500 DLHs

       d. Fixed overhead variance analysis:

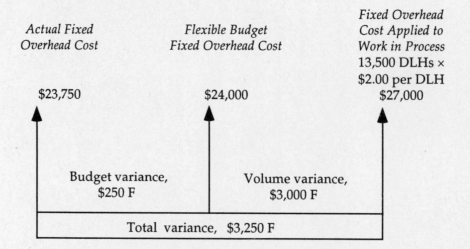

Actual Fixed Overhead Cost	Flexible Budget Fixed Overhead Cost	Fixed Overhead Cost Applied to Work in Process 13,500 DLHs × $2.00 per DLH
$23,750	$24,000	$27,000

Budget variance, $250 F   Volume variance, $3,000 F

Total variance, $3,250 F

Chapter 12

Segment Reporting and Decentralization

Chapter Study Suggestions

The first part of the chapter covers segment reporting. Before you start reading this part of the chapter, study Exhibits 12-2 and 12-3. Notice particularly that on a segmented report the company is divided into progressively smaller parts. Make sure you fully understand the difference between traceable and common costs, and the difference between segment margin and contribution margin. You should memorize the format for a segment report.

The second part of the chapter covers return on investment (ROI) and residual income. Memorize the formulas for ROI and residual income since they are used extensively in the homework material.

The appendix to the chapter covers transfer pricing. The key ideas in this appendix are the lower limits and the upper limits on the transfer price. Make sure you understand how these limits are determined.

CHAPTER HIGHLIGHTS

A. A *responsibility accounting* system functions best in a decentralized organization. A *decentralized organization* is one in which decision making is spread throughout the organization, with managers at all levels making decisions. In a decentralized organization the responsibility accounting system is structured around cost centers, profit centers, and investment centers.

    1. A *cost center* is any responsibility center where a manager has control over cost but not over revenues or investments. A cost center manager is usually held responsible for minimizing cost while providing quality goods and services as requested.

    2. The manager of a *profit center* has control over both cost and revenue. A profit center manager is usually held responsible for maximizing profit.

    3. The manager of an *investment center* has control over cost, revenue, and investments in operating assets. An investment center manager is ordinarily evaluated on the basis of return on investment or residual income, as explained later.

B. To operate effectively, the manager needs much more information than is provided by a single income statement. The manager needs information that focuses on the segments of the organization.

    1. A *segment* is any part or activity of an organization about which the manager seeks cost or revenue data. Examples of segments include sales territories, manufacturing divisions, departments, and groups or lines of products.

    2. Segmented reports for the use of managers should be prepared in the contribution format with which you are already largely familiar.

    3. Exhibit 12-2 contains an illustration of a series of segmented reports. Notice that as you go from one segmented report to another in the exhibit, you are looking at smaller and smaller pieces of the company.

    4. By preparing segmented reports such as those illustrated in Exhibit 12-2, the manager may uncover problems and opportunities that otherwise would have remained hidden from view. For example, some product lines may be unprof-

itable; some sales territories may have a poor sales mix; other sales territories may be using ineffective promotional strategies, etc. Such problems can be spotted with segmented reports.

C. Two general guidelines should be used in assigning costs to the various segments when the contribution approach is used.

    1. First, costs are assigned according to cost behavior patterns; that is, according to whether they are variable or fixed.

    2. Second, costs are assigned according to whether they are traceable or common to the various segments.

      a. Only *traceable costs* should be charged to the segments. The traceable costs of a segment consist of those costs, including fixed costs, that arise because of the existence of the segment. The general rule is to treat as traceable costs only those costs that would disappear over time if the segment itself disappeared.

      b. *Common costs* should not be charged to the segments. Common costs are costs that support more than one segment, but are not traceable, in whole or in part, to any one of those segments. Common costs would not disappear over time if a segment were eliminated and therefore should not be allocated to segments for decision-making purposes. For example, the cost of the company's executive jet is a common cost of the products the company sells. Even if a product were dropped entirely, it is unlikely that there would be any significant change in the costs of owning and operating the executive jet.

D. The format of a segmented income statement is:

	Total	Segment A	Segment B
Sales	$XXX	$XXX	$XXX
Less variable expenses	XXX	XXX	XXX
Contribution margin	XXX	XXX	XXX
Less traceable fixed expenses	XXX	XXX	XXX
Segment margin	XXX	$XXX	$ XXX
Less common fixed expenses not traceable to individual segments	XXX		
Net Income.	$ XXX		

1. A segmented income statement empha-sizes the distinctions between variable and fixed costs and between traceable and common costs.

2. As an organization is segmented into smaller and smaller pieces, some costs that were previously traceable will become common to the smaller segments. There are limits to how finely a cost can be divided.

3. The *segment margin* shows the profitability of a segment after it has covered all of the costs which can be traced directly to it.

4. Common costs should not be allocated to segments, since such an allocation would convey the misleading impression to management that the cost can be avoided by eliminating the seg-ment.

E. Performance in an investment center is often measured by *return on investment (ROI)*, which is defined as:

$$ROI = \frac{\text{Net operating income}}{\text{Average operating assets}}$$

You won't actually use the above formula very much. Instead, you will use the following formula for ROI that is expressed in terms of margin and turnover:

$$ROI = \text{Margin} \times \text{Turnover}$$

where:

$$\text{Margin} = \frac{\text{Net operating income}}{\text{Sales}}$$

$$\text{Turnover} = \frac{\text{Sales}}{\text{Average operating assets}}.$$

1. *Net operating income* is income before interest and taxes.

2. *Operating assets* include cash, accounts receivable, inventory, and all other assets held for productive use within the organization. Operat-ing assets do *not* include, for example, invest-ments in other companies and investments in undeveloped land. Assets that are common to all divisions (such as assets associated with corpo-rate headquarters) should not be allocated to the divisions when making ROI computations.

3. A company's return on investment can be improved by (1) increasing sales, (2) reducing

expenses, or (3) reducing assets, holding all other things constant.

4. ROI is criticized for several reasons. One of the most important criticisms is that a division manager who is evaluated based on ROI will tend to reject projects whose ROIs are less than the division's current ROI but greater than the com-pany's minimum rate of return. This would not be in the best interests of the overall organization since a project whose rate of return exceeds the minimum rate of return should ordinarily be accepted.

F. Another approach to measuring performance in an investment center is known as residual income.

1. *Residual income* is the net operating income that an investment center earns above the mini-mum required rate of return on operating assets.

$$\text{Residual income} = \text{Net operating income} - \left(\begin{array}{c} \text{Required rate of return} \times \text{Average operating assets} \end{array} \right)$$

2. The residual income approach to per-formance evaluation encourages investment in worthwhile projects that would be rejected under ROI.

3. A major disadvantage of the residual income approach is that it can't be easily used to compare divisions of different sizes. Larger divi-sions naturally tend to have larger residual incomes, all other things the same.

Appendix 12A: Transfer Pricing

A. It is fairly common for one part of a company to provide goods or services to another part of the company. For example, the General Motors truck division sells delivery trucks to the Chevrolet Division. The price that is charged for such a sale inside a company is called a *transfer price*.

1. If the divisions are profit or investment centers, then the selling division would like the transfer price to be high and the purchasing divi-sion would like the price to be low.

2. Three general approaches are used in set-ting transfer prices: (1) allow the managers involved to negotiate their own transfer price, (2)

set the transfer price equal to cost, or (3) set the transfer price equal to a market price.

B. When an organization relies on negotiated transfer prices, managers are free to work out transfer prices on their own. The managers of two divisions involved in the proposed transfer can choose whether to agree to the transfer or not. If they do agree to a transfer, then they must agree on the transfer price. Presumably, neither manager would agree to a transfer price unless it increases his or her division's profits.

1. From the viewpoint of the selling division, the transfer price must cover at least variable costs plus any opportunity costs. This sets a limit on how low the transfer price can go in negotiations.

$$\frac{\text{Transfer}}{\text{price}} \geq \frac{\text{Variable}}{\text{cost}} + \frac{\text{Opportunity}}{\text{cost}}$$

a. There is an opportunity cost if there is a constraint. In that case, filling the purchasing division's order would result in lost sales to other customers.

b. The opportunity cost can be computed as follows:

$$\frac{\text{Opportunity}}{\text{cost}} = \frac{\begin{array}{c}\text{Total contribution margin}\\ \text{on lost sales}\end{array}}{\text{Number of units transferred}}$$

2. If the purchasing division can buy what it needs from an outside supplier (vendor), then the manager of the purchasing division clearly would not want to pay a higher price within the company. From the viewpoint of the purchasing division, the upper limit on the transfer price is given by:

$$\frac{\text{Transfer}}{\text{price}} \leq \frac{\text{Cost of buying from}}{\text{an outside supplier}}$$

3. If the lower limit on the transfer price is less than the upper limit, it is possible for the two managers to pick a transfer price that would increase both of their divisions' net incomes by going through with the transfer.

4. In principle, negotiated transfer prices should work. If it is in the best interests of the company for the transfer to be made, it will always be possible for the managers to find a transfer price that would make them both better off.

5. However, in practice, managers may not understand what is in their own best interests or they may be uncooperative. In either case, negotiations my drag on and even fail. Perhaps for that reason, most companies use transfer pricing rules based on either cost or market price instead of relying on negotiations.

C. Cost-based transfer prices are convenient to use, but may lead to bad decisions.

1. If variable cost is used as the transfer price, it will understate the real cost to the company of the transfer when there is no idle capacity and there are opportunity costs. In essence, the manager of the purchasing division will be getting the transferred good or service at a discounted price below true cost. This can lead to unwise decisions such as pricing products too low.

2. If full absorption cost is used as the transfer price, the cost will never reflect the true cost to the company of making the transfer. If the transfer has no effect on total fixed costs, then the true cost to the company is variable cost plus, possibly, opportunity cost. This would very rarely equal full cost.

3. When the transfer price is set equal to cost, the only division that will show any profit on the transaction is the one that makes a final sale to an outside party. Other divisions will show no profits for their efforts.

4. When transfers are priced at the selling division's cost, there is no incentive to control costs. The selling division simply passes its costs on to the next division. For this reason, if transfer prices are based on cost, standard costs rather than actual costs should be used.

D. Market prices are often used as transfer prices. This solution works very well when the selling division has no idle capacity. However, when the selling division has idle capacity, the market price overstates the real cost of the transfer.

REVIEW AND SELF TEST
Questions and Exercises

True or False

Enter a T or an F in the blank to indicate whether the statement is true or false.

___ 1. Common costs should be allocated to product line segments on the basis of sales dollars.

___ 2. The terms "traceable cost" and "variable cost" are synonymous.

___ 3. As an organization is broken down into smaller segments, costs that were traceable to the larger segments may become common to the smaller segments.

___ 4. A decentralized organization is one in which decision making is confined to top management.

___ 5. Residual income is equal to the difference between total revenues and operating expenses.

___ 6. Using ROI to evaluate managers may lead managers to reject investment opportunities that would be beneficial to the company as a whole.

___ 7. A profit center manager is responsible for generating revenue, but is not responsible for controlling costs.

___ 8. A reduction in operating assets will increase a division's ROI if sales and expenses remain unchanged.

___ 9. In computing residual income, expenses incurred in operating corporate headquarters should be allocated to the separate divisions on the basis of the contribution margins of the divisions.

___ 10. Under the residual income approach, the manager seeks to maximize the rate of return on operating assets.

___ 11. An increase in total sales would typically increase the turnover of assets but it would have no effect on the margin.

___ 12. (Appendix 12A) When a division is operating at capacity, the cost of transferring a product or service to another division includes an element of opportunity cost.

___ 13. (Appendix 12A) Transfer prices based on actual cost are superior in that they provide incentive for the control of costs between transferring divisions.

Multiple Choice

Choose the best answer or response by placing the identifying letter in the space provided.

___ 1. Armco, Inc., produces and sells five product lines. Which of the following costs would typically be a traceable fixed cost of a product line? a) advertising costs of the product line; b) the salary of the company's president; c) depreciation of facilities jointly used to produce several product lines; d) responses a, b, and c, are all correct.

___ 2. If a segment has a negative segment margin: a) the segment should be dropped; b) the segment should be retained only if it has a positive contribution margin; c) the segment is not covering its own traceable costs, but it still may be of benefit to the company; d) none of these.

___ 3. Rumberger, Inc. sells two products: X and Y. Data concerning the company for July follow:

	Product X	Product Y
Sales	$200,000	$300,000
Variable expenses	50,000	100,000
Traceable fixed expenses	80,000	150,000

In addition, there were common fixed expenses of $70,000 in July. What was the segment margin for Product X? a) $70,000; b) $120,000; c) $150,000; d) $38,000.

___ 4. Refer to the data for Rumberger, Inc. in exercise (3) above. What was the net income for the entire company? a) $120,000; b) $(4,000); c) $70,000; d) $50,000.

___ 5. Refer to the data for Rumberger, Inc. in exercise (3) above. Suppose advertising for Prod-

151

uct Y is increased by $20,000 per month, which results in increased sales of $90,000 per month. This should have the following effect on Product Y's monthly segment margin: a) increase by $70,000; b) increase by $40,000; c) increase by $60,000; d) decrease by $20,000.

___ 6. Refer to the data for Rumberger, Inc. in exercise (5) above. What would be the effect of the increase in advertising and sales of Product Y on the company's overall net income? a) increase by $70,000; b) increase by $40,000; c) increase by $60,000; d) decrease by $20,000.

___ 7. If the level of inventory in a company is reduced, and if sales and expenses remain unchanged, one would expect the company's ROI to: a) increase; b) decrease; c) remain unchanged; d) it is impossible to tell what would happen to ROI.

___ 8. A company reported the following results:

Average operating assets	$ 45,000
Sales	180,000
Contribution margin	21,600
Net operating income	9,000

The company's ROI would be: a) 48%; b) 12%; c) 20%; d) 30%.

___ 9. The purpose of the residual income approach is to: a) maximize a segment's overall rate of return; b) maximize the ROI that a segment is able to get on its operating assets; c) maximize the total amount of the residual income; d) none of these.

___ 10. A company reported the following results:

Average operating assets	$300,000
Stockholders' equity	50,000
Sales	900,000
Net operating income	75,000
Minimum required rate of return	18%

The company's residual income would be: a) $25,000; b) $15,000; c) $21,000; d) 475,000.

___ 11. (Appendix 12A) Division A produces a part that it sells to outside customers. Data concerning this part appear below:

Selling price to outside customers ...	$60
Variable cost per unit	$40
Total fixed cost	$100,000
Capacity in units	20,000

Division B of the same company now purchases 5,000 units of a similar part from an outside supplier at a price of $58 per unit. Division B wants to purchase these 5,000 units from Division A instead, but Division A has no idle capacity. Division A should insist on a transfer price of at least: a) $60; b) $58; c) $40; d) $45.

___ 12. (Appendix 12A) Refer to the data in question (11) above. If Division A has idle capacity, the manager of Division A should insist that the transfer price be at least: a) $60; b) $40; c) between $45 and $58; d) between $40 and $58.

12-1.   The following data, pertain to Bylund Company's operations for July.

	Total	Product X	Product Y
Number of units sold		10,000	12,000
Selling price per unit		$20.00	$25.00
Variable cost per unit:			
Production		9.00	10.00
Selling and administrative		3.00	3.75
Fixed costs:			
Production	$ 155,000		
Selling and administrative	20,000		

Of the fixed costs, only $50,000 of the fixed production costs are traceable to the production of Product X and $75,000 are traceable to Product Y.

a.   Prepare a segmented income statement for Bylund Company using the following form:

BYLUND COMPANY
Income Statement
For the Month Ended July 31

	Total		Product X		Product Y	
	Amount	%	Amount	%	Amount	%
Sales	$_____ ___		$_____ ___		$_____ ___	
Less variable expenses:						
Production	$_____ ___		$_____ ___		$_____ ___	
Selling and administrative	$_____ ___		$_____ ___		$_____ ___	
Total variable expenses	$_____ ___		$_____ ___		$_____ ___	
Contribution margin	$_____ ___		$_____ ___		$_____ ___	
Less traceable fixed expenses	$_____ ___		$_____ ___		$_____ ___	
Product line segment margin	$_____ ___		$_____ ___		$_____ ___	
Less common fixed expenses not						
traceable to individual products:						
Production	$_____ ___					
Selling and administrative	$_____ ___					
Total common fixed expenses	$_____ ___					
Net income	$_____ ___					

b. Should either Product X or Product Y be dropped? Why?

_____

_____

_____

_____

c. Product X can be enhanced by incurring an additional $25,000 in fixed production costs. Instead of raising the price of Product X to reflect the enhancement, Bylund Company would seek to increase sales. If sales increased by $80,000, should the product be enhanced?

_____

_____

_____

_____

_____

_____

_____

_____

12-2. Fill in the missing data for Biggerstaff, Inc.

	Total		Southwest Division		Central Division	
	Amount	%	Amount	%	Amount	%
Sales	$1,000,000	___	$ _____	___	$ _____	___
Variable expenses	$_____	___	$ _____	___	$ _____	___
Contribution margin	$_____	___	$ 360,000	60	$ _____	___
Traceable fixed expenses	$_____	___	$ 150,000	___	$ 200,000	___
Division segment margin	$_____	___	$ _____	___	$ 120,000	30
Common fixed expenses not traceable to individual divisions	$_____	___				
Net income	$ 40,000	___				

Hint: The contribution margin ratio for the Southwest Division can be used to determine its sales.

12-3. Frankel Company has the following data for its Connectors Division for last year:

Sales	$2,000,000
Net operating income	160,000
Average operating assets	800,000
Minimum rate of return	16%

a.   Compute the return on investment (ROI) for the Connectors Division, using margin and turnover.

b.   Compute the residual income for the Connectors Division.

12-4. Fill in the missing information for the three different companies below:

	Company 1	Company 2	Company 3
Sales	$600,000	$600,000	$_____
Net operating income	60,000	_____	27,000
Average operating assets	300,000	200,000	_____
Margin	_____	7.5%	_____
Turnover	_____	_____	1.8
Return on investment (ROI)	_____	_____	27%

Chapter 12

12-5. (Appendix 12A) Perchon Company's Regulator Division produces a small valve used by other companies as a key part in their products. Cost and sales data relating to the valve are given below:

Selling price per unit $50
Variable costs per unit 30
Fixed costs per unit 12*

*Based on the Regulator Division's capacity of 40,000 valves per year.

Perchon Company's Boiler Division is introducing a new product that will use a valve such as the one produced in the Regulator Division. An outside supplier has quoted the Boiler Division a price of $48 per valve for the 10,000 valves the Boiler Division needs every year. The Boiler Division would like to purchase the valves from the Regulator Division instead if an acceptable transfer price can be worked out.

a. Assume that the Regulator Division is presently selling all the valves it can produce to outside customers. What is the lowest transfer price below which the selling division should not go?

b. From the standpoint of the entire company, should the Boiler Division purchase the valves from the Regulator Division or from the outside supplier? Explain.

_____

_____

_____

_____

c. Assume the Regulator Division is presently selling 35,000 valves per year to outside customers. What would be the impact on Perchon Company's overall profits if all 10,000 valves were acquired from the Regulator Division rather than from the outside supplier?

d. Assume that the Regulator Division has ample idle capacity to handle all the Boiler Division's needs. What is the lowest transfer price below which the selling division should not go?

Answers to Questions and Exercises

True or False

1. F Common costs should never be allocated to segments since such allocated costs could be misleading and lead managers to believe that they could be avoided by dropping the segment.

2. F A traceable cost can be either variable or fixed.

3. T As an organization is divided into smaller and smaller segments, there are limits to how finely a cost can be divided.

4. F In a decentralized organization, decision making is spread through all levels of management.

5. F Residual income is the difference between net operating income and the minimum return that must be generated on operating assets.

6. T This is a major criticism of the ROI method.

7. F A profit center is responsible for controlling costs as well as generating revenues.

8. T A reduction in assets will result in an increase in the turnover figure, and an increase in the ROI.

9. F Common expenses, such as those associated with operating corporate headquarters, should not be allocated to segments when making either residual income or ROI computations.

10. F Under the residual income approach, the manager seeks to maximize the residual income figure.

11. F The margin would also typically increase, since the net operating income would generally increase more rapidly than sales due to the effects of operating leverage discussed in an earlier chapter.

12. T The opportunity cost is the contribution margin lost from giving up outside sales.

13. F The opposite is true. When actual cost is used as a transfer price there is little or no incentive to control costs since whatever cost is incurred can simply be transferred on to the next division.

Multiple Choice

1. a The cost of advertising a specific product could be eliminated if the product were dropped.

2. c A negative segment margin means that a segment is not covering its own traceable costs. However, the segment may still be of value to the company if it is necessary to the sale of other products.

3. a The segment margin for Product X can be read directly from the segmented income statement that appears below:

	Total	Product X	Product Y
Sales	$500,000	$200,000	$300,000
Variable expenses	150,000	50,000	100,000
Contribution margin	350,000	150,000	200,000
Traceable fixed expenses	230,000	80,000	150,000
Segment margin	120,000	$70,000	$50,000
Common fixed expenses	70,000		
Net income	$50,000		

4. d See the segmented income statement above in the answer to exercise (3).

5. b The following statement will help in solving this exercise:

	Product Y	Percentage of Sales
Sales	$300,000	100 %
Variable expenses	100,000	$33\frac{1}{3}$ %
Contribution margin	200,000	$66\frac{2}{3}$ %
Traceable fixed expenses	150,000	50 %
Segment margin	$50,000	$16\frac{2}{3}$ %

Using the contribution margin ratio method, the $90,000 increase in sales should lead to a $60,000 (= 66 2/3% X $90,000) increase in contribution mar-

157

gin. This would be offset by the $20,000 increase in advertising expenses, a traceable fixed expense, to yield a net $40,000 increase in segment margin.

6. b   Since there is no mention of any change in common fixed expenses, the change in the company's overall net income should be the same as the change in Product Y's segment margin.

7. a   If the level of inventory is reduced, then operating assets are reduced. The result will be a higher turnover figure and an increase in the ROI.

8. c   The computations are:

$$ROI = \frac{\$9,000}{\$180,000} \times \frac{\$180,000}{\$45,000} = 5\% \times 4 = 20\%$$

9. c   Residual income has nothing to do with ROI; moreover, as residual income increases ROI frequently decreases (as shown in examples in the chapter).

10. c   The computations are:

Average operating assets $300,000
Net operating income .... $ 75,000
Minimum required return
   (18% × $300,000) 54,000
Residual income .... $ 21,000

11. a   The computations are:

Transfer price = Variable costs +
                         Opportunity cost
Transfer price = $40 + ($60 − $40)
Transfer price = $60

12. b   The computations are:

Transfer price = Variable costs +
                         Opportunity cost
Transfer price = $40 + $ 0
Transfer price = $40

Exercises

12-1.

a.

BYLUND COMPANY
Income Statement
For the Month Ended July 31

	Total		Product X		Product Y	
	Amount	%	Amount	%	Amount	%
Sales	$500,000	100	$200,000	100	$300,000	100
Less variable expenses:						
Production	210,000	42	90,000	45	120,000	40
Selling and administrative	75,000	15	30,000	15	45,000	15
Total variable expenses	285,000	57	120,000	60	165,000	55
Contribution margin	215,000	43	80,000	40	135,000	45
Less traceable fixed expenses	125,000	25	50,000	25	75,000	25
Product line segment margin	90,000	18	$ 30,000	15	$ 60,000	20
Less common fixed expenses not						
traceable to individual products:						
Production	30,000					
Selling and administrative	20,000					
Total common fixed expenses ..	50,000					
Net Income	$ 40,000					

b.   Neither product should be dropped. They are both covering all of their own traceable costs and are contributing to covering the fixed common costs and to overall profits of the company.

c.   Increase in sales $80,0000
      Contribution margin ratio .... × 40%
      Increase in contribution margin .... $ 32,000
      Increase in fixed production costs .... $ 25,000
      Increase in net income .... $ 7,000

      Yes, the product should be enhanced

12-2.

	Total		Southwest Division		Central Division	
	Amount	*%*	*Amount*	*%*	*Amount*	*%*
Sales	$1,000,000	100	$600,000[5]	100	$400,000[6]	100
Variable expenses	320,000[10]	32	240,000[7]	40	80,000[9]	20
Contribution margin	680,000[11]	68	360,000	60	320,000[8]	80
Traceable fixed expenses	350,000[2]	35	150,000	25	200,000	50
Division segment margin	330,000[3]	33	$210,000[1]	35	$120,000	30
Common fixed expenses not traceable to divisions	290,000[4]	29				
Net income	$ 40,000	4				

Note: This problem can be solved in many different ways. The following is one sequence that can be followed:
1. $360,000 - $150,000 = $210,000
2. $150,000 + $200,000 = $350,000
3. $210,000 + $120,000 = $330,000
4. $330,000 + $40,000 = $290,000
5. $360,000 ÷ 60% = $600,000
6. $1,000,000 - $600,000 = $400,000
7. $600,000 - $360,000 = $240,000
8. $200,000 + $120,000 = $320,000
9. $400,000 - $320,000 = $80,000
10. $240,000 + $80,000 = $320,000
11. $360,000 + $320,000 = $680,000

12-3. a. $\text{Margin} = \dfrac{\text{Net operating income}}{\text{Sales}} = \dfrac{\$160,000}{\$2,000,000} = 8\%$

$\text{Turnover} = \dfrac{\text{Sales}}{\text{Average operating assets}} = \dfrac{\$2,000,000}{\$800,000} = 2.5$

ROI = Margin × Turnover
= 8% × 2.5 = 20%

b.
Average operating assets	$800,000
Net operating income	$160,000
Minimum required return (16% × $800,000)	128,000
Residual income	$ 32,000

12-4.

	Company 1	Company 2	Company 3
Sales	$600,000*	$600,000*	$180,000
Net operating income	60,000*	45,000	27,000*
Average operating assets	300,000*	200,000*	100,000
Margin	10%	7.5%*	15%
Turnover	2	3.0	1.8*
Return on investment (ROI)	20%	22.5%	27%*

*Given

12-5.
  a. If the Regulator Division transfers a valve to the Boiler Division, it cannot be sold on the outside market. Therefore, the Regulator Division loses $50 in revenue. Thus, the lowest transfer price the Regulator Division could accept is $50. This is verified by using the formula approach as follows:

$$\frac{\text{Transfer}}{\text{price}} \geq \frac{\text{Variable}}{\text{cost}} + \frac{\text{Total contribution margin on lost sales}}{\text{Number of units transferred}}$$

$$\frac{\text{Transfer}}{\text{price}} \geq \$30 + \frac{(\$50 - \$30) \times 10,000}{10,000} = \$30 + (\$50 - \$30) = \$50$$

  b. The valves should be purchased from the outside supplier, since the price will be only $48 per valve. In contrast, the company will give up $50 in revenue for each valve transferred internally rather than sold on the outside market.

  c.
Regulator Division capacity	40,000 valves
Less Boiler Division's requirements	10,000 valves
Valves available for sale to outsiders	30,000 valves

Potential sales to outsiders	35,000 valves
Valves available for sale to outsiders	30,000 valves
Lost sales	5,000 valves

Cost of transferring internally:	
Variable cost $30 × 10,000	$300,000
Lost contribution margin ($50 − $30) × 5,000	100,000
Total cost of transferring internally	$400,000
Cost of purchasing from an outside supplier	$480,000

Profits will be $80,000 higher if the valves are acquired internally rather than purchased outside.

  d. Transfer Price = $30 + $0 = $30
      There is no lost contribution margin, since the Regulator Division has idle capacity.

Chapter 13

Relevant Costs for Decision Making

Chapter Study Suggestions

The concept of relevant costs is covered in the first few pages of the chapter. Study these pages carefully, since this basic idea is used throughout the chapter.

A number of specific decision-making situations are covered in the chapter. The same principles are used in each situation to identify the relevant costs.

CHAPTER HIGHLIGHTS

A. Every decision involves a choice from among at least two alternatives. A *relevant cost* or benefit is a cost or benefit that differs between alternatives. If a cost or benefit does not differ between alternatives, it is not relevant in the decision and can be ignored. *Avoidable cost, differential cost,* and *incremental cost* are synonyms for relevant cost.

1. Two broad classifications of costs are irrelevant in decisions: (a) sunk costs; and (b) future costs that do not differ between alternatives. *Sunk costs* are not relevant since they have already been incurred and therefore cannot differ between alternatives.

2. To make a decision, you should:

a. Eliminate the costs and benefits that do not differ between alternatives. These irrelevant costs consist of sunk costs and future costs that do not differ between alternatives.

b. Make a decision based on the remaining cost and benefit data. These data consist of the costs and benefits that differ between alternatives.

3. Costs that are relevant in one situation may not be relevant in another situation. There are no rules for identifying what costs are relevant and what costs are irrelevant except that costs that do not differ between alternatives are irrelevant.

B. As stated above, sunk costs are never relevant since they are not avoidable; that is, they can never differ between alternatives.

1. The book value of old equipment is a sunk cost. Hence, it is not relevant in decision making. Periodic depreciation based on the book value of old equipment is also irrelevant.

2. However, depreciation is a sunk cost only if it relates to old equipment (e.g., equipment that has already been purchased). Thus, depreciation on new equipment would be a relevant cost.

3. Even though the book value of old equipment is not relevant in a decision, the resale value of old equipment may be relevant. For example, if you are considering whether to replace an old machine, its resale value is rele-

vant. If the machine were not replaced, the resale value would not be realized.

C. As stated above, future costs that do not differ between alternatives are not relevant costs.

1. For example, maintenance costs are irrelevant to the decision of which machine to purchase if maintenance costs will be the same regardless of which machine is purchased.

2. Relevant costs should be isolated in cost analysis for three reasons:

a. In any given situation, the irrelevant costs greatly outnumber the relevant costs. Focusing just on the relevant costs simply takes less time and effort.

b. The use of irrelevant costs intermingled with relevant costs may draw the decision-maker's attention away from the really critical data.

c. People often make mistakes when they include irrelevant costs in an analysis. They often incorrectly calculate the amount of the irrelevant cost under the alternatives and it may appear that the amount of the irrelevant cost differs between the alternatives when in fact it does not. It is particularly easy to make this mistake when dealing with fixed costs that are stated on a per unit basis. This makes the fixed costs appear as if they are variable costs that change if the number of units produced and sold changes.

D. *Adding or dropping a segment* such as a product line is one of the decision-making situations covered in the chapter. In making this decision, compare the contribution margin of the segment to the fixed costs that could be avoided by dropping the segment.

1. If the contribution margin lost by dropping a segment is greater than the fixed costs that can be avoided, then the segment should be retained.

2. If the contribution margin lost by dropping a segment is less than the fixed costs that can be avoided, then the segment should be dropped.

3. Exhibit 13-3 illustrates an alternative approach to deciding whether to retain or drop a

product line or other segment of a company. In this approach two income statements are prepared —one for each alternative.

4. The decision to keep or drop a product line or other segment of a company is often clouded by the allocation of common fixed costs as discussed in Chapter 12.

    a. Allocations of common costs can make a product line or other segment *appear* to be unprofitable, when in fact the segment may be contributing substantially to the overall profits of the company.

    b. Common fixed costs should never be allocated to segments of a company; segments should be charged only with those costs that are directly traceable to them, as shown in Exhibit 13-4 and discussed in Chapter 12.

E. A decision to produce a part internally rather than to buy it from a supplier is called a *make or buy decision*. The relevant costs in such a decision, as always, are the costs that differ between the alternatives.

    1. Exhibit 13-5 contains an example of a make or buy decision. Notice from the exhibit that the costs that are relevant in a make or buy decision are the costs that *differ* between the make or buy alternatives.

    2. Opportunity cost may be a key factor in a make or buy decision as well as in other decisions.

    a. If there are no alternative uses of the capacity that is currently being used to make a part or a product, then the opportunity cost is zero and it does not need to be considered.

    b. On the other hand, if buying from outside the company would release capacity that could be used to produce something else, then there is an opportunity cost involved in using that capacity to make parts internally. This opportunity cost is the segment margin that could be obtained from the alternative use of the capacity. The opportunity cost should be included in the analysis.

F. Another decision concerns *special orders*. A company may have an opportunity to sell products under special circumstances that don't affect regular sales. For example, a company may receive an order on a one-time basis from an overseas customer in a market the company does not ordinarily sell in. Such a special order should be accepted if the incremental revenue from the special order exceeds the incremental (i.e., avoidable) costs of the order. Any opportunity costs should be taken into account.

G. A *constraint* is a scarce resource that limits output. When the constraint is a machine or a workstation, it is called a *bottleneck*. For example, a company may be able to sell 1,000 units of a product per week, but have a machine that is capable of only producing 800 units a week. The machine would be a bottleneck and time on the machine would be a scarce resource that is a constraint.

    1. When there is a production constraint, demand exceeds capacity. In that case, managers must decide what the company will *not* do since it cannot do everything.

    2. If the problem is how to best utilize a scarce resource, fixed costs are likely to be constant and therefore irrelevant. Maximizing the company's total contribution margin is equivalent to maximizing the company's profit. Given capacity and the company's fixed costs, the problem is how to best use that capacity to maximize total contribution margin and profit.

    3. The key to the efficient utilization of a scarce resource is *the contribution margin per unit of the constrained resource*. The products with the greatest contribution margin per unit of the constrained resource are the most profitable; they generate the greatest profit from a given amount of the constrained resource. These products should be emphasized over products with a lower contribution margin per unit of the constrained resource.

    4. Since the constraint limits the output of the entire organization, there can be a tremendous payoff to increasing the amount of the available scarce resource. This is called "elevating the constraint" and can be accomplished in a variety of ways including working overtime on the bottleneck, buying another machine, subcontracting work, and so on.

    5. The contribution margin per unit of the constrained resource is also a measure of opportunity cost. For example, when considering

whether to accept an order for a product that uses the constrained resource, the opportunity cost of using the constrained resource should be considered. That opportunity cost is the lost contribution margin for the job that would be displaced if the order were accepted.

H. In some industries, such as petroleum refining, a number of end products are produced from a single raw material input. Such products are known as *joint products*. The *split-off point* is that point in the manufacturing process at which the joint products can be recognized as separate products.

1. Decisions as to whether a joint product should be sold at the split-off point or processed further and then sold are known as "sell or process further" decisions.

2. Costs incurred up to the split-off point are called *joint product costs*. These costs are irrelevant in decisions regarding whether a product should be processed further after the split-off point, since they will be incurred regardless of what is done after the split-off point.

3. It is profitable to continue processing joint products after the split-off point so long as the incremental revenue from such processing exceeds the incremental processing costs.

REVIEW AND SELF TEST
Questions and Exercises

True or False

Enter a T or an F in the blank to indicate whether the statement is true or false.

___ 1. All costs are relevant in a decision except costs that do not differ between alternatives.

___ 2. In a decision, variable costs are relevant costs and fixed costs are irrelevant.

___ 3. Sunk costs may be relevant in a decision.

___ 4. Depreciation is a relevant cost if it relates to equipment that has not yet been purchased.

___ 5. Future costs are always relevant in decision-making.

___ 6. Costs that are relevant in one decision are not necessarily relevant in another decision.

___ 7. If a company is able to avoid more in fixed costs than it loses in contribution margin by dropping a product, then it will be better off financially if the product is eliminated.

___ 8. Allocation of common fixed costs to product lines and to other segments of a company helps the manager to see if the product line or segment is profitable.

___ 9. If a product has a negative segment margin, the product should be discontinued.

___ 10. Opportunity cost may be a key factor in a make or buy decision.

___ 11. If there is a constrained resource, a company should emphasize the product that has the highest contribution margin per unit.

___ 12. A joint product should continue to be processed after the split-off point so long as the incremental revenue from such processing exceeds the incremental processing costs.

___ 13. Joint product costs are irrelevant in decisions regarding what to do with joint products after the split-off point.

Multiple Choice

Choose the best answer or response by placing the identifying letter in the space provided.

___ 1. All of the following costs are relevant in a make or buy decision except: a) the opportunity cost of space; b) costs that are avoidable by buying rather than making; c) variable costs of producing the item; d) costs that are differential between the make and buy alternatives; e) all of the above costs are relevant.

___ 2. One of Simplex Company's products has a contribution margin of $50,000 and fixed costs totaling $60,000. If the product is dropped, $40,000 of the fixed costs will continue unchanged. As a result of dropping the product, the company's net operating income should: a) decrease by $50,000; b) increase by $30,000; c) decrease by $30,000; d) increase by $10,000.

___ 3. Halley Company produces 2,000 parts each year that are used in one of its products. The unit product cost of this part is:

Variable manuf. cost	$ 7.50
Fixed manuf. cost	6.00
Unit product cost	$13.50

The part can be purchased from an outside supplier for $10 per unit. If the part is purchased from the outside supplier, two-thirds of the fixed manufacturing costs can be eliminated. The effect on net operating income from purchasing the part would be a: a) $3,000 increase; b) $1,000 decrease; c) $7,000 increase; d) $5,000 decrease.

___ 4. Product A has a contribution margin of $8 per unit, a contribution margin ratio of 50%, and requires 4 machine-hours to produce. Product B has a contribution margin of $12 per unit, a contribution margin ratio of 40%, and requires 5 machine-hours to produce. If the constraint is machine-hours, then the company should emphasize: a) Product A; b) Product B.

___ 5. Sunderson Products, Inc. has received a special order for 1,000 units of a sport-fighting kite. The customer has offered a price of $9.95 for each kite. The unit costs of the kite, at its normal sales level of 30,000 units per year, are detailed below:

Variable production costs	$5.25
Fixed production costs	2.35
Variable selling costs	0.75
Fixed selling and admin. costs	3.45

There is ample idle capacity to produce the special order without any increase in total fixed costs. The variable selling costs on the special order would be $0.15 per unit instead of $0.75 per unit. The special order would have no impact on the company's other sales. What effect would accepting this special order have on the company's net operating income? a) $1,850 increase; b) $1,850 decrease; c) $4,550 increase; d) $4,550 decrease.

___ 6. Products A and B are joint products. Product A can be sold for $1,200 at the split-off point, or processed further at a cost of $600 and then sold for $1,700. Product B can be sold for $3,000 at the split-off point, or processed further at a cost of $800 and then sold for $4,000. The company should process further: a) Product A; b) Product B; c) both products; d) neither of the products.

Exercises

13-1.   The most recent income statement for the men's formal wear department of Merrill's Department Store is given below:

Sales		$500,000
Less variable expenses		200,000
Contribution margin		300,000
Less fixed expenses:		
Salaries and wages	$150,000	
Insurance on inventories	10,000	
Depreciation of fixtures	65,000*	
Advertising	100,000	325,000
Net operating income (loss)		$ (25,000)

*Six year remaining useful life, with little or no current resale value.

Due to its poor showing, management is thinking about dropping the men's formal wear department. If the department is dropped, a make-work position will be found for one long-time employee who is due to retire in several years. That employee's salary is $30,000. The fixtures in the department would have no resale value and would be hauled to the county dump.

Prepare an analysis, using the following form, to determine whether the department should be dropped.

Contribution margin lost if the department is dropped ...... $ _____

Less avoidable fixed costs:

_____ .... $ _____

_____ .... _____

_____ .... _____   _____

Increase (decrease) in operating income .... $_____

Based on this analysis, should the men's formal wear department be dropped?

Redo the analysis, using the alternate format shown below:

	Keep Department	Drop Department	Difference: Income Increase or (Decrease)
Sales	$500,000	$_____	$_____
Less variable expenses	200,000	_____	_____
Contribution margin	300,000	_____	_____
Less fixed expenses:			
Salaries and wages	150,000	_____	_____
Insurance on inventories	10,000	_____	_____
Depreciation of equipment	65,000	_____	_____
Advertising	100,000	_____	_____
Total fixed expenses	325,000	_____	_____
Net operating income (loss)	$ (25,000)	$_____	$_____

13-2.   Watson Company produces two products from a common input. Data relating to the two products are given below:

	Product A	Product B
Sales value at the split-off point	$60,000	$120,000
Allocated joint product costs	45,000	90,000
Sales value after further processing	90,000	200,000
Cost of further processing	20,000	85,000

Determine which of the products should be sold at the split-off point, and which should be processed further before sale. Use the form that appears below.

	Product A	Product B
Sales value after further processing	$_____	$_____
Sales value at the split-off point	_____	_____
Incremental revenue from further processing	_____	_____
Less cost of further processing	_____	_____
Profit (loss) from further processing	$_____	$_____

13-3. Petre Company is now making a small part that is used in one of its products. The company's accounting department reports the following costs of producing the part internally:

	Per Part
Direct materials	$15
Direct labor	10
Variable manufacturing overhead	2
Fixed manufacturing overhead, traceable	4
Fixed manufacturing overhead, allocated common	5
Unit product cost	$36

A total of 75% of the traceable fixed manufacturing overhead cost consists of depreciation of special equipment, and 25% consists of supervisory salaries. The special equipment has no resale value. The supervisory salaries could be avoided if production of the part were discontinued.

An outside supplier has offered to sell the parts to Petre Company for $30 each, based on an order of 5,000 parts per year. Should Petre Company accept this offer, or continue to make the parts internally? Assume that direct labor is a variable cost. Use the following form in your answer:

	Per Unit Differential Cost		5,000 Parts	
	Make	Buy	Make	Buy
Outside purchase price		$_____		$_____
Cost of making internally:				
_____	$_____		$_____	
_____	_____		_____	
_____	_____		_____	
_____	_____		_____	
_____	_____		_____	
Total cost	$_____	$_____	$_____	$_____

13-4.   Kuski Corporation makes two models of its hair dryer at a facility in Lexington. The copper-winding machine has been the constraint in the factory in the past. The capacity of this machine is 9,600 minutes per month. Data concerning these two products appear below:

	Standard	*Premium*
Unit selling price	$14.00	$20.00
Variable cost per unit	5.00	8.00
Copper-winding machine time per unit	0.5 minute	0.6 minute
Monthly demand per month	12,000 units	8,000 units

a.   Determine if the copper-winding machine is currently a constraint. In other words, does demand exceed capacity? Use the form below to answer this question

	Standard	*Premium*	*Total*
_____	_____	_____	
_____	_____	_____	
Copper-winding time required to satisfy demand	_____	_____	_____

b.   Compute the contribution margin per copper-winding minute for the two products using the following form:

	Standard	*Premium*
Unit selling price	_____	_____
Variable cost per unit	_____	_____
Contribution margin per unit	_____	_____
Copper-winding machine time per unit	_____	_____
Contribution margin per minute	_____	_____

c.   Assuming that the copper-winding machine is the company's constraint, how many units of each product should be made in order to maximize net operating income?

13-5. **Critical thought writing exercise:** "The easiest way to distinguish between relevant and irrelevant costs is by cost behavior; variable costs are relevant costs and fixed costs are irrelevant costs." Explain why you do or do not agree with this statement.

_____

_____

_____

_____

_____

_____

_____

_____

_____

Answers to Questions and Exercises

True or False

1. T Costs that differ between alternatives are relevant. Costs that do not differ between alternatives are not relevant.

2. F Fixed costs can be relevant and variable costs can be irrelevant. What is relevant and what is irrelevant depends on the situation.

3. F Sunk costs are never relevant since they have already been incurred and thus can't be avoided by choosing one alternative over another.

4. T Depreciation on equipment that has not yet been purchased is avoidable and therefore relevant.

5. F Future costs are relevant only if they differ between alternatives; future costs that do not differ between alternatives are irrelevant.

6. T For example, a product line manager's salary would be relevant in a decision to drop the product line, but would not be relevant in a decision about how much to spend on advertising.

7. T If the avoidable fixed costs exceed the lost contribution margin, profits would increase if the product line were dropped.

8. F Allocation of common fixed costs to product lines and to other segments of a company can easily result in misleading data and can make a product line appear to be unprofitable when in fact it may be one of a company's best products.

9. F Even if a product line has a negative segment margin, the product's costs must still be analyzed to determine if the product should be dropped. For example, depreciation on special equipment with no resale value would be traceable to the product line, but would not be relevant in a decision to drop the product line.

10. T Opportunity cost can be a key factor in *any* decision involving a constrained resource.

11. F The product with the highest contribution margin per unit of the constrained resource should be emphasized. A product might have a high contribution margin per unit but require a disproportionately large amount of the constrained resource.

12. T Processing further under these conditions will increase profits.

13. T At the split-off point, joint product costs have already been incurred and are not affected by what is done with the joint products from that point forward.

Multiple Choice

1. e These costs are all relevant because they all differ between the alternatives.

2. c The computations are:

Contribution margin lost .... $(50,000)
Less avoidable fixed costs 20,000*
Decrease in operating income ..... $(30,000)
*$60,000 – $40,000 = $20,000

3. a The computations are:

	Differential Cost Make	Buy
Variable manuf. costs	$ 7.50	—
Avoidable fixed manufacturing cost	4.00	—
Outside purchase price ..	—	$10.00
Total relevant cost	$11.50	$10.00

2,000 units × $1.50 = $3,000

4. b The computations are:

	A	B
Contribution margin per unit (a)	$8.00	$12.00
Machine-hours to produce (b)	4.00	5.00
CM per machine-hour (a) ÷ (b)	$2.00	$ 2.40

5. c   The computations are:

Incremental revenue	
($9.95 × 1,000)	$9,950
Incremental costs:	
Variable production	
($5.25 × 1,000)	5,250
Variable selling	
($0.15 × 1,000)	150
Increase in operating income	$4,550

6. b   The computations are:

	A	B
Sales value after		
further processing	$1,700	$4,000
Sales value at split-off	1,200	3,000
Incremental sales value	500	1,000
Incremental processing cost ..	600	800
Advantage (disadvantage)		
of further processing	$ (100)	$ 200

Exercises

13-1.

Contribution margin lost if the department is dropped		$(300,000)
Less avoidable fixed costs:		
Salaries and wages ($150,000 - $30,000)	$120,000	
Insurance on inventories	10,000	
Advertising	100,000	230,000
Decrease in overall company net operating income		$ (70,000)

Based on the analysis above, the department should not be dropped. The solution using the alternate format appears below:

	Keep Department	Drop Department	Difference: Income Increase or (Decrease)
Sales	$500,000	$ -0-	$(500,000)
Less variable expenses	200,000	-0-	200,000
Contribution margin	300,000	-0-	$(300,000)
Less fixed expenses:			
Salaries and wages	150,000	30,000	120,000
Insurance on inventories	10,000	-0-	10,000
Depreciation of fixtures	65,000	65,000*	-0-
Advertising	100,000	-0-	100,000
Total fixed expenses	325,000	95,000	230,000
Net operating income (loss)	$(25,000)	$(95,000)	$ (70,000)

* If the department were dropped, the remaining book value of the fixtures would be written off immediately. If the department were not dropped, the remaining book value would be written off over a number of years in the form of depreciation charges. In either case, the entire remaining book value will eventually flow through the income statement as charges in one form or another.

13-2.

	Product A	Product B
Sales value after further processing	$ 90,000	$200,000
Sales value at the split-off point	60,000	120,000
Incremental revenue from further processing	30,000	80,000
Less cost of further processing	20,000	85,000
Profit (loss) from further processing	$ 10,000	$ (5,000)

174

13-3.

	Per Unit Differential Costs		5,000 Parts	
	Make	Buy	Make	Buy
Outside purchase price		$30		$150,000
Cost of making internally:				
Direct materials	$15		$ 75,000	
Direct labor	10		50,000	
Variable manufacturing overhead	2		10,000	
Fixed manufacturing overhead, traceable	1*		5,000	
Fixed manufacturing overhead, allocated common	-	-	-	-
Total	$28	$30	$140,000	$150,000
Difference in favor of making		$2		$10,000

*$4 × 25% = $1. The depreciation on the equipment and the common fixed overhead would not be avoidable costs.

13-4.

a. Demand exceeds capacity for the copper-winding machine, as shown below:

	Standard	Premium	Total
Monthly demand per month (a)	12,000 units	8,000 units	
Copper-winding machine time per unit (b)	0.5 min./unit	0.6 min./unit	
Copper-winding time required to satisfy demand (a) × (b)	6,000 min.	4,800 min.	10,800 min.

b.

	Standard	Premium
Unit selling price	$14.00	$20.00
Variable cost per unit	5.00	8.00
Contribution margin per unit (a)	$ 9.00	$12.00
Copper-winding machine time per unit (b)	0.5 min.	0.6 min.
Contribution margin per minute (a) ÷ (b) ..	$ 18/min.	$ 20/min.

c. Since the contribution margin per copper-winding minute is higher for the premium model than for the standard model, the premium model should be emphasized. The optimal plan is to produce all 8,000 units of the premium model and use the remaining capacity to make 9,600 units of the standard model.

Total copper-winding time available	9,600 minutes
Time required to produce 8,000 units of the premium model	4,800 minutes
Time remaining with which to make the standard model (a)	4,800 minutes
Time required to make one unit of the standard model (b)	0.5 minute/unit
Number of units of the standard model produced (a) ÷ (b)	9,600 units

13-5.   This statement is false. Variable costs are not automatically relevant costs, and fixed costs are not automatically irrelevant costs. Whether a cost is relevant or not depends on whether the cost differs between alternatives. A fixed cost may differ between alternatives, such as in an equipment replacement decision. On the other hand, a variable cost may not be avoidable in a particular decision situation and therefore not relevant to the decision. For example, the variable costs in already manufactured obsolete goods would not be relevant in a decision as to whether the goods should be sold at a discount price or simply junked. The variable production costs would be the same under either alternative.

Chapter 14

Capital Budgeting Decisions

Chapter Study Suggestions

To understand the material in this chapter, it is essential that you have a solid understanding of the concept of present value. If you have not worked with present value before, carefully study Appendix 14A, "The Concept of Present Value."

Once you understand present value, you will be ready to tackle the capital budgeting methods in the chapter. The first of these methods is called the net present value method. Follow through each number in Exhibits, 14-1 and 14-4 and trace the factors back to the tables given at the end of the chapter.

The second capital budgeting method is called the internal rate of return method. It is illustrated in Example D. This method is similar to the net present value method in that both methods are based on discounting future cash flows.

Two other methods of making capital budgeting decisions are presented in the chapter. These are the payback method and the simple rate of return method. Formulas are provided for both methods. Pay particular attention to the formula for the simple rate of return—it can be tricky to apply.

CHAPTER HIGHLIGHTS

A. The term *capital budgeting* is used to describe planning major outlays on projects that commit the company for some time into the future such as purchasing new equipment, building a new facility, or introducing a new product.

1. Capital budgeting usually involves investment; i.e., committing funds now so as to obtain cash inflows in the future.

2. Capital budgeting decisions fall into two broad categories:

    a. *Screening decisions:* Potential projects are categorized as acceptable or unacceptable.

    b. *Preference decisions*: Projects must be ranked because there are insufficient funds to support all of the acceptable.

3. The time value of money should be considered. A dollar in the future is worth less than a dollar today for the simple reason that a dollar today can be invested to yield more than a dollar in the future.

    a. *Discounted cash flow methods* give full recognition to the time value of money.

    b. There are two methods that use discounted cash flows—the *net present value method* and the *internal rate of return method*.

B. The net present value method is illustrated in Example A (Exhibit 14-1) and in Example C (Exhibit 14-4). The basic steps in this method are:

1. Determine the required investment.

2. Determine the future cash inflows and outflows that result from the investment.

3. Use the *present value tables* to find the appropriate *present value factors*.

    a. The values (or factors) in the present value tables depend upon the discount rate and the number of periods (usually years).

    b. The *discount rate* in present value analysis is the company's required rate of return, which is often the company's cost of capital. The *cost of capital* is the average rate of return the company must pay its long-term creditors and shareholders for the use of their funds. The

details of the cost of capital are covered in finance classes.

4. Multiply the cash flows by their present value factors and sum the results. The end result (which is net of the initial investment) is called the *net present value* of the project.

5. In a screening decision, if the net present value is positive, the investment is acceptable. If the net present value is negative, the investment should be rejected.

C. Discounted cash flow analysis is based entirely on *cash flows*—not on accounting net income. Accounting net income must be ignored in cash flow analysis.

1. Typical cash flows associated with an investment are:

    a. Outflows: initial investment (including installation costs); increased working capital needs; repairs and maintenance; and incremental operating costs.

    b. Inflows: include incremental revenues; reductions in costs; salvage value; and release of working capital at the end of the project.

2. Depreciation is not a cash flow and therefore is not part of the analysis. (However, depreciation can affect taxes, which is a cash flow. This aspect of depreciation is covered in Chapter 15.)

3. Quite often, a project requires an infusion of cash (i.e., working capital) in order to finance inventories, receivables, and other working capital items. Typically, at the end of the project these working capital items can be liquidated (i.e., the inventory can be sold) and the cash that had been invested in these items can be recovered. Thus, working capital is counted as a cash outflow at the beginning of a project and as a cash inflow at the end of the project.

4. We usually assume that all cash flows, other than the initial investment, occur at the *end* of a period.

D. The internal rate of return method is another discounted cash flow method used in capital budgeting decisions.

1. The *internal rate of return* is the rate of return promised by an investment project over its useful life; it is the discount rate for which the net present value of a project is zero.

2. When the cash flows are the same every year, the following formula can be used to find the internal rate of return:

$$\frac{\text{Factor of the}}{\text{internal rate of return}} = \frac{\text{Investment required}}{\text{Net annual cash inflows}}$$

3. For example, assume an investment of $3,791 is made in a project that will last five years and has no salvage value. Also assume that the annual cash inflow from the project will be $1,000.

$$\frac{\text{Factor of the}}{\text{internal rate of return}} = \frac{\$3,791}{\$1,000} = 3.791$$

Since this is a project with a five-year life, we will use the 5-year row in Table 14C-4 in Appendix 14C, which provides the present value factors for an annuity. (This is an annuity since the same cash inflow is received at the end of every year beginning with the first year.) Scanning along the 5-year row, it can be seen that this factor represents a 10% rate of return. Therefore, the internal rate of return is 10%. (You may want to verify that this calculation is correct by computing the net present value of the investment, which should be zero.)

4. If the present value factor computed above falls between two factors in the present value table, interpolation is used to estimate the true internal rate of return. The interpolation process is illustrated in the chapter.

5. If the cash inflows are not the same every year, the internal rate of return is found using trial and error. The internal rate of return is whatever discount rate makes the net present value of the project equal zero.

6. In a screening decision, the internal rate of return is compared to the required rate of return. If the internal rate of return is less than the required rate of return, the project is rejected. If it is greater than or equal to the required rate of return, the project is accepted.

E. Two common approaches used in the net present value method are the *total-cost* approach and the *incremental-cost* approach.

1. The total-cost approach is the most flexible and the most widely used method. Exhibit 14-7 shows this approach. Note in Exhibit 14-7 that *all* cash inflows and *all* cash outflows are included in the solution under each alternative.

2. The incremental-cost approach is a simpler and more direct route to a decision since it ignores all cash flows that are the same under both alternatives. The incremental-cost approach focuses on differential costs. Exhibit 14-8 shows this approach.

3. If done correctly, both the total-cost and incremental-cost approaches will lead to the same decision.

F. Sometimes no revenue or cash inflow is directly involved in a decision. In this situation, the alternative with the *least cost* should be selected. The least cost alternative can be determined using either the total-cost approach or the incremental approach. Exhibits 14-9 and 14-10 illustrate least-cost decisions.

G. It is often difficult to quantify all the costs and benefits involved in a decision. An investment in automation provides a good example.

1. The reduction in direct labor cost from automation may be easy to quantify. Intangible benefits, such as greater throughput or greater flexibility in operations, are usually very difficult to quantify. It would be a mistake to ignore these intangible benefits simply because they are difficult to quantify.

2. The difficulty can often be resolved by computing how large the intangible benefits would have to be to make the investment attractive. The steps in this approach are:

a. Compute the net present value of the tangible costs and benefits. If the result is positive, the investment is accepted immediately since the intangible benefits simply make it even more attractive.

b. If the net present value of the tangible costs and benefits is negative, compute the additional net annual cash inflows that would make the net present value positive.

c. If the intangible benefits are likely to be at least as large as the required additional net annual cash inflows computed in (2), then accept the project.

H. Preference decisions involve ranking investment projects. Such a ranking is necessary whenever there are limited funds available for investment.

1. Preference decisions are sometimes called *ranking* decisions or *rationing* decisions because they ration limited investment funds among competing investment opportunities.

2. When using the internal rate of return to rank competing investment projects, the preference rule is: *The higher the internal rate of return, the more desirable the project.*

3. If the net present value method is used to rank competing investment projects, the net present value of one project should not be compared directly to the net present value of another project, unless the investments in the projects are of equal size.

a. To make a valid comparison between projects that require different investment amounts, a *profitability index* is computed. The formula for the profitability index is:

$$\text{Profitability index} = \frac{\text{Present value of cash inflows}}{\text{Investment required}}$$

This is basically an application of the idea from Chapter 13 of utilization of a scarce resource. In this case, the scarce resource is the investment funds. The profitability index is similar to the contribution margin per unit of the scarce resource.

b. The preference rule when using the profitability index is: *The higher the profitability index, the more desirable the project.*

I. Which method of discounted cash flow analysis—the present value method or the internal rate of return method—is better? The present value method has several major advantages for both screening decisions and preference decisions.

1. The internal rate of return method assumes that any cash flows received during the life of the project can be reinvested at an interest rate equal to the internal rate of return. This assumption is questionable if the internal rate of

return is high. In contrast, the net present value method assumes that any cash flows received during the life of the project are reinvested at an interest rate equal to the discount rate. Ordinarily, this is a more realistic assumption.

2. It is usually easier to compute the net present value of a project than to compute the internal rate of return. The net present value method does not involve trial-and-error.

J. There are two other capital budgeting methods considered in the chapter. These methods do not involve discounting cash flows One of these is the payback method.

1. The *payback method* computes the time period required for an investment project to recoup its own initial cost out of the cash receipts it generates. The payback period is expressed in years.

a. When the cash inflows from the project are the same every year, the following formula can be used to compute the payback period:

$$\text{Payback period} = \frac{\text{Investment required}}{\text{Net annual cash inflows}}$$

b. If new equipment is replacing old equipment, the "investment required" should be reduced by any salvage value obtained from the disposal of old equipment. And in this case, in computing the "net annual cash inflows," only the incremental cash inflow provided by the new equipment over the old equipment should be used.

2. The payback period is not a measure of profitability. Rather it is a measure of how long it takes for a project to recoup its own investment cost.

3. Major defects in the payback method are that it ignores the time value of money, and that it ignores all cash flows that occur once the initial cost has been recovered. Therefore, this method is very crude and should be used only with a great deal of caution. Nevertheless, the payback method can be useful in industries where project lives are very short and uncertain.

K. Another capital budgeting method that does not involve discounted cash flow is the simple rate of return method.

1. The *simple rate of return* method focuses on accounting net income, rather than on cash flows. The formula for its computation is:

$$\text{Simple rate of retun} = \frac{\text{Incremental revenue} - \text{Incremental expenses}}{\text{Initial investment}}$$

If new equipment is replacing old equipment, then the "initial investment" in the new equipment is the cost of the new equipment reduced by any salvage value obtained from the old equipment.

2. Like the payback method, the simple rate of return method is that it does not consider the time value of money. Therefore, the rate of return computed by this method will not be an accurate guide as to the profitability of an investment project.

Appendix 14A: The Concept of Present Value

A. Since most business investments extend over long periods, it is important to recognize the time value of money in capital budgeting analysis. Essentially, a dollar received today is more valuable than a dollar received in the future for the simple reason that a dollar received today can be invested—yielding more than a dollar in the future.

B. Present value analysis recognizes the time value of money in capital budgeting decisions.

1. Present value analysis involves expressing a future cash flow in terms of present dollars.

When a future cash flow is expressed in terms of its present value, the process is called *discounting*.

2. Use Table 14C-3 in Appendix 14C to determine the present value of a single sum to be received in the future. This table contains factors for various rates of interest for various periods, which when multiplied by a future sum, will give the sum's present value.

3. Use Table 14C-4 in Appendix 14C to determine the present value of an *annuity*, or stream, of cash flows. This table contains factors that, when multiplied by the stream of cash flows, will give the stream's present value. Be careful to note that this annuity table is for a very specific type of annuity in which the first payment occurs at the end of the first year.

Appendix 14B: Inflation and Capital Budgeting

A. Inflation has an impact on the numbers that are used in a capital budgeting analysis—both the cash flows and the discount rate.

B. Under certain conditions, it doesn't make any difference whether you adjust both the cash flows and the discount rate for inflation or whether you do not adjust either of them for inflation. However, you must be consistent. If there is any adjustment made for inflation, both the cash flows and the discount rate must be adjusted for inflation.

C. For the sake of simplicity, we assume in Chapters 14 and 15 that there is no inflation.

REVIEW AND SELF TEST
Questions and Exercises

True or False

Enter a T or an F in the blank to indicate whether the statement is true or false.

____ 1. Under the net present value method, the present value of all cash inflows associated with an investment project are compared to the present value of all cash outflows, with the difference, or net present value, determining whether or not the project is acceptable.

____ 2. One key shortcoming of discounted cash flow methods is that they do not provide for the recovery of the original investment.

____ 3. Cash outlays for noncurrent assets such as machines would be considered in a capital budgeting analysis, but not cash outlays for current assets such as inventory.

____ 4. The internal rate of return is the discount rate for which a project's net present value is zero.

____ 5. The internal rate of return method is simpler to use and makes more realistic assumptions than the net present value method.

____ 6. In present value analysis, the higher the discount rate, the higher is the present value of a given future cash inflow.

____ 7. When comparing two investment alternatives, the total-cost approach provides the same ultimate answer as the incremental-cost approach.

____ 8. If an investment in automated equipment can't be justified by a reduction in direct labor cost, then the investment probably shouldn't be made.

____ 9. In ranking investment projects, a project with a high net present value should be ranked above a project with a lower net present value.

____ 10. In preference decision situations, the net present value and internal rate of return methods may yield conflicting rankings of projects.

____ 11. The simple rate of return method explicitly takes depreciation into account.

____ 12. The payback method does not consider the time value of money.

____ 13. The present value of a cash inflow to be received in 5 years is greater than the present value of the same sum to be received in 10 years.

Multiple Choice

Choose the best answer or response by placing the identifying letter in the space provided.

The following data relate to questions 1 and 2.

Peters Company is considering the purchase of a machine to further automate its production line. The machine would cost $30,000, and have a ten-year life with no salvage value. It would save $8,000 per year in labor costs, but would increase power costs by $1,000 annually. The company's discount rate is 12%.

____ 1. The present value of the net annual cost savings would be: a) $39,550; b) $45,200; c) $5,650; d) $70,000.

____ 2. The net present value of the proposed machine would be: a) $(15,200); b) $5,650; c) $9,550; d) $30,000.

____ 3. Acme Company is considering investing in a new machine that costs $84,900, and which has a useful life of 12 years with no salvage value. The machine will generate $15,000 annually in net cash inflows. The internal rate of return on the machine is: a) 8%; b) 10%; c) 12%; d) 14 %.

____ 4. White Company's required rate of return and discount rate is 12%. The company is considering an investment opportunity that would yield a return of $10,000 in five years. What is the most that the company should be willing to invest in this project? a) $36,050; b) $5,670; c) $17,637; d) $2,774.

___ 5. Dover Company is considering an investment project in which a working capital investment of $30,000 would be required. The investment would provide cash inflows of $10,000 per year for six years. If the company's discount rate is 18%, and if the working capital is released at the end of the project, then the project's net present value is: a) $4,980; b) $(4,980); c) $16,080; d) $(12,360).

___ 6. Whiting Company has completed a net present value analysis for a project that shows a $113,000 *negative* net present value. This project involves a purchase of automated equipment that would have a 10-year useful life. The company's required rate of return and discount rate is 12%.

What amount of cash inflow each year would have to be provided by the intangible benefits associated with the project in order for the project to be acceptable? a) $11,300; b) $13,560; c) $18,000; d) $20,000

___ 7. Frumer Company has purchased a machine that cost $30,000, that will save $6,000 per year in cash operating costs, and that has an expected life of 15 years with zero salvage value. The payback period on the machine will be: a) 2 years; b) 7.5 years; c) 5 years; d) 0.2 years.

___ 8. Refer to the data in question (7) above. The simple rate of return on the machine is approximately: a) 20%; b) 13.3%; c) 18%; d) 10%.

Exercises

14-1. You have recently won $100,000 in a contest. You have been given the option of receiving $100,000 today or receiving $12,000 at the end of each year for the next 20 years.

a. If you can earn 8% on investments, which of these two options would you select? (Note: The net present value method assumes that any cash flows are reinvested at a rate of return equal to the discount rate. Therefore, to answer this question you can compare the net present values of the cash flows under the two alternatives using 8% as the discount rate.)

Item	Year(s)	Amount of Cash Flows	8% Factor	Present Value of Cash Flows
Receive the annuity	_____	_____	_____	$_____
Receive the lump sum	_____	_____	_____	_____
Net present value in favor of _____ .				$_____

b. If you can earn 12% on investments, which of these two options would you select?

Item	Year(s)	Amount of Cash Flows	12% Factor	Present Value of Cash Flows
Receive the annuity	_____	$ _____	_____	$_____
Receive the lump sum	_____	_____	_____	_____
Net present value in favor of _____ .				$_____

14-2.   Lynde Company has been offered a contract to provide a key replacement part for the Army's main attack helicopter. The contract would expire in eight years. The projected cash flows that result from the contract are given below:

Cost of new equipment $300,000
Working capital needed 100,000
Net annual cash inflows 85,000
Salvage value of equipment in eight years 50,000

The company's required rate of return and discount rate is 16%. The working capital would be released for use elsewhere at the end of the project.
   Complete the analysis below to determine whether the contract should be accepted.

Item	Year(s)	Amount of Cash Flows	16% Factor	Present Value of Cash Flows
Cost of new equipment	____	$_____	_____	$_____
Working capital needed	____	_____	_____	_____
Net annual cash inflows	____	_____	_____	_____
Salvage value of equipment	____	_____	_____	_____
Working capital released	____	_____	_____	_____
Salvage value of equipment	____	_____	_____	_____
Net present value				$_____

Should the contract be accepted? Explain.

_____
_____
_____
_____
_____
_____
_____

14-3. Swift Company is considering the purchase of a new machine that will cost $20,000. The machine will provide revenues of $9,000 per year. Out-of-pocket operating costs will be $6,000 per year. The new machine will have a useful life of 10 years and will have zero salvage value. The company's required rate of return is 12%.

    a. What is the internal rate of return? (Interpolate if necessary.)

        Annual revenue .... $_____

        Annual operating costs .... _____

        Net annual cash inflow .... $_____

$$\text{Factor of the internal rate of return} = \frac{\text{Investment required}}{\text{Net annual cash inflows}}$$

$$\frac{\rule{3cm}{0.4pt}}{\rule{3cm}{0.4pt}} = \rule{2cm}{0.4pt}$$

	Present Value Factor	
_____% factor	_____	_____
True factor	_____	
_____% factor		_____
Difference	============	============

Internal rate of return = ____% + (————— × 2%) =

    b. Should the company buy the new machine? Why or why not?

_____

_____

_____

_____

_____

_____

_____

14-4. Harlan Company would like to purchase a new machine that makes wonderfully smooth fruit sorbet that the company can sell in the premium frozen dessert sections of supermarkets. The machine costs $450,000 and has a useful life of ten years with a salvage value of $50,000. Annual revenues and expenses resulting from the new machine follow:

Sales revenue		$300,000
Less operating expenses:		
Advertising	$100,000	
Salaries of operators	70,000	
Maintenance	30,000	
Depreciation	40,000	240,000
Net income		$ 60,000

a. Harlan Company will not invest in new equipment unless it promises a payback period of 4 years or less. Compute the payback period on the sorbet machine.

Computation of the net annual cash inflow:

Net income .... $_____

Add: Noncash deduction for depreciation .... _____

Net annual cash inflow .... $_____

Computation of the payback period:

$$\text{Payback period} = \frac{\text{Investment required}}{\text{Net annual cash inflows}}$$

$$\frac{\rule{3cm}{0.4pt}}{\rule{3cm}{0.4pt}} = \text{_____ years}$$

b. Compute the simple rate of return on the investment in the new machine.

$$\frac{\text{Simple rate}}{\text{of retun}} = \frac{\text{Incremental revenue} - \text{Incremental expenses}}{\text{Initial investment}}$$

$$\frac{\rule{3cm}{0.4pt}}{\rule{3cm}{0.4pt}} = \text{_____ \%}$$

14-5. **Critical thought writing exercise:** As the discount rate increases, the present value of a given future sum also increases. Do you agree? Why or why not?

_____

_____

_____

_____

_____

_____

_____

_____

_____

_____

_____

_____

_____

Answers to Questions and Exercises

True or False

1. **T** Exhibit 14-4 illustrates this point.

2. **F** Discounted cash flow methods do provide for recovery of original investment, as illustrated in Exhibit 14-3.

3. **F** All cash flows should be included in a capital budgeting analysis.

4. **T** This statement is true by definition; the principle is illustrated in Exhibit 14-5.

5. **F** The opposite is true—the net present value method is the method that is simpler to use and the assumption about the rate of return on cash flows thrown off by the investment is more realistic.

6. **F** The opposite is true—the higher the discount rate, the lower is the present value of a given future cash inflow.

7. **T** The total-cost approach and the incremental-cost approach are just different ways of obtaining the same result.

8. **F** Only rarely will a reduction in direct labor cost justify an investment in automated equipment. Typically, the investment is justified by intangible benefits such as greater throughput or greater flexibility.

9. **F** Net present value shouldn't be used to rank projects when investment funds are limited, since one project may have a higher net present value than another simply because it is larger. The profitability index should be used to compare projects.

10. **T** See the example in the text in the section "Comparing the Preference Rules."

11. **T** This point is illustrated in formulas (3) and (4) in the text.

12. **T** A major defect of the payback method is that dollars are given the same weight regardless of when they are received.

13. **T** When discounting the shorter the time period, the greater the present value.

Multiple Choice

1. **a** The computations are:

Savings in labor costs	$ 8,000
Less increased power costs	1,000
Net cost savings.........................	$ 7,000
Present value factor for 12% for 10 years (Table 14C-4)	× 5.650
Present value of cost savings...	$39,550

2. **c** The computations are:

Investment in the machine.......	$(30,000)
Present value of cost savings ..	39,550
Net present value......................	$ 9,550

3. **d** The computations are:

$$\frac{\text{Factor of the}}{\substack{\text{internal} \\ \text{rate of return}}} = \frac{\text{Investment required}}{\substack{\text{Net annual} \\ \text{cash inflows}}}$$

$$\frac{\$84,900}{\$15,000} = 5.660$$

Looking at the 12-year row in the annuity Table 14C-4, a factor of 5.660 equals a return of 14%.

4. **b** The computations are:

Return in 5 years.....................	$10,000
Factor for 12% for 5 years (Table 14C-3).........................	× 0.567
Present value	$ 5,670

This is the maximum amount the company is willing to invest. If it were to invest more than $5,670, the net present value of the investment would be negative.

5. **c** The computations are:

	Year(s)	Amount	18% Factor	Present Value
Working capital investment	Now	$(30,000)	1.000	$(30,000)
Cash inflow	1-6	10,000	3.498	34,980
Working capital released	6	30,000	0.370	11,100
Net present value				$ 16,080

6. d   The computation is:

$$\frac{\text{Net present value, \$(113,000)}}{\text{Present value factor, 5.650}} = \$20,000$$

7. c   The computation is:

$$\frac{\text{Payback}}{\text{period}} = \frac{\text{Investment required}}{\text{Net annual}}$$
$$\frac{}{\text{cash inflows}}$$

$$= \frac{\$30,000}{\$6,000} = 5 \text{ years}$$

8. b   The computation is:

$$\frac{\text{Simple rate}}{\text{of return}} = \frac{\text{Incremental}}{\text{revenues}} - \frac{\text{Incremental}}{\text{expenses}}$$
$$\frac{}{\text{Initial investment}}$$

$$= \frac{\$6,000^* - \$2,000^{**}}{\$30,000} = 13.3\%$$

* The "incremental revenue" is the cost savings of \$6,000 per year.
** The incremental expense is the annual depreciation charge of \$2,000 = \$30,000 ÷ 15 years.

Exercises

14-1.   a.   The annuity is preferable if the discount rate is 8%:

Item	Year(s)	Amount of Cash Flows	8% Factor	Present Value of Cash Flows
Receive the annuity	1-20	$ 12,000	9.818	$117,816
Receive the lump sum	Now	100,000	1.000	100,000
Net present value in favor of the annuity				$ 17,816

b.   The lump sum is preferable if the discount rate is 12%:

Item	Year(s)	Amount of Cash Flows	12% Factor	Present Value of Cash Flows
Receive the annuity	1-20	$ 12,000	7.469	$ 89,628
Receive the lump sum	Now	100,000	1.000	100,000
Net present value in favor of the lump sum				$ 10,372

14-2.

Item	Year(s)	Amount of Cash Flows	16% Factor	Present Value of Cash Flows
Cost of new equipment	Now	($300,000)	1.000	($300,000)
Working capital needed	Now	(100,000)	1.000	(100,000)
Net annual cash receipts	1-8	85,000	4.344	369,240
Salvage value of equipment	8	50,000	0.305	15,250
Working capital released	8	100,000	0.305	30,500
Net present value				$ 14,990

Yes, the contract should be accepted. The net present value is positive, which means that the contract will provide more than the company's 16% required rate of return.

14-3. a.
Annual revenue $9,000
Annual operating costs 6,000
Incremental cash inflow ... $3,000

$$\text{Factor of the internal rate of return} = \frac{\text{Investment required}}{\text{Net annual cash inflows}}$$

$$= \frac{\$20,000}{\$3,000} = 6.667$$

Since the 6.667 factor falls between the 8% and 10% rates of return in Table 14C-4, it will be necessary to interpolate to find the exact rate of return:

	Present Value Factor	
8% factor	6.710	6.710
True factor	6.667	
10% factor		6.145
Difference	0.043	0.565

$$\text{Internal rate of return} = 8\% + \left(\frac{0.043}{0.565} \times 2\%\right) = 8.15\%$$

b. No, the machine should be rejected since the 8.15% internal rate of return is less than the 12% required rate of return.

14-4. a. The net annual cash inflow would be:

Net income .... $ 60,000
Add: Noncash deduction for depreciation 40,000
Net annual cash inflow $100,000

The payback period would be:

$$\frac{\text{Payback}}{\text{period}} = \frac{\text{Investment required}}{\text{Net annual cash inflows}} = \frac{\$450,000}{\$100,000} = 4.5 \text{ years}$$

The machine would not be purchased since it will not provide the 4 year payback period required by the company.

b. The simple rate of return would be:

$$\frac{\text{Simple rate}}{\text{of return}} = \frac{\text{Incremental revenues} - \text{Incremental expenses}}{\text{Initial investment}} = \frac{\$300,000 - \$240,000}{\$450,000} = 13.3\%$$

14-5. No. As the discount rate increases, the present value of a given future sum decreases. As the discount rate increases, less must be set aside today to yield a given future sum. This is the power of compounding interest. For example, the factor for a discount rate of 12% for a single sum to be received ten years from now is 0.322, whereas the factor for a discount rate of 14% over the same period is 0.270. If the sum to be received in ten years is $10,000, the present value in the first case is $3,220, but only $2,700 in the second case. Thus, as the discount rate increases, the present value of a given sum decreases.

Chapter 15

Income Taxes in Capital Budgeting Decisions

Chapter Study Suggestions

This chapter builds on the discounted cash flow methods introduced in Chapter 14. The key to the chapter is Exhibit 15-3 that shows the adjustments required for cash expenses and receipts and for depreciation deductions for capital budgeting purposes. Exhibit 15-7 provides a comprehensive illustration of the computation of net present value. Study this exhibit and the related text material with special care; the computations in the exhibit are complex and will take some time to digest.

CHAPTER HIGHLIGHTS

A. Income taxes affect cash flows and therefore should usually be considered in capital budgeting. However, nonprofit entities such as hospitals, schools, or governmental units are not subject to income taxes and may use the simpler approach in Chapter 14 that ignores taxes.

B. Both the costs and benefits of a project should be estimated on an after-tax basis.

1. The true cost of a tax-deductible item is the amount of the payment net of any reduction in income taxes due to the payment. An expenditure net of its tax effects is known as an *after-tax cost*. For example, assume that a company needs to overhaul a machine at a cost of $6,000. The cost of the overhaul is a tax-deductible expense. If the income tax rate is 30%, the after-tax cost of the overhaul is:

Cost of overhaul	$6,000
Reduction in taxes due to the overhaul	
(30% × $6,000)	(1,800)
After-tax cost	$4,200

2. The net after-tax cost (cash outflow) for any tax-deductible expenditure can be computed as follows:

$$\text{After - tax cost} = (1 - \text{Tax rate}) \times \frac{\text{Tax deductible}}{\text{cash expense}}$$

3. Not all cash outflows are tax deductible expenses.

    a. An investment in working capital is not tax-deductible; it is not an expense.

    b. The cost of a depreciable asset *is not* tax deductible in the period in which it is purchased. However, depreciation on the asset *is* tax deductible. (See section D below.)

C. As with cash expenditures, taxable cash receipts must be placed on an after-tax basis.

1. A cash receipt net of its tax effect is known as an *after-tax benefit*. For example, assume that a company receives $100,000 from sale of services. If the tax rate is 30%, the after-tax benefit is:

Revenue	$ 100,000
Income tax payment required	
(30% × $100,000)	(30,000)
After-tax benefit	$ 70,000

2. The net after-tax cash inflow from revenue or other taxable cash receipts can be computed as follows:

$$\text{After - tax benefits} = (1 - \text{Tax rate}) \times \frac{\text{Taxable cash}}{\text{receipt}}$$

3. This formula can be used for a project that does not bring in any additional revenue but saves cost. The cost savings can be treated the same as a cash receipt. The formula can also be applied to net taxable cash receipts, which is the difference between taxable cash receipts and tax-deductible cash expenses.

4. Not all cash receipts are taxable. For example, the release of working capital at the termination of an investment project is not a taxable cash inflow.

D. Depreciation is not a cash outflow. However, depreciation deductions do affect the amount of taxes that a company will pay.

1. The depreciation deduction acts as a *tax shield*. Depreciation deductions shield revenues from taxation and lower the amount of income taxes that a company has to pay.

2. The formula used to compute the tax savings from the depreciation tax shield is:

$$\frac{\text{Tax savings from the}}{\text{depreciation tax shield}} = \text{Tax rate} \times \frac{\text{Depreciation}}{\text{deduction}}$$

E. In the United States, taxpayers must use the Modified Accelerated Cost Recovery System (MACRS) to depreciate assets for tax purposes. MACRS does not have to be used for financial reporting purposes and usually isn't.

1. Under MACRS, assets are placed into one of eight property classes. Each property class has its own depreciation table. See Exhibit 15-4 in the text for details.

2. Under MACRS, the *half-year convention* must be used. Only one half year's depreciation can be taken in the first and last year of the asset's life. In effect, this adds a full year to the recovery period, as shown in Exhibit 15-5.

3. Under MACRS, salvage value is not considered in computing depreciation deductions; the entire cost of an asset is depreciated.

4. There are two methods of determining the depreciation deduction: the MACRS tables and the optional straight-line method.

    a. The MACRS tables, which are based on accelerated depreciation methods, are reproduced in Exhibit 15-5.

    b. Under the optional straight-line method, taxpayers can depreciate an asset evenly over its property class life—with the exception of the first and last years which are depreciated at half the usual rate.

    c. Generally, the MACRS tables should be used since they allow more rapid write-offs of the original cost of assets and therefore usually yield a higher present value.

5. If an asset is disposed of after it has been fully depreciated for tax purposes, any proceeds are fully taxable since the MACRS tables and the optional straight-line methods assume zero salvage value.

F. Exhibit 15-7 contains a comprehensive example of income taxes and capital budgeting. Follow this example carefully step by step.

1. All cash flows involving tax-deductible expenses and taxable receipts are placed on an after-tax basis by multiplying the cash flow by one minus the tax rate.

2. Also notice that the depreciation deductions are multiplied *by the tax rate itself* to determine the tax savings (cash inflow) resulting from the tax shield.

3. *These two above points should be studied with great care until both are thoroughly understood.*

REVIEW AND SELF TEST
Questions and Exercises

True or False

Enter a T or an F in the blank to indicate whether the statement is true or false.

___ 1. The after-tax cost of a tax-deductible item is computed by multiplying the amount of the tax deduction by the tax rate.

___ 2. The half-year convention must be used with the MACRS tables, but not with the optional straight-line method.

___ 3. Since salvage value is not considered when computing depreciation under MACRS, any salvage value received on sale of an asset after it has been fully depreciated is taxed as income.

___ 4. The MACRS tables allow a greater total amount of depreciation to be taken over the life of an asset than is allowed under the optional straight-line method.

___ 5. The release of working capital at the end of an investment project is a taxable cash inflow.

___ 6. A company can use one depreciation method for tax purposes and an entirely different method in preparing financial statements.

___ 7. In general, a larger present value of tax savings from the depreciation tax shield will result from using the MACRS tables than from the optional straight-line method.

___ 8. Under the optional straight-line method, an asset is depreciated over its useful life rather than over its MACRS property class life.

___ 9. The depreciation method that is used for financial statement purposes should also be used in net present value analysis.

Multiple Choice

Choose the best answer or response by placing the identifying letter in the space provided.

___ 1. A project is being considered for which the annual cash operating expenses are $20,000. If the company's tax rate is 30%, what is the after-tax cost of these operating expenses? a) $6,000; b) $14,000; c) $20,000; $60,000.

___ 2. A project is being considered for which the annual cash revenues are $80,000. If the company's tax rate is 30%, what is the after-tax benefit of the revenues? a) $0; b) $24,000; c) $56,000; d) $80,000.

___ 3. Kinnard Inc.'s depreciation deduction is $50,000 and its tax rate is 30%. The company's tax savings from the depreciation tax shield is: a) $15,000; b) $35,000; c) $50,000; d) $30,000.

___ 4. Leeds Company has purchased a machine that cost $90,000, has an $8,000 salvage value, and is in the MACRS 5-year property class. The machine was purchased on December 1 of the current year. If the optional straight-line method is used, the depreciation in the first year will be: a) $1,600; b) $18,000; c) $16,400; d) $9,000.

___ 5. Refer to the data in question (4) above. If the MACRS tables are used to compute depreciation deductions, the depreciation in the *second* year will be: a) $9,000; b) $16,400; c) $28,800; d) $18,000.

___ 6. Polar Company is studying a project that would require a $200,000 working capital investment. If the company's tax rate is 30%, then the initial investment in working capital should be shown in the capital budgeting analysis as a cash outflow of: a) $200,000; b) $140,000; c) $60,000; d) $0.

___ 7. Refer to the data in question (6) above. The working capital would be released for use elsewhere at the end of the project in four years. The company's after-tax cost of capital is 10%. What is the approximate present value of the after-tax cash flows associated with the release of the working capital? a) $200,000; b) $95,600; c) $136,600; d) $0.

Exercises

15-1.   Martin Company is acquiring a new copier for use in its office. The following data relate to the new copier:

Cost of the new copier	$150,000
Annual savings in cash operating costs	40,000
Salvage value of the new copier	6,000
Overhaul of the new copier required in the third year	5,000
Life of the new copier	8 years

The new copier would replace an old machine that has a remaining book value (for tax purposes) of $18,000. The old machine can be sold now for $10,000. The company's tax rate is 30%.

a.   Compute the after-tax savings in annual cash operating costs. $_____

b.   Compute the after-tax cost of the overhaul required in the third year. $_____

c.   Compute the tax savings from the depreciation tax shield for each year and in total. The company uses the MACRS tables and the copier is in the 5-year property class.

Year	Cost	MACRS Percentage	Depreciation Deduction	Tax Rate	Tax Shield: Income Tax Savings
1	$150,000	_____	_____	0.30	_____
2	_____	_____	_____	_____	_____
3	_____	_____	_____	_____	_____
4	_____	_____	_____	_____	_____
5	_____	_____	_____	_____	_____
6	_____	_____	_____	_____	_____
Total					_____

d.   Compute the after-tax benefit from the salvage value of the new copier. $_____

e. Compute the after-tax cash inflow from sale of the old machine. (This is a tough question. See the computations in Exhibit 15-8 in the text for an example.)

Cash received from the sale .... $ _____

Tax savings from loss on sale:

     Current book value .... $ _____

     Sale price now ....   _____

     Loss on disposal ....   _____

     Multiply by the tax rate ....   _____ × 0.30

       Tax savings from loss ....   _____

Total cash inflows .... $ _____

15-2. Marvel Company has $60,000 to invest and is considering two alternatives:

	Investment X	Investment Y
Cost of equipment	$60,000	—
Working capital needed	—	$60,000
Annual cash inflows	20,000	20,000
Salvage value	3,000	—
Life of the project	5 years	5 years

The company's after-tax cost of capital is 12%, and the tax rate is 30%.

Compute the net present value of each investment using the form that appears below. The equipment is in the MACRS 3-year property class. The company uses the optional straight-line method of depreciation for tax purposes.

Items and computations	Year(s)	(1) Amount	(2) Tax effect	(1) × (2) After-tax cash flows	12 percent factor	Present value of cash flows
Investment X:						
Cost of equipment	____	____	____	____	____	____
Annual cash inflows	____	____	____	____	____	____
Depreciation deductions:						

Year	Cost	Dep'n percentage	Dep'n deduction						
1	____	____	____	____	____	____	____	____	____
2	____	____	____	____	____	____	____	____	____
3	____	____	____	____	____	____	____	____	____
4	____	____	____	____	____	____	____	____	____

Salvage value	____	____	____	____	____	____
Net present value						══════
Investment Y:						
Working capital needed	____	____	____	____	____	____
Annual cash inflows	____	____	____	____	____	____
Working capital released	____	____	____	____	____	____
Net present value						══════

15-3.   **Critical thought writing exercise:** On an income statement, cash expenses and depreciation expenses are added together and deducted from revenues to determine net income. Assume that a company has cash operating expenses of $50,000 and depreciation expenses of $20,000. Can these amounts be added together and treated as one in a capital budgeting analysis, or should they be kept separate? Explain your answer.

_____

_____

_____

_____

_____

_____

_____

_____

_____

_____

Answers to Questions and Exercises

True or False

1. F The after-tax cost of a tax deductible cash expense is determined by multiplying it by *one minus* the tax rate.

2. F The half-year convention must be observed with both the MACRS tables and the optional straight-line method.

3. T The salvage value is fully taxable as income since the taxpayer will already have fully depreciated the asset.

4. F The same total amount of depreciation (equal to the original cost of the asset) is taken regardless of the depreciation method used. This point is illustrated in Exhibit 15-6 (where a total of $300,000 depreciation is taken under both methods).

5. F The release of working capital is a return of the taxpayer's original investment (which itself is not a tax deduction) and thus would not be taxable as income.

6. T The depreciation method used for tax purposes has no bearing on the method(s) that can be used in preparing financial statements.

7. T The MACRS tables accelerate the depreciation deductions, bringing earlier tax benefits. From a present value point of view, earlier tax benefits are preferred to later tax benefits. This point is illustrated in Exhibit 15-6.

8. F Under the optional straight-line method, a taxpayer depreciates an asset over its MACRS property class life which may differ from the asset's useful life.

9. F In net present value analysis, a taxpayer should use the depreciation method that is used for tax purposes. The only bearing depreciation has on discounted cash flow analysis is the reduction in tax payments.

Multiple Choice

1. b $(1 - 0.30) \times \$20,000 = \$14,000$

2. c $(1 - 0.30) \times \$80,000 = \$56,000$

3. a $0.30 \times \$50,000 = \$15,000$

4. d The computations are:
$\$90,000 \div 5 \text{ years} = \$18,000$;
$\$18,000 \times 1/2 = \$9,000$.

5. c From Exhibit 15-5, the depreciation rate for the second year for the 5-year property class is 32%. Therefore, the second year's depreciation would be 32% of $90,000 or $28,800.

6. a Working capital represents an investment, not an expense, so there is no effect on taxes. This point is discussed in connection with Exhibit 15-7.

7. c The release of working capital does not affect taxes. Therefore, the entire $200,000 represents an after-tax cash flow. The present value factor for four periods at 10% per period is 0.683, so the present value of the $200,000 is 0.683 × $200,000 or $136,600.

Exercises

15-1. a. After-tax benefit = (1 – Tax rate) × Taxable cash receipt
             = (1 – 0.30) × $40,000 = $28,000

       b. After-tax cost = (1 – Tax rate) × Tax deductible cash expense
             = (1 - 0.30) × $5,000 = $3,500

       c.

Year	Cost (1)	MACRS Percentage (2)	Depreciation Deduction (1) × (2) = (3)	Tax Rate (4)	Tax Shield: Income Tax Savings (3) × (4)
1	$150,000	20.0	$30,000	0.30	$ 9,000
2	$150,000	32.0	48,000	0.30	14,400
3	$150,000	19.2	28,800	0.30	8,640
4	$150,000	11.5	17,250	0.30	5,175
5	$150,000	11.5	17,250	0.30	5,175
6	$150,000	5.8	8,700	0.30	2,610
					$45,000

       d. After-tax benefit = (1 – Tax rate) × Taxable cash receipt
             = (1 - 0.30) × $6,000 = $4,200

       e. Cash flow from disposal of the old machine:

Cash received from sale		$10,000
Tax savings from loss on sale:		
Current book value	$18,000	
Sale price now	10,000	
Loss on disposal	8,000	
Multiply by the tax rate	× 0.30	
Tax savings from loss		2,400
Total net cash inflow		$12,400

15-2.

Items and computations	Year(s)	(1) Amount	(2) Tax effect	(1) ×(2) After-tax cash flows	12 percent factor	Present value of cash flows
Investment X:						
Cost of equipment	Now	$(60,000)	—	$(60,000)	1.000	$(60,000)
Annual cash inflows	1-5	20,000	1 – 0.30	14,000	3.605	50,470
Depreciation deductions:						

Year	Cost	Dep'n percentage	Dep'n deduction						
1	$60,000	16.7%	$10,000	1	10,000	0.30	3,000	0.893	2,679
2	60,000	33.3	20,000	2	20,000	0.30	6,000	0.797	4,782
3	60,000	33.3	20,000	3	20,000	0.30	6,000	0.712	4,272
4	60,000	16.7	10,000	4	10,000	0.30	3,000	0.636	1,908

	Year(s)	Amount	Tax effect	After-tax cash flows	12 percent factor	Present value of cash flows
Salvage value	5	3,000	1 – 0.30	2,100	0.567	1,191
Net present value						$ 5,302
Investment Y:						
Working capital needed	Now	$(60,000)	—	$(60,000)	1.000	$(60,000)
Annual cash inflows	1-5	20,000	1 – 0.30	14,000	3.605	50,470
Working capital released	5	60,000	—	60,000	0.567	34,020
Net present value						$ 24,490

15-3.   The two amounts should be kept separate. The after-tax cash flows are very different for cash expenses and for depreciation. The after-tax cash outflows for deductible cash expenses are measured by multiplying the cash expenses by one minus the tax rate. By contrast, depreciation expenses trigger a cash inflow through the depreciation tax shield. The amount of the inflow is measured by multiplying the depreciation expenses by the tax rate itself.

Chapter 16

Service Department Costing:
An Activity Approach

Chapter Study Suggestions

There are three key exhibits in this chapter—Exhibits 16-2, 16-4, and 16-7. Exhibit 16-2 illustrates the direct method and Exhibit 16-4 illustrates the step method of allocating service department costs to operating departments. Follow the computations in the exhibits step-by-step, and note the difference in the way the two methods handle the cost data.

Exhibit 16-7 expands on Exhibits 16-2 and 16-4 by showing how breaking costs down into their variable and fixed components can make the allocations more meaningful. Spend the bulk of your study time on the sections titled, "Allocating costs by behavior," and "A summary of cost allocation guidelines." Then note from Exhibit 16-7 how the ideas in these two sections are implemented in an extended allocation problem. This is a very important exhibit, since it is the basis for many of the longer, more difficult homework problems.

CHAPTER HIGHLIGHTS

A. The two broad classes of departments within an organization are operating departments and service departments.

1. *Operating departments* include those departments or units where the central purposes of the organization are carried out. Examples of such departments or units include the surgery department in a hospital, the shoe department in a department store, and producing departments in a manufacturing firm.

2. *Service departments* do not engage directly in operating activities. Rather, they provide service or assistance to other departments. Examples of service departments include the cafeteria in a hospital, the billing department in a department store, and the purchasing department in a factory.

3. The costs of service departments are typically allocated to operating departments. These allocated costs are then added to the overhead costs of the operating departments and included in predetermined overhead rates.

B. Three major methods are used to allocate service department costs—the direct method, the step method, and the reciprocal method. The methods differ mainly in how they treat services that service departments provide to each other. These services are called *interdepartmental services* or *reciprocal services*.

C. The *direct method* is the simplest, but the least accurate, of the three methods. When the direct method is used, reciprocal services are ignored and service department costs are allocated directly to operating departments. For example, a hospital's custodial staff cleans administrative offices as well as operating rooms and hospital wards. However, in the direct method none of the custodial costs are allocated to the administrative department. Instead, all the custodial costs are allocated *directly* to the operating departments.

D. The *step method* is slightly more complex than the direct method, but it is also more accurate.

1. In the step method, service department costs are allocated in a specific order. Usually, service departments are ranked in terms of the amount of service they provide to other service departments, with the service department that provides the greatest service to the other service departments allocated first.

2. The costs of the first service department are allocated to all the other departments, both service and operating departments. After the first service department's costs have been allocated, it is ignored in subsequent allocations.

3. Then the costs of the next service department are allocated to the *remaining* service departments as well as to the operating departments. However, any services provided by the second service department to the first service department are ignored. No costs are allocated back to the first service department.

4. The allocation proceeds in this manner, stepping through all the service departments. In each step, a service department's costs are allocated to the remaining service departments as well as to the operating departments. After a service department's costs have been allocated, the service department is ignored.

5. By following this procedure, the step method takes into account some of the reciprocal services, but not all of them.

E. Under both the direct and step methods, the service department whose cost is being allocated is never included in the allocation base. For example, when allocating the costs of a cafeteria on the basis of meals served, the meals served to cafeteria workers themselves are always ignored.

F. The *reciprocal method* is the most complex, and the most accurate method of the three methods for allocating service department costs. The reciprocal method takes all of the reciprocal services fully into account. However, the reciprocal method is seldom used in practice because of its complexity. This method is covered in more advanced textbooks.

G. Service department costs should be separated into fixed and variable elements and allocated separately to other departments. This procedure provides data that are more useful for planning and controlling operations.

1. The variable costs of providing services should be charged to other departments using as an allocation base whatever causes the variable cost to vary. For example, if maintenance costs increase and decrease in proportion to machine hours, then machine hours should be used as the allocation base for maintenance costs.

a. At the beginning of the period, charges to departments for the variable costs of a service department should be computed by multiplying the *budgeted* rate for the service by the *budgeted* use of the service. These allocations, or charges, are used for planning and for computing departmental predetermined overhead rates.

b. At the end of the period, charges to the departments for the variable costs of a service department should be computed by multiplying the *budgeted* rate (*not actual* rate) for the service by *actual* activity. These charges are used for performance evaluation. If actual rates were used, the other departments would implicitly be held responsible for inefficiencies in the service department.

2. The fixed costs of service departments are incurred in order to have the *capacity* to provide service during a period. This capacity may or may not be fully utilized. The fixed costs of service departments should be allocated to consuming departments in proportion to the capacity they require, not the capacity they use. Thus, the fixed costs should be allocated in *predetermined, lump-sum* amounts.

a. When allocating fixed costs, the *budgeted* (not actual) costs should be allocated on the basis of either *long-run average* activity or *peak period* requirements (not budgeted or actual activity). The reason for this is that the level of the fixed costs is determined by management's planning for the long run average or for peak period activity. Management wants to make sure that there is enough capacity to handle peak period or long run average needs.

b. Once set, lump-sum allocations of fixed costs will not change between the beginning and the end of the period.

c. A company should not allocate fixed costs with a variable allocation base such as sales dollars. An inequity may arise since fixed costs allocated to one department will be affected by what happens in other departments.

3. Any difference between the actual service department costs and the costs charged to the operating departments at the end of the period should be retained in the service department as a spending variance.

REVIEW AND SELF TEST
Questions and Exercises

True or False

Enter a T or an F in the blank to indicate whether the statement is true or false.

___ 1. The direct method of allocating service department costs fully accounts for all reciprocal services among service departments.

___ 2. When allocating a service department's costs under the direct method, one should never include the service department being allocated in the allocation base. (e.g., The meals served to cafeteria workers should not be included in the allocation base for the cafeteria.)

___ 3. When allocating a service department's costs under the step method, one *should* include the service department being allocated in the allocation base.

___ 4. The direct method of cost allocation is much simpler than the step method, in that services provided between service departments are ignored.

___ 5. The reciprocal method is generally considered to be more accurate than the step method of service department allocation.

___ 6. When the direct method is used, the order in which service departments are allocated makes a difference in the costs that are allocated to a particular operating department.

___ 7. In allocating costs by the step method, the allocation sequence typically begins with the service department that provides the greatest amount of service to other departments.

___ 8. Variable costs of service departments should be allocated to operating departments in predetermined, lump-sum amounts.

___ 9. Budgeted costs, rather than actual costs, should always be allocated from service departments to operating departments.

___ 10. Sales dollars is a good allocation base because sales dollars are easy to work with and show a department's "ability to pay."

Multiple Choice

Choose the best answer or response by placing the identifying letter in the space provided.

The following data are used in multiple choice questions 1 through 6:

Oscar Company has two service departments, Personnel and Custodial, and two operating departments, A and B. Budgeted data for the current year appear below:

| | Service Departments | | Operating Departments | |
	Personnel	Custodial	A	B
Overhead costs	$800	$600	$2,000	$5,000
Employees	2	18	30	50
Space occupied in thousands of sq. ft.	20	10	40	80

Personnel costs are allocated on the basis of employees. Custodial costs are allocated on the basis of space occupied. The company makes no distinction between fixed and variable costs in its service department allocations.

___ 1. If the direct method of service department allocation is used, how much Personnel Department cost would be allocated to Operating Department A? a) $240; b) $300; c) $0; d) $800.

___ 2. If the direct method of service department allocation is used, how much Personnel Department cost would be allocated back to the Personnel Department? a) $16; b) $800; c) $0; d) $200.

___ 3. If the direct method of service department allocation is used, what would be the total overhead cost in Operating Department B after the allocations have been completed? a) $5,900; b) $900; c) $5,000; d) $6,400.

___ 4. If the step method of service department allocation is used and Personnel Department costs are allocated first, how much Personnel Department cost would be allocated to the Custodial Department? a) $146.94; b) $0; c) $144; d) $200.

___ 5. If the step method of service department allocation is used and Personnel Department costs are allocated first, how much Custodial Department cost would be allocated to the Personnel Department? a) $80; b) $0; c) $99.59; d) $150.

___ 6. If the step method of service department allocation is used and Personnel Department costs are allocated first, how much Custodial Department cost would be allocated to Operating Department A? a) $0; b) $150; c) $248.94; d) $171.43.

The following data are used in multiple choice questions 7 through 11:

Data for Wasatch Company's two operating departments follow:

	Budgeted Machine Hours	Peak Period Requirement
Operating Department #1	15,000	40%
Operating Department #2	25,000	60
Total machine hours	40,000	100%

The Wasatch Company has a Repair Department that serves these two operating departments. The variable repair costs are budgeted at $0.20 per machine hour. Fixed costs are budgeted at $12,000 per year. Fixed Repair Department costs are allocated to operating departments on the basis of peak period requirements.

At the end of the year, the actual machine hours worked by the operating departments were 16,000 hours for Department #1 and 24,000 hours for Department #2. The actual Repair Department costs were $8,600 variable and $13,000 fixed.

___ 7. The amount of variable repair cost allocated to Department #1 at the beginning of the year should be: a) $3,000; b) $5,000; c) $4,800; d) $7,200.

___ 8. The amount of fixed repair cost allocated to Department #2 at the beginning of the year should be: a) $3,000; b) $5,000; c) $4,800; d) $7,200.

___ 9. The amount of variable repair cost allocated to Department #1 at the end of the year should be: a) $4,800; b) $5,200; c) $3,200; d) $7,200.

___ 10. The amount of fixed repair cost allocated to Department #2 at the end of the year should be: a) $4,800; b) $7,800; c) $3,200; d) $7,200.

___ 11. The amount of actual repair costs not allocated to the operating departments and retained in the Repair Department at the end of the year as a spending variance should be: a) $600; b) $1,600; c) $1,000; d) $1,400.

Exercises

16-1.   Piney Company has three service departments and two operating departments. Cost and other data relating to these departments follow:

	Service Departments			Operating Departments	
	Janitorial	Cafeteria	Engineering	Assembly	Finishing
Overhead costs	$60,000	$42,600	$75,000	$230,000	$300,000
Square feet	1,500 sq. ft.	2,000 sq. ft.	1,000 sq. ft.	4,000 sq. ft.	3,000 sq. ft.
Number of employees	15	12	50	200	400

The company allocates Janitorial costs on the basis of square feet. The Cafeteria and Engineering costs are allocated on the basis of the number of employees. The company makes no distinction between variable and fixed service department costs in its allocations of service department costs.

Allocate service department costs to the operating departments using the step method. The company allocates service department costs in the following order: Janitorial, Cafeteria, then Engineering.

	Service Departments			Operating Departments	
	Janitorial	Cafeteria	Engineering	Assembly	Finishing
Overhead costs	$ 60,000	$ 42,600	$ 75,000	$ 230,000	$ 300,000
Allocations:					
Janitorial	_____	_____	_____	_____	_____
Cafeteria		_____	_____	_____	_____
Engineering			_____	_____	_____
Total	$_____	$_____	$_____	$_____	$_____

16-2.   Refer to the data in Exercise 16-1. Allocate the service department costs to the operating departments using the direct method.

	Service Departments			Operating Departments	
	Janitorial	Cafeteria	Engineering	Assembly	Finishing
Overhead costs	$ 60,000	$ 42,600	$ 75,000	$ 230,000	$ 300,000
Allocations:					
Janitorial	_____			_____	_____
Cafeteria		_____		_____	_____
Engineering			_____	_____	_____
Total	$_____	$_____	$_____	$_____	$_____

16-3.   The municipal motor pool provides cars on loan to city employees who must travel on official business. The city has three departments that use this service—Public Safety, General Administration, and Sanitation. Data concerning these departments' annual use of the motor pool (in thousands of miles driven) appear below:

	Public Safety	General Administration	Sanitation
Budgeted use (thousands of miles)	600	800	200
Actual use (thousands of miles)	500	900	250
Peak period requirements	35%	50%	15%

The motor pool's budgeted annual fixed costs are $330,000. Peak period requirements determine the level of the fixed costs. Budgeted variable costs are $80 per thousand miles driven.

a.   How much of the motor pool's budgeted costs should be allocated to Public Safety at the beginning of the year for planning purposes?

b.   Suppose the motor pool's actual costs for the year were $345,000 for fixed costs and $138,000 for variable costs. How much of this actual cost should be allocated to Public Safety at the end of the year for performance evaluation purposes?

16-4.   **Critical thought writing exercise:** "Since sales dollars is a measure of ability to pay, it is probably the most equitable base for allocating service department costs to operating departments." Explain why you do or do not agree with this statement.

_____

_____

_____

_____

_____

_____

_____

_____

Answers to Questions and Exercises

True or False

1. F   The direct method entirely ignores reciprocal services among service departments.

2. T   If the service department being allocated is included in the allocation base, then some of the cost will be allocated back to the service department.

3. F   See the answer to (2) above.

4. T   See Exhibit 16-2.

5. T   The reciprocal method fully accounts for all reciprocal services among service departments.

6. F   The order of allocation doesn't make any difference in the direct method. The order of allocation does, however, make a difference in the step method.

7. T   This statement describes the procedure followed using the step method.

8. F   Fixed costs—not variable costs—should be allocated in predetermined, lump-sums.

9. T   Budgeted, rather than actual, costs should be allocated in order to avoid passing inefficiencies on from one department to another.

10. F   As discussed in the text, sales dollars is a poor allocation base.

Multiple Choice

1. b   Allocation base = 30 + 50 = 80
       Allocation: (30/80) × $800 = $300

2. c   Even though the Personnel Department has two employees, none of its costs are charged to itself in the direct method or in the step method.

3. a   Original overhead cost in
       Operating Department B $5,000
       Allocated Personnel Dept. cost:
       (50/80) × $800   500
       Allocated Custodial Dept. cost:
       (80/120) × $600   400
       Total $5,900

4. a   Allocation base = 18 + 30 + 50 = 98
       Allocation: (18/98) × $800 = $146.94

5. b   In the step method, once a service department's costs have been allocated, the department is ignored in subsequent allocations.

6. c   This problem requires two steps:

       Original Custodial cost $600.00
       Allocated from Personnel* 146.94
       Custodial cost to be allocated $746.94
       *See the answer to question (4) above.

       Allocation base = 40 + 80 = 120
       Allocation: (40/120) × $746.94 = $248.98

7. a   15,000 hours × $0.20 = $3,000.

8. d   60% × $12,000 = $7,200.

9. c   16,000 hours × $0.20 = $3,200.
       The budgeted rate is still used.

10. d   Fixed costs should be allocated in predetermined, lump-sum amounts and the allocation at the end of the year should be the same as at the beginning of the year.

11. b   The computations are:

       Actual costs
       ($8,600 + $13,000) $21,600
       Allocated costs:
       Variable* $8,000
       Fixed**   12,000   20,000
       Unallocated .... $ 1,600

       *(16,000 hrs. + 24,000 hrs.) × $0.20 = $8,000
       ** The budgeted amount

Exercises

16-1.

	Service Departments			Operating Departments	
	Janitorial	*Cafeteria*	*Engineering*	*Assembly*	*Finishing*
Overhead costs	$60,000	$42,600	$75,000	$230,000	$300,000
Allocations:					
Janitorial [1]	(60,000)	12,000	6,000	24,000	18,000
Cafeteria [2]		(54,600)	4,200	16,800	33,600
Engineering [3]			(85,200)	28,400	56,800
Total	$ -0-	$ -0-	$ -0-	$299,200	$408,400

[1] $\dfrac{\text{Janitorial cost}}{\text{Total square feet}} = \dfrac{\$60,000}{10,000 \text{ square feet}} = \$6 \text{ per square foot}$

[2] $\dfrac{\text{Cafeteria cost}}{\text{Number of employees}} = \dfrac{\$54,600}{650 \text{ employees}} = \$84 \text{ per employee}$

[3] $\dfrac{\text{Engineering cost}}{\text{Number of employees}} = \dfrac{\$85,200}{600 \text{ employees}} = \$142 \text{ per employee}$

16-2.

	Service Departments			Operating Departments	
	Janitorial	*Cafeteria*	*Engineering*	*Assembly*	*Finishing*
Overhead costs	$60,000	$42,600	$75,000	$230,000	$300,000
Allocation:					
Janitorial [1]	(60,000)			34,286	25,714
Cafeteria [2]		(42,600)		14,200	28,400
Engineering [3]			(75,000)	25,000	50,000
Total	$ -0-	$ -0-	$ -0-	$303,486	$404,114

[1] $\dfrac{\text{Janitorial cost}}{\text{Total square feet}} = \dfrac{\$60,000}{7,000 \text{ square feet}} = \$8.57 \text{ per square foot}$

[2] $\dfrac{\text{Cafeteria cost}}{\text{Number of employees}} = \dfrac{\$42,600}{600 \text{ employees}} = \$71 \text{ per employee}$

[3] $\dfrac{\text{Engineering cost}}{\text{Number of employees}} = \dfrac{\$75,000}{600 \text{ employees}} = \$125 \text{ per employee}$

16-3.   a.   Variable cost allocation:
             Budgeted rate × Budgeted activity
                 $80 per thousand miles × 600 thousand miles ... $ 48,000
             Fixed cost allocation:
             Budgeted fixed cost × Percentage of peak period needs
                 $330,000 × 35%   115,500
             Total $163,500

        b.   Variable cost allocation:
             Budgeted rate × Actual activity
                 $80 per thousand miles × 500 thousand miles ... $ 40,000
             Fixed cost allocation:
             Budgeted fixed cost × Percentage of peak period needs
                 $330,000 × 35%   115,500
             Total $155,500

        Note that the fixed cost allocation is the same at the end of the period as it was
        at the beginning of the period.

16-4.   Sales dollars is not a good base for allocating service department costs to other departments.
This is because there generally is no cause-and-effect relationship between sales in operating departments and the costs incurred in the service departments. Thus, if sales dollars is used to allocate service
department costs to other departments, inequities can result in the allocations. The amount of cost allocated to a given department will depend in large part on what is happening in other departments. A
drop in sales in one department will result in it being relieved of allocated costs, and these costs will be
shifted to other departments. As a consequence, the better departments will be penalized for lack of
effectiveness elsewhere that is beyond their control.

Chapter 17

"How Well Am I Doing?"—
Statement of Cash Flows

Chapter Study Suggestions

This chapter explains how to prepare a statement of cash flows. The statement of cash flows is constructed by examining changes in balance sheet accounts. There are three key exhibits in the chapter. The first, Exhibit 17-2, indicates which changes in the various balance sheet items are considered to be sources of cash and which are considered to be uses of cash. The second key exhibit is Exhibit 17-7, which provides guidelines for classifying transactions as operating, investing, and financing activities. Once transactions have been classified as sources or uses and as operating, investing, or financing activities, it is fairly straightforward to put together a statement of cash flows. However, you must keep track of many details. Therefore, we recommend a systematic approach based on a worksheet such as the one in Exhibit 17-10.

CHAPTER HIGHLIGHTS

A. The purpose of the statement of cash flows is to highlight the major activities that have provided and used cash during the period.

B. The term *cash* on the statement of cash flows is broadly defined to include both cash and cash equivalents. Cash equivalents consist of short-term, highly liquid investments such as treasury bills, commercial paper, and money market funds that are made solely for the purpose of generating a return on cash that is temporarily idle.

C. A period's net cash flow is equal to the change in the cash account during the period. Exhibit 17-1 shows that the change in cash during a period can be expressed in terms of the changes in all of the noncash balance sheet accounts. The statement of cash flows is based on this fact. The statement is basically a listing of changes in the nocash balance sheet accounts.

D. Changes in noncash account balances can be classified as *sources* and *uses*. On the statement of cash flows, sources positively affect cash flow and uses negatively affect cash flow.

1. The following are classified as sources:

   a. Net income.

   b. Decreases in noncash assets.

   c. Increases in liabilities.

   d. Increases in capital stock accounts.

2. The following are classified as uses:

   a. Increases in noncash assets.

   b. Decreases in liabilities.

   c. Decreases in capital stock accounts.

   d. Dividends paid to shareholders.

3. The sources and uses usually make intuitive sense. For example, an increase in inventory (a noncash asset) implicitly requires cash and is considered to be a use.

E. The FASB requires that the statement of cash flows be divided into three sections. These sections relate to *operating activities, investing activities, and financing activities.*

1. As a general rule, operating activities are those activities that enter into determination of net income. These activities include:

   a. Net income (or net loss).

   b. Changes in current assets.

   c. Changes in noncurrent assets that affect net income, such as depreciation and amortization.

   d. Changes in current liabilities (except for debts to lenders and dividends).

   e. Changes in noncurrent liabilities that affect net income, such as interest on debt.

2. Investing activities consist of changes in noncurrent assets that are not included in net income.

3. Financing activities consist of transactions involving borrowing from creditors (other than the payment of interest), and transactions involving the owners of a company. Specific financing activities include:

   a. Changes in current liabilities that are debts to lenders rather than obligations to suppliers, employees, or government.

   b. Changes in noncurrent liabilities that are not included in net income.

   c. Changes in capital stock accounts.

   d. Dividends paid to the company's shareholders.

F. Companies sometimes acquire assets or dispose of liabilities through *direct exchange transactions.*

1. Examples include issuing capital stock in exchange for property and equipment and converting long-term debt into common stock.

2. Direct exchanges that affect only non-current balance sheet accounts are not reported on the statement of cash flows itself. Instead, they are disclosed in a separate schedule accompanying the statement of cash flows.

G. In some cases, the net change in an account is shown on the statement of cash flows. In other cases, the increases and decreases are disclosed separately. The treatment depends on whether the change appears in the operating activities section or in the investing and financing activities sections.

1. For both financing and investing activities, items on the statement of cash flows must be presented in gross amounts rather than in net amounts. For example, if a company buys $100,000 of new equipment and sells $30,000 of used equipment, both amounts must be disclosed rather than the net effect of a $70,000 increase in the equipment account.

2. For operating activities, only the net change in an account is shown on the statement of cash flows.

H. The net result of the cash inflows and outflows arising from operating activities is referred to as the *net cash provided by operating activities*. This figure can be computed using the *direct method* or the *indirect method*.

1. Under the direct method, the income statement is reconstructed on a cash basis from top to bottom. This method is discussed in Appendix 17A.

2. Under the indirect method, the net cash provided by operations is computed by starting with net income and adjusting it to a cash basis. The steps to follow in this adjustment process are shown in Exhibit 17-8.

3. The direct and indirect methods yield exactly the same figure for the net cash provided by operating activities.

I. Carefully study Exhibit 17-10, which illustrates the mechanics of putting together a worksheet. Make sure you understand each of the entries on this worksheet. Once this worksheet has been completed, the statement of cash flows can be easily constructed.

J. Carefully study Exhibit 17-12, which illustrates the format of the statement of cash flows. Trace each of the entries from the worksheet in Exhibit 17-10 to the statement of cash flows in Exhibit 17-12.

Appendix 17A: The Direct Method

A. The direct method reconstructs the income statement from the top down.

1. To adjust revenue to a cash basis:

- Subtract (add) any increase (decrease) in accounts receivable.

2. To adjust cost of goods sold to a cash basis:

- Add (subtract) any increase (decrease) in inventory.
- Subtract (add) any increase (decrease) in accounts payable.

3. To adjust operating expenses to a cash basis:

- Add (subtract) any increase (decrease) in prepaid expenses.
- Subtract (add) any increase (decrease) in accrued liabilities.
- Subtract the period's depreciation and amortization charges.

4. To adjust income tax expense to a cash basis:

- Subtract (add) any increase (decrease) in taxes payable.
- Subtract (add) any increase (decrease) in deferred taxes.

REVIEW AND SELF TEST
Questions and Exercises

True or False

Enter a T or an F in the blank to indicate whether the statement is true or false.

___ 1. Dividends received on stock held as an investment are included in the operating activities section of the statement of cash flows.

___ 2. Interest paid on amounts borrowed is included in the financing activities section of the statement of cash flows.

___ 3. Lending money to another entity (such as to a subsidiary) is classified as a financing activity.

___ 4. Paying cash dividends to the company's stockholders is classified as a financing activity.

___ 5. Transactions involving all forms of debt, including accounts payable, short-term borrowing, and long-term borrowing, are classified as financing activities on the statement of cash flows.

___ 6. For both financing and investing activities, items on the statement of cash flows should be presented gross rather than net.

___ 7. The direct and indirect methods can yield different figures for the net cash provided by operating activities.

___ 8. Only changes in noncurrent accounts are analyzed for a statement of cash flows.

___ 9. If a company is profitable, the net cash flow must be positive.

___ 10. (Appendix 17A) The income statement is reconstructed on a cash basis from top to bottom under the direct method of computing the net cash provided by operating activities.

___ 11. (Appendix 17A) In computing the net cash provided by operating activities, depreciation is added to net income under the indirect method, but it is deducted from operating expenses under the direct method.

Multiple Choice

Choose the best answer or response by placing the identifying letter in the space provided.

___ 1. For purposes of constructing a statement of cash flows, an increase in inventory would be classified as: a) a source and an operating activity; b) a use and an operating activity; c) a source and an investing activity; d) a use and an investing activity.

___ 2. An increase in accounts payable would be classified as: a) a source and an operating activity; b) a use and an operating activity; c) a source and a financing activity; d) a use and a financing activity.

___ 3. An increase in bonds payable would be classified as: a) a source and an investing activity; b) a use and an investing activity; c) a source and a financing activity; d) a use and a financing activity.

___ 4. An increase in long-term investments would be classified as: a) a source and an investing activity; b) a use and an investing activity; c) a source and a financing activity; d) a use and a financing activity.

___ 5. Cash dividends paid to the company's stockholders would be classified as: a) a source and an operating activity; b) a use and an operating activity; c) a source and a financing activity; d) a use and a financing activity.

___ 6. An increase in the company's common stock account would be classified as: a) a source and an investing activity; b) a use and an investing activity; c) a source and a financing activity; d) a use and a financing activity.

Exercises

17-1. Ingall Company's comparative balance sheet and income statement for the most recent year follow:

INGALL COMPANY
Comparative Balance Sheet
(dollars in millions)

	Ending Balance	Beginning Balance
Assets		
Cash	$ 14	$ 10
Accounts receivable	21	15
Inventory	50	43
Prepaid expenses	2	6
Plant and equipment	190	140
Less accumulated depreciation	(65)	(54)
Long-term investments	70	90
Total assets	$282	$250
Liabilities and Stockholders' Equity		
Accounts payable	$ 26	$ 25
Accrued liabilities	10	12
Taxes payable	13	18
Bonds payable	50	40
Deferred income taxes	36	31
Common stock	80	70
Retained earnings	67	54
Total liabilities and stockholders' equity	$282	$250

INGALL COMPANY
Income Statement
(dollars in millions)

Sales	$230
Less cost of goods sold	120
Gross margin	110
Less operating expenses	70
Net operating income	40
Gain on sale of long-term investments	5
Income before taxes	45
Less income taxes	14
Net income	$ 31

Notes: Dividends of $18 million were declared and paid during the year. The gain on sale of long-term investments was from the sale of investments for $25 million in cash. These investments had an original cost of $20 million. There were no retirements or disposals of plant or equipment during the year.

Using the blank form on the following page, prepare a worksheet like Exhibit 17-10 for Ingall Company.

INGALL COMPANY
Statement of Cash Flows Worksheet

	Change	Source or use?	Cash Flow Effect	Adjust- ments	Adjusted Effect	Classi- fication
Assets (except cash and cash equivalents)						
Current assets:						
Accounts receivable	_____	_____	_____		_____	_____
Inventory	_____	_____	_____		_____	_____
Prepaid expenses	_____	_____	_____		_____	_____
Noncurrent assets:						
Plant and equipment	_____	_____	_____		_____	_____
Long-term investments	_____	_____	_____	_____	_____	_____
Liabilities, Contra-Assets, and Stockholders' Equity						
Contra-assets:						
Accumulated depreciation	_____	_____	_____		_____	_____
Current liabilities:						
Accounts payable	_____	_____	_____		_____	_____
Accrued liabilities	_____	_____	_____		_____	_____
Taxes payable	_____	_____	_____		_____	_____
Noncurrent liabilities:						
Bonds payable	_____	_____	_____		_____	_____
Deferred income taxes	_____	_____	_____		_____	_____
Stockholders' equity:						
Common stock	_____	_____	_____		_____	_____
Retained earnings						
Net income	_____	_____	_____		_____	_____
Dividends	_____	_____	_____		_____	_____
Additional Entries						
Proceeds from sale of long-term investments				_____	_____	_____
Gain on sale of long-term investments				_____	_____	_____
Total (net cash flow)			=======	=======	=======	

17-2. Determine Ingall Company's net cash provided by operating activities using the indirect method.

Net income .... $_____

Adjustments to convert net income to a cash basis:

    Depreciation charges .... _____

    _____ in accounts receivable .... _____

    _____ in inventory .... _____

    _____ in prepaid expenses .... _____

    _____ in accounts payable .... _____

    _____ in accrued liabilities .... _____

    _____ in taxes payable .... _____

    _____ in deferred taxes .... _____

    Gain on sale of long-term investments .... _____

Net cash flow provided by (used in) operations .... $_____

17-3.   (Appendix 17A) Using the direct method, determine Ingall Company's net cash provided by operating activities.

Sales .... $ 230

Adjustments to convert sales to a cash basis:

    _____ in accounts receivable .... _____ $ _____

Cost of goods sold .... $ 120

Adjustments to convert cost of goods sold to a cash basis:

    _____ in inventory .... _____

    _____ in accounts payable .... _____   _____

Operating expenses .... $ 70

Adjustments to convert operating expenses to a cash basis:

    _____ in prepaid expenses .... _____

    _____ in accrued liabilities .... _____

    Depreciation charges .... _____   _____

Income taxes .... $ 14

Adjustments to convert income taxes to a cash basis:

    _____ in taxes payable .... _____

    _____ in deferred taxes .... _____   _____

Net cash provided by (used in) operating activities .... $_____

17-4. Prepare a statement of cash flows for Ingall Company using the form below.

INGALL COMPANY
Statement of Cash Flows

Operating activities

Net cash provided by (used in) operating activities .... $_____

Investing activities

_____........................ $_____

_____........................ _____

Net cash provided by (used in) investing activities............................ _____

Financing activities

_____........................ $_____

_____........................ _____

_____........................ _____

Net cash provided by (used in) financing activities .... _____

Net increase (decrease) in cash .... _____

Cash balance, beginning .... _____

Cash balance, ending .... $_____

Answers to Questions and Exercises

True or False

1. T Dividends received enter into the determination of net income and therefore are included in operating rather than investing activities.

2. F Interest paid on amounts borrowed is included in operating activities since interest enters into net income.

3. F Lending money to another entity is classified as an investing activity.

4. T Dividends do not affect net income and therefore are not considered to be an operating activity.

5. F Transactions involving accounts payable are included among operating activities—not financing activities.

6. T Only transactions involving operating activities are presented in net amounts.

7. F The direct and indirect methods will always yield exactly the same figure for the net cash provided by operating activities.

8. F Changes in all noncash accounts, current as well as noncurrent, are analyzed when preparing a statement of cash flows.

9. F The net cash flow may be negative even if a company is profitable. For example, a profitable company may make a major investment using cash reserves it has accumulated in the past.

10. T See Exhibit 17A-1 for an example.

11. T Subtracting depreciation from an expense is equivalent to adding it to net income.

Multiple Choice

1. b Inventory is a current asset. Increases in current assets are classified as uses. Changes in current assets are considered to be the result of operating activities.

2. a Accounts payable is a current liability. Increases in current liabilities are classified as sources. Changes in current liabilities are considered to be the result of operating activities.

3. c Bonds payable is a noncurrent liability. An increase in a noncurrent liability is considered to be a source. A change in a noncurrent liability is considered to be a financing activity unless it enters into net income.

4. b Long-term investments is a noncurrent asset account. An increase in a noncurrent asset is considered to be a use. A change in a noncurrent asset is considered to be an investing activity unless it directly enters into the determination of net income.

5. d Dividends are considered to be a use. They are classified as a financing activity since they do not enter into the determination of net income.

6. c An increase in the common stock account is considered to be a source and a financing activity.

Exercises

17-1. The completed worksheet for Ingall Company appears below:

	Change	Source or use?	Cash Flow Effect	Adjust-ments	Adjusted Effect	Classi-fication*
Assets (except cash and cash equivalents)						
Current assets:						
Accounts receivable	+6	Use	-6		-6	Operating
Inventory	+7	Use	-7		-7	Operating
Prepaid expenses	-4	Source	+4		+4	Operating
Noncurrent assets:						
Plant and equipment	+50	Use	-50		-50	Investing
Long-term investments	-20	Source	+20	-20	0	Investing
Liabilities, Contra-Assets, and Stockholders' Equity						
Contra-assets:						
Accumulated depreciation	+11	Source	+11		+11	Operating
Current liabilities:						
Accounts payable	+1	Source	+1		+1	Operating
Accrued liabilities	-2	Use	-2		-2	Operating
Taxes payable	-5	Use	-5		-5	Operating
Noncurrent liabilities:						
Bonds payable	+10	Source	+10		+10	Financing
Deferred income taxes	+5	Source	+5		+5	Operating
Stockholders' equity:						
Common stock	+10	Source	+10		+10	Financing
Retained earnings						
Net income	+31	Source	+31		+31	Operating
Dividends	-18	Use	-18		-18	Financing
Additional Entries						
Proceeds from sale of long-term investments				+25	+25	Investing
Gain on sale of long-term investments				-5	-5	Operating
Total (net cash flow)			+4	0	+4	

Note: The most difficult part of this worksheet is the adjustment for the sale of the long-term investments. Basically, the adjustment moves the gain on the sale from the operating activities section to the investing section. It would be wise to pay particular attention to this entry and how it affects the statement of cash flows.

17-2.   The operating activities section of the statement of cash flows constructed using the indirect method appears below:

Net income	$31
Adjustments to convert net income to a cash basis:	
Depreciation charges	11
Increase in accounts receivable	(6)
Increase in inventory	(7)
Decrease in prepaid expenses	4
Increase in accounts payable	1
Decrease in accrued liabilities	(2)
Decrease in taxes payable	(5)
Increase in deferred taxes	5
Gain on sale of long-term investments	(5)
Net cash flow provided by operations	$27

Note that the gain on sale of long-term investments is deducted from net income. This removes the gain from the operating activities section of the statement of cash flows. The gain will show up implicitly in the investing activities section of the statement of cash flows. See the solution to 17-4 below.

17-3.   The direct method can be used to arrive at the same answer as in 17-2 above.

Sales	$230	
Adjustments to convert sales to a cash basis:		
Increase in accounts receivable	(6)	$224
Cost of goods sold	120	
Adjustments to convert cost of goods sold to a cash basis:		
Increase in inventory	7	
Increase in accounts payable	(1)	126
Operating expenses	70	
Adjustments to convert operating expenses to a cash basis:		
Decrease in prepaid expenses	(4)	
Decrease in accrued liabilities	2	
Depreciation charges	(11)	57
Income taxes	14	
Adjustments to convert income taxes to a cash basis:		
Decrease in taxes payable	5	
Increase in deferred taxes	(5)	14
Net cash provided by operating activities		$ 27

17-4.

INGALL COMPANY
Statement of Cash Flows

Operating activities
Net cash provided by operating activities .... $ 27

Investing activities
    Proceeds from sale of long-term investments $25
    Increase in plant and equipment .... (50)
Net cash used for investing activities .... (25)

Financing activities
    Increase in bonds payable 10
    Increase in common stock 10
    Dividends .... (18)
Net cash provided by financing activities 2

Net increase in cash 4
Cash balance, beginning 10
Cash balance, ending $14

Chapter 18

"How Well Am I Doing?"— Financial Statement Analysis

Chapter Study Suggestions

The chapter is divided into two parts. The first part discusses the preparation and use of statements in comparative and common-size form. This part of the chapter is easy and involves nothing more complicated than computing percentages. Your study in this part should be focused on Exhibits 18-1, 18-2, and 18-4 in the text. These exhibits show how statements in comparative and common-size form are prepared.

The second part of the chapter deals with ratio analysis. Altogether, seventeen ratios are presented in this part of the chapter. You should memorize the formula for each ratio since it is likely that you will be expected to know these formulas on exams. This may at first seem like an overwhelming task, but most of the ratios are intuitive and easy to compute. You should also learn how to interpret each ratio. Exhibit 18-7 in the text provides a compact summary of the ratios.

CHAPTER HIGHLIGHTS

A. Financial statement analysis is concerned with assessing the financial condition of the firm.

　　1. To be most useful, financial statement analysis should involve comparisons. Comparisons can be made from one year to another, as well as to other firms within the same industry.

　　2. The analyst must be careful not to rely just on financial statement analysis in making a judgment about a firm.

　　　　a. The ratios should be viewed as a starting point for analysis rather than as an end in themselves. They indicate what should be pursued in greater depth.

　　　　b. One problem is that companies may use different accounting methods such as LIFO or FIFO and these differences in accounting methods may make comparisons difficult.

　　　　c. Another problem is that the ratios are based on accounting data which show what has happened in the past. This may not be a reliable guide to what is going to happen in the future.

B. Three common analytical techniques for financial statement analysis are: 1) dollar and percentage changes on statements (horizontal analysis); 2) common-size statements (vertical analysis); and 3) ratios.

　　1. Horizontal analysis involves placing two or more yearly statements side by side and analyzing changes between years. These comparisons are made both in terms of dollars and in terms of percentage changes from year to year.

　　　　a. Showing changes in dollar form helps identify the most significant changes.

　　　　b. Showing changes in percentage form helps to identify the most unusual changes.

　　　　c. Trend percentages are often computed. Each item, such as sales or net income, is stated as a percentage of the same item in a base year.

　　2. A common-size statement shows items in percentages rather than in dollars. Balance Sheet items are stated as a percentage of Total Assets and Income Statement items are stated as a percentage of sales. Preparation of common-size statements is known as vertical analysis. Showing the balance sheet and the income statement in common-size form helps the analyst see the relative importance of the various items.

　　3. The *gross margin percentage* is a particularly important item on the common-size income statement. It is defined as follows:

$$\text{Gross margin percentage} = \frac{\text{Gross margin}}{\text{Sales}}$$

The gross margin percentage is used as a rough measure of the overall profitability of a company's products. However, caution is advised. In manufacturing firms, the gross margin percentage should increase as sales increase since fixed production costs are spread across more units.

　　4. In addition to horizontal and vertical analysis, stockholders, short-term creditors, and long-term creditors use a variety of ratios to help them evaluate companies. Ratios that are designed to meet the needs of these three different groups are discussed in sections C, D, and E below.

C. Several ratios provide measures of how well the company is doing from the shareholders' perspective.

　　1. *Earnings per share* is an important measure of the annual earnings available for common shareholders. The formula is:

$$\frac{\text{Earnings}}{\text{per share}} = \frac{\text{Net income - Preferred dividends}}{\text{Average number of common shares outstanding}}$$

Preferred dividends are subtracted from net income since they are not an expense on the income statement but reduce the earnings that can be distributed to common shareholders.

　　2. The *price-earnings ratio* shows the relation between the market price of a share of stock and the stock's current earnings per share. The price-earnings ratio is computed as follows:

$$\text{Price - earnings ratio} = \frac{\text{Market price per share}}{\text{Earnings per share}}$$

Price-earnings ratios differ from one company to another although they tend to be similar for companies in the same industry. One of the biggest factors affecting the price-earnings ratio is future earnings growth. If investors believe high future earnings growth is likely for a company, they will bid up the price of its stock and hence it will have a high price-earnings ratio.

3. The *dividend payout ratio* gauges the proportion of current earnings being paid out as dividends. The formula is:

$$\text{Dividend payout ratio} = \frac{\text{Dividends per share}}{\text{Earnings per share}}$$

A company with a high dividend payout ratio is paying out most of its earnings to shareholders as dividends rather than reinvesting the earnings in the company.

4. The d*ividend yield ratio* measures the cash yield on the common stockholder's investment. The ratio is computed as follows:

$$\text{Dividend yield ratio} = \frac{\text{Dividends per share}}{\text{Market price per share}}$$

Investors hope to profit from both dividends and increases in the market value of the stock they own. The dividend yield measures only the contribution of the dividends. Note that the current market price per share is used in this ratio and not the price the investor originally paid for the shares.

5. The *return on total assets* is a measure of how effectively a company has used its assets. The formula is:

$$\text{Return on total assets} = \frac{\text{Net income} + \left[\begin{array}{c}\text{Interest expense} \times \\ (1 - \text{Tax rate})\end{array}\right]}{\text{Average total assets}}$$

a. Note that interest expense is placed on an after-tax basis by multiplying it by one minus the tax rate before being added back to net income.

b. Interest expense is added back to net income to show earnings *before* any distributions have been made to either creditors or shareholders. This adjustment results in a total return on assets that measures operating performance independently of how the assets were financed.

6. The *return on common stockholders' equity* measures a company's ability to generate income. The formula is:

$$\text{Return on common stockholders' equity} = \frac{\text{Net income} - \text{Preferred dividends}}{\text{Average common stockholders' equity}}$$

As with earnings per share, preferred dividends are subtracted from net income since preferred dividends reduce the earnings available to common shareholders. The return on common stockholders' equity is often higher than the return on total assets because of financial leverage.

a. *Financial leverage* involves purchasing assets with funds obtained from creditors or from preferred stockholders at a fixed rate of return. If the assets in which the funds are invested earn a greater return than the fixed rate of return required by the suppliers of the funds, then financial leverage is *positive*. Financial leverage is *negative* if the assets earn a return that is less than the fixed rate of return required by creditors.

b. Sources of leverage include long-term debt, preferred stock, and current liabilities.

c. Long-term debt is usually a more effective source of financial leverage than preferred stock since interest on long-term debt is tax-deductible, whereas dividends on preferred stock are not.

d. If a company has positive financial leverage, its common stockholders are likely to benefit if the company takes on debt.

7. The *book value per share* measures the common stockholders' equity on a per share basis. The formula is:

$$\text{Book value per share} = \frac{\text{Common stockholders' equity}}{\text{Number of common shares outstanding}}$$

a. Note that the denominator in this ratio is the number of common shares outstanding at the end of the year—not the average number of shares outstanding over the year as in the earnings per share calculation.

b. The book value per share is usually less than the market value per share. Market value reflects investors' expectations concerning future earnings and dividends. By contrast, book value measures financial effects of already completed transactions and hence looks to the past. Because of this, book value is of limited usefulness.

D. Short-term creditors are concerned with being paid on time and are far more concerned with a company's financial assets and cash flows than with its accounting net income.

1. *Working capital* measures the excess of current assets over current liabilities.

$$\text{Working capital} = \frac{\text{Current}}{\text{assets}} - \frac{\text{Current}}{\text{liabilities}}$$

Negative working capital signals that current assets are insufficient to cover current liabilities.

2. The *current ratio* is also a widely used measure of short-term debt-paying ability. The formula is:

$$\text{Current ratio} = \frac{\text{Current assets}}{\text{Current liabilities}}$$

The current ratio, as well as working capital, should be interpreted with care. The *composition* of the assets and liabilities is very important. A high current ratio does not necessarily mean that the company is easily able to pay its current liabilities. For example, most of the current assets may be inventory that is difficult to sell quickly.

3. The *acid-test* or *quick ratio* is designed to measure how well a company can meet its short-term obligations using only its *most liquid* current assets. The formula is:

$$\text{Acid-test ratio} = \frac{\text{Cash} + \text{Marketable securities} + \text{Current receivables}}{\text{Current liabilities}}$$

Current receivables includes accounts receivable and short-term notes receivable. The current assets in this ratio do not include inventories or prepaid assets since they may be difficult to convert into cash.

4. The *accounts receivable turnover* ratio measures the relation between sales on account and accounts receivable. The formula is:

$$\text{Accounts receivable turnover} = \frac{\text{Sales on account}}{\text{Average accounts receivable balance}}$$

The higher this ratio, the quicker accounts receivable are collected. This is easier to see if the accounts receivable turnover is divided into 365 days. This gives the *average collection period* which is computed as follows:

$$\text{Average collection period} = \frac{365 \text{ days}}{\text{Accounts receivable turnover}}$$

As its name implies, the average collection period indicates the average number of days required to collect credit sales. Ordinarily a short average collection period is desirable.

5. The *inventory turnover* ratio relates cost of goods sold to the average inventory balance using the following formula:

$$\text{Inventory turnover} = \frac{\text{Cost of goods sold}}{\text{Average inventory balance}}$$

The higher this ratio, the quicker inventory is sold. This is easier to see if the inventory turnover is divided into 365 days. The resulting figure is called the *average sale period* and measures how many days on average it takes to sell inventory. The formula is:

$$\text{Average sale period} = \frac{365 \text{ days}}{\text{Inventory turnover}}$$

The average sale period can differ dramatically from one industry to another. For example, the average sale period is much shorter in a florist shop than in a jewelry shop. Florists have to sell their inventory quickly or it will perish.

E. Long-term creditors are concerned with both the near-term and the long-term ability of a firm to repay its debts.

1. The *times interest earned ratio* gauges the ability of a firm to pay interest. The formula is:

$$\text{Times interest earned} = \frac{\text{Earnings before interest expense and income taxes}}{\text{Interest expense}}$$

Generally, the higher the times interest earned, the greater the ability of the company to make interest payments.

2. The *debt-to-equity ratio* relates debt to equity using the following formula:

$$\text{Debt-to-equity ratio} = \frac{\text{Total liabilities}}{\text{Stockholders' equity}}$$

The lower this ratio, the greater the excess of assets over liabilities. Therefore creditors generally prefer a low debt-to-equity ratio since this provides a large cushion of protection.

REVIEW AND SELF TEST
Questions and Exercises

True or False

Enter a T or an F in the blank to indicate whether the statement is true or false.

___ 1. Horizontal analysis uses dollar and percentage changes from year to year to highlight trends.

___ 2. Common-size statements focus on companies of similar size and operations.

___ 3. The current ratio is current assets less current liabilities.

___ 4. Trend percentages in financial statements would be an example of vertical analysis.

___ 5. A common-size statement shows items in percentage form, with each item stated as a percentage of a total of which that item is a part.

___ 6. The earnings per share figure is computed after deducting preferred dividends from the net income of a company.

___ 7. If earnings remain unchanged and the price-earnings ratio goes up, then the market price of the stock must have gone down.

___ 8. Dividing the market price of a share of stock by the dividends per share gives the price-earnings ratio.

___ 9. Book value per share is not a good predictor of future earnings potential.

___ 10. The acid test ratio excludes inventories from current assets.

___ 11. When computing the return on total assets, after-tax interest expense is subtracted from net income.

___ 12. Inventory turnover is computed by dividing sales by average inventory.

___ 13. If a company's return on total assets is substantially higher than its cost of borrowing, then the common stockholders would normally want the company to have a high debt-to-equity ratio.

Multiple Choice

Choose the best answer or response by placing the identifying letter in the space provided.

___ 1. Artway Company's net income last year was $200,000. It paid dividends of $50,000 to the owners of the company's preferred stock. There were 10,000 shares of common stock outstanding throughout the year. What was the company's earnings per share for the year? a) $20; b) $5; c) $15; d) $25.

___ 2. Carston Company's earnings per share is $3.50 and its market price per share is $28. There are 1 million shares of common stock outstanding. What is the company's price-earnings ratio? a) 43.75; b) 4.375; c) 80.0; d) 8.0.

___ 3. Refer to the data for Carston Company in question 2 above. Assume in addition that the company pays an annual dividend of $2.17 per share. What is the company's dividend payout ratio? a) 62%; b) 7.75%; c) 217%; d) 8.9%.

___ 4. Refer again to the data for Carston Company in questions 2 and 3 above. What is the company's dividend yield ratio? a) 62%; b) 7.75%; c) 217%; d) 8.9%.

___ 5. Darsden Company's net income last year was $800,000; its average assets were $4,000,000; its interest expense was $200,000; and its tax rate was 30%. What was the company's return on total assets? a) 23.5%; b) 25%; c) 16.5%; d) 30%.

___ 6. Kristal Company's net income last year was $600,000. The company paid preferred dividends of $200,000 to the owners of its preferred stock. The average common stockholders' equity was $5,000,000. What was the company's return on common stockholders' equity? a) 12%; b) 4%; c) 10%; d) 8%.

___ 7. Harrison Company's common stockholders' equity is $24 million. There are 6 million shares of common stock and 2 million shares of preferred stock outstanding. What is the company's book value per share? a) $3.00; b) $4.00; c) $6.00; d) $2.40.

___ 8. J.J. Company's current assets are $6 million and its current liabilities are $2 million. What is the company's working capital? a) $6 million; b) $2 million; c) $4 million; d) $8 million.

___ 9. Refer to the data for J.J. Company in question 8 above. What is the company's current ratio? a) 3.0 to 1; b) 2.0 to 1; c) 0.33 to 1; d) 0.50 to 1.

___ 10. Refer to the data for J.J. Company in question 8 above. Assume in addition that the company has $1 million in cash and marketable securities and $1.2 million in current receivables. What is the company's acid-test ratio? a) 0.8 to 1; b) 1.0 to 1; c) 1.2 to 1; d) 1.1 to 1.

___ 11. Proctor Company had $25 million of credit sales last year and its average accounts receivable balance was $5 million. What was the company's average collection period? a) 73 days; b) 5 days; c) 20 days; d) 84 days.

___ 12. Larimart Company's cost of goods sold last year was $750,000 and its average inventory balance was $300,000. What was the company's average days to sell inventory? a) 2.5 days; b) 5 days; c) 146 days; d) 912.5 days.

___ 13. Bresser Company's earnings before taxes last year was $42,000 and its interest expense was $6,000. What was the company's times interest earned? a) 12.5 times; b) 1.25 times; c) 80 times; d) 8.0 times.

___ 14. Nupper Company's total liabilities are $320,000 and its stockholders' equity is $400,000. What is the company's debt-to-equity ratio? a) 0.2 to 1; b) 1.25 to 1; c) 0.8 to 1; d) 5 to 1.

___ 15. The acid-test ratio: a) can be expected to be less than the current ratio; b) can be expected to be greater than the current ratio; c) could be either greater or less than the current ratio; d) none of these.

Exercises

18-1. The financial statements of Amfac, Inc., are given below for the just completed year (This Year) and for the previous year (Last Year):

AMFAC, INC.
Balance Sheet
December 31

Assets

	This Year	Last Year
Cash	$ 8,000	$ 10,000
Accounts receivable, net	36,000	34,000
Inventory	40,000	32,000
Prepaid expenses	2,000	1,000
Plant and equipment, net	214,000	173,000
Total Assets	$300,000	$250,000

Liabilities & Equities

Current liabilities	$ 40,000	$ 30,000
Long-term liabilities	60,000	40,000
Preferred stock	50,000	50,000
Common stock	30,000	30,000
Retained earnings	120,000	100,000
Total liabilities and equity	$300,000	$250,000

AMFAC, INC.
Income Statement
For the Year Ended December 31

	This Year
Sales (all on account)	$450 000
Cost of goods sold	270,000
Gross margin	180,000
Operating expenses	129,000
Net operating income	51,000
Interest expense	6,000
Net income before taxes	45,000
Income taxes (30%)	13,500
Net Income	$ 31,500

Preferred dividends were $4,000 this year.

Compute the following ratios for this year:

a. Current ratio.

b. Acid-test ratio.

c. Debt-to-equity ratio.

d. Average collection period.

e. Inventory turnover.

f. Times interest earned.

g. Return on total assets.

h. Return on common stockholders' equity.

i. Is financial leverage positive or negative? Explain.

_____

_____

_____

_____

18-2.   Cartwright Company has reported the following data relating to sales and accounts receivable in its most recent annual report

	Year 5	Year 4	Year 3	Year 2	Year 1
Sales	$700,000	$675,000	$650,000	$575,000	$500,000
Accounts receivable	$ 72,000	$ 60,000	$ 52,000	$ 46,000	$ 40,000

Express the data above in trend percentages. Use Year 1 as the base year.

	Year 5	Year 4	Year 3	Year 2	Year 1
Sales	_____	_____	_____	_____	_____
Accounts receivable	_____	_____	_____	_____	_____

Comment on the significant information revealed by your trend percentages:

_____

_____

_____

_____

18-3. Consider the following comparative income statements of Eldredge Company, a jewelry design and manufacturing company:

ELDREDGE COMPANY
Income Statements
For the Years Ended December 31

	This Year	Last Year
Sales	$600,000	$500,000
Cost of goods sold	420,000	331,000
Gross margin	180,000	169,000
Operating expenses:		
Selling expenses	87,000	72,500
Administrative expenses	46,800	51,000
Total operating expenses	133,800	123,500
Net operating income	46,200	45,500
Interest expense	1,200	1,500
Net income before taxes	45,000	44,000
Income taxes	13,500	13,200
Net Income	$ 31,500	$ 30,800

a. Express the income statements for both years in common-size percentages. Round percentages to one decimal point.

	This Year	Last Year
Sales	_____	_____
Cost of goods sold	_____	_____
Gross margin	_____	_____
Operating expenses:		
Selling expenses	_____	_____
Administrative expenses	_____	_____
Total operating expenses	_____	_____
Net operating income	_____	_____
Interest expense	_____	_____
Net income before taxes	_____	_____
Income taxes	_____	_____
Net Income	_____	_____

b. Comment briefly on the changes between the two years.

_____

_____

_____

_____

Answers to Questions and Exercises

True or False

1. T   This is true by definition.

2. F   A common-size statement shows items in percentage form. Each item is stated as a percentage of some total of which that item is a part.

3. F   The current ratio is current assets *divided* by current liabilities.

4. F   Trend percentages would be an example of horizontal analysis.

5. T   This point is discussed in connection with question 2 above.

6. T   The net income available to the common shareholders is the amount that remains after paying preferred dividends.

7. F   The opposite is true. If the price-earnings ratio goes up, then the stock is selling for a higher market price per dollar of earnings.

8. F   Dividing the market price of a share of stock by the earnings per share gives the price-earnings ratio.

9. T   Book value per share is the balance sheet carrying value of completed transactions—it tells little about the future.

10. T   Inventories are excluded because they may be difficult to quickly convert to cash.

11. F   When computing the total return on assets, the after-tax interest expense is *added back* to net income to remove its effect.

12. F   Inventory turnover is computed by dividing cost of goods sold by average inventory.

13. T   If a company's return on total assets is higher than its cost of borrowing, then financial leverage is positive. Common stockholders would want the company to use this positive financial leverage to their advantage by having a high amount of debt in the company.

Multiple Choice

1. c   The computations are:

$$\text{Earnings per share} = \frac{\text{Net income - Preferred dividends}}{\text{Average number of common shares outstanding}}$$

$$\frac{\$200,000 - \$50,000}{10,000} = \$15$$

2. d   The computations are:

$$\text{Price - earnings ratio} = \frac{\text{Market price per share}}{\text{Earnings per share}}$$

$$\frac{\$28.00}{\$3.50} = 8.0$$

3. a   The computations are:

$$\text{Dividend payout ratio} = \frac{\text{Dividends per share}}{\text{Earnings per share}}$$

$$\frac{\$2.17}{\$3.50} = 62.0\%$$

4. b   The computations are:

$$\text{Dividend yield ratio} = \frac{\text{Dividends per share}}{\text{Market price per share}}$$

$$\frac{\$2.17}{\$28.00} = 7.75\%$$

5. a   The computations are:

$$\text{Return on total assets} = \frac{\text{Net income} + \left[\begin{array}{c}\text{Interest expense} \times \\ (1 - \text{Tax rate})\end{array}\right]}{\text{Average total assets}}$$

$$\frac{\$800,000 + \left[\begin{array}{c}\$200,000 \times \\ (1 - 0.30)\end{array}\right]}{\$4,000,000} = 23.5\%$$

6. d   The computations are:

$$\text{Return on common stockholers' equity} = \frac{\text{Net income} - \text{Preferred dividends}}{\text{Average common stockholders' equity}}$$

$$\frac{\$600,000 - \$200,000}{\$5,000,000} = 8\%$$

7. b The computations are:

$$\text{Book value per share} = \frac{\text{Common stockholders' equity}}{\text{Number of common shares outstanding}}$$

$$\frac{\$24,000,000}{6,000,000} = \$4.00 \text{ per share}$$

8. c The computations are:

$$\text{Working capital} = \text{Current assets} - \text{Current liabilities}$$
$$\$6,000 - \$2,000 = \$4,000,000$$

9. a The computations are:

$$\text{Current ratio} = \frac{\text{Current assets}}{\text{Current liabilities}}$$

$$\frac{\$6,000,000}{\$2,000,000} = 3.0 \text{ to } 1$$

10. d The computations are:

$$\text{Acid-test ratio} = \frac{\text{Cash + Marketable securities + Current receivables}}{\text{Current liabilities}}$$

$$\frac{\$1,000,000 + \$1,200,000}{\$2,000,000} = 1.1 \text{ to } 1$$

11. a The computations are:

$$\text{Accounts receivable turnover} = \frac{\text{Sales on account}}{\text{Average accounts receivable balance}}$$

$$\frac{\$25,000,000}{\$5,000,000} = 5.0 \text{ to } 1$$

$$\text{Average collection period} = \frac{365 \text{ days}}{\text{Accounts receivable turnover}}$$

$$\frac{365 \text{ days}}{5.0} = 73 \text{ days}$$

12. c The computations are:

$$\text{Inventory turnover} = \frac{\text{Cost of goods sold}}{\text{Average inventory balance}}$$

$$\frac{\$750,000}{\$300,000} = 2.5 \text{ to } 1$$

$$\text{Average sale period} = \frac{365 \text{ days}}{\text{Inventory turnover}}$$

$$\frac{365 \text{ days}}{2.5} = 146 \text{ days}$$

13. d The computations are:

$$\text{Times interest earned} = \frac{\text{Earnings before interest expense and income taxes}}{\text{Interest expense}}$$

$$\frac{\$42,000 + \$6,000}{\$6,000} = 8.0 \text{ times}$$

14. c The computations are:

$$\text{Debt-to-equity ratio} = \frac{\text{Total liabilities}}{\text{Stockholders' equity}}$$

$$\frac{\$320,000}{\$400,000} = 0.8 \text{ to } 1$$

15. a The acid-test ratio will always be less than the current ratio because it contains fewer assets in the numerator but the same amount of liabilities in the denominator.

Exercises

18-1.

a. $\text{Current ratio} = \dfrac{\text{Current assets}}{\text{Current liabilities}} = \dfrac{\$8,000 + \$36,000 + \$40,000 + \$2,000}{\$40,000} = 2.15 \text{ to } 1$

b. $\begin{array}{l}\text{Acid - test} \\ \text{ratio}\end{array} = \dfrac{\begin{array}{c}\text{Cash } + \text{ Marketable securities} \\ + \text{ Current receivables}\end{array}}{\text{Current liabilities}} = \dfrac{\$8,000 + \$36,000}{\$40,000} = 1.10 \text{ to } 1$

c. $\begin{array}{l}\text{Debt - to - equity} \\ \text{ratio}\end{array} = \dfrac{\text{Total liabilities}}{\text{Stockholders' equity}} = \dfrac{\$40,000 + \$60,000}{\$50,000 + \$30,000 + \$120,000} = 0.50 \text{ to } 1$

d. $\begin{array}{l}\text{Accounts receivable} \\ \text{turnover}\end{array} = \dfrac{\text{Sales on account}}{\begin{array}{c}\text{Average accounts} \\ \text{receivable balance}\end{array}} = \dfrac{\$450,000}{(\$36,000 + \$34,000)/2} = 12.9 \text{ times (rounded)}$

$\begin{array}{l}\text{Average collection} \\ \text{period}\end{array} = \dfrac{365 \text{ days}}{\text{Accounts receivable turnover}} = \dfrac{365 \text{ days}}{12.9} = 28 \text{ days (rounded)}$

e. $\begin{array}{l}\text{Inventory} \\ \text{turnover}\end{array} = \dfrac{\text{Cost of goods sold}}{\text{Average inventory balance}} = \dfrac{\$270,000}{(\$40,000 + \$32,000)/2} = 7.5 \text{ times}$

f. $\begin{array}{l}\text{Times interest} \\ \text{earned}\end{array} = \dfrac{\begin{array}{c}\text{Earnings before interest expense} \\ \text{and income taxes}\end{array}}{\text{Interest expense}} = \dfrac{\$51,000}{\$6,000} = 8.5 \text{ times}$

g. $\begin{array}{l}\text{Return on} \\ \text{total assets}\end{array} = \dfrac{\text{Net income} + \left[\begin{array}{c}\text{Interest expense} \times \\ (1 - \text{Tax rate})\end{array}\right]}{\text{Average total assets}} = \dfrac{\$31,500 + \left[\begin{array}{c}\$6,000 \times \\ (1 - 0.30)\end{array}\right]}{(\$300,000 + \$250,000)/2} = 13.0\% \text{ (rounded)}$

h.

	End of Year	Beginning of Year
Total stockholders' equity	$200,000	$180,000
Less preferred stock	50,000	50,000
Common stockholders' equity	$150,000	$130,000

$\begin{array}{l}\text{Return on common} \\ \text{stockholers' equity}\end{array} = \dfrac{\begin{array}{c}\text{Net income} - \\ \text{Preferred dividends}\end{array}}{\begin{array}{c}\text{Average common} \\ \text{stockholders' equity}\end{array}} = \dfrac{\$31,500 - \$4,000}{(\$150,000 + \$130,000)/2} = 19.6\% \text{ (rounded)}$

i. Financial leverage is positive, since the return on the common stockholders' equity is greater than the return on total assets.

18-2.

	Year 5	Year 4	Year 3	Year 2	Year 1
Sales	140%	135%	130%	115%	100%
Accounts receivable	180%	150%	130%	115%	100%

Sales grew by about 15% per year through Year 3, and then dropped off to about a 5% growth rate for the next two years. The accounts receivable grew at about a 15% rate through Year 3, but then rather than dropping off to about a 5% rate, the accounts receivable grew at an even faster rate through Year 5. This suggests that the company may be granting credit too liberally and is having difficulty collecting.

18-3.

a.

ELDREDGE COMPANY
Common-Size Comparative Income Statements
For the Years Ended December 31

	This Year	Last Year
Sales	100.0	100.0
Cost of goods sold	70.0	66.2
Gross margin	30.0	33.8
Operating expenses:		
Selling expenses	14.5	14.5
Administrative expenses	7.8	10.2
Total operating expenses	22.3	24.7
Net operating income	7.7	9.1
Interest expense	0.2	0.3
Net income before taxes	7.5	8.8
Income taxes	2.2	2.6
Net Income	5.3	6.2

b. Cost of goods sold and administrative expenses were the two primary areas affecting the percentage decrease in net income. Cost of goods sold increased from 66.2% of sales in to 70.0% of sales—an increase of 3.8%age points. On the other hand, administrative expenses dropped from 10.2% of sales to only 7.8% of sales—a decrease of 2.4 percentage points. The net effect was a decrease in net income as a percentage of sales, which fell from 6.2% of sales to only 5.3% of sales. The increase in the cost of goods sold as a percentage of sales is puzzling since sales increased. Ordinarily, cost of goods sold as a percentage of sales should decrease as sales increase because fixed production costs are spread across more units.

Appendix A

Pricing Products and Services

Study Suggestions

This appendix covers four approaches to pricing—the economists approach, the absorption costing approach, target costing, and time and material pricing. Time and material pricing is really a variation of the absorption costing approach for service companies. You should memorize the five highlighted equations in the text that describe the first three approaches.

APPENDIX HIGHLIGHTS

A. Some companies have little control over the prices they charge, whereas others have significant latitude in their pricing.

   1. Companies that are small players in highly competitive markets for standard products typically have little control over the prices they charge. For example, prices for agricultural commodities like corn, wheat, and soybeans are set by the interplay of worldwide supply and demand. Individual farmers have no control over the prices of these commodities.

   2. A company that sells a product that is different from the products offered by other companies or that supplies a big chunk of the market typically has some control over its price.

B. *Cost-plus pricing* is the most common approach to setting prices. Under this approach, a markup is added to a cost base to arrive at the target selling price. The formula is:

   Target selling price = Cost + (Markup% × Cost)

What is the cost base? How is the markup percentage determined?

   1. In *the economists' approach*, the cost base is variable cost and the markup percentage is determined by how sensitive unit sales are to changes in price.

   2. In the *absorption costing approach*, the cost base is the product's absorption costing unit product cost and the markup percentage is a function of a number of factors.

C. The economists' approach recognizes that pricing involves a delicate trade-off. The higher the price, the higher the revenue per unit sold, but the lower the number of units sold. The markup over cost should depend on how sensitive customers are to price. If customers are not particularly sensitive to price, the markup can be high. If they are very sensitive to price, the markup over cost should be low.

   1. The *price elasticity of demand*, ε_d, measures the sensitivity of unit sales to a change in price. The formula in the text for price elasticity is:

$$\varepsilon_d = \frac{\ln(1+\% \text{ change in quantity sold})}{\ln(1+\% \text{ change in price})}$$

   a. The natural log, ln(), can be computed using the LN or lnx key on your calculator.

   b. For example, suppose that management believes that a 5% increase in price would result in an 8% drop in unit sales.

$$\varepsilon_d = \frac{\ln(1+(-0.08))}{\ln(1+(+0.05))} = \frac{\ln(0.92)}{\ln(1.05)} = \frac{-0.08338}{0.04879} = -1.71$$

   c. Because of the way the price elasticity of demand has been defined, it is always negative and less than -1 in realistic situations. (The reasons for this are technical.) The greater the absolute value of ε_d, the greater the elasticity of demand. For example, suppose a 5% increase in price results in a 10% drop in unit sales rather than an 8% drop:

$$\varepsilon_d = \frac{\ln(1+(-0.10))}{\ln(1+(+0.05))} = \frac{\ln(0.90)}{\ln(1.05)} = \frac{-0.10536}{0.04879} = -2.16$$

   d. As in the above example, when customers are more sensitive to price (i.e., there is a greater reaction to a price change), the absolute value of the price elasticity of demand is greater.

   e. The above formula may be different from the formula you learned if you took an economics class. While the simpler formula found in most introductory economics texts has its uses, it is not of much help in setting prices.

   2. If the price elasticity of demand is constant for a product and the cost of making and selling the product is a combination of variable and fixed costs, the price that would maximize the company's profit is given by the following formula:

$$\text{Profit-maximizing price} = \left(\frac{\varepsilon_d}{1+\varepsilon_d}\right) \begin{array}{l}\text{Variable cost}\\ \text{per unit}\end{array}$$

   a. For example, suppose the variable cost per unit is $1 and the price elasticity of demand is -1.71. The profit-maximizing price is computed as follows:

$$\text{Profit-maximizing price} = \left(\frac{-1.71}{1+(-1.71)}\right)\$1$$
$$= 2.41 \times \$1 = \$2.41$$

In this case the markup over variable cost is 141%.

b.   Or suppose the variable cost per unit is $1 and the price elasticity of demand is -2.16. The profit-maximizing price is computed as follows:

$$\text{Profit-maximizing price} = \left(\frac{-2.16}{1+(-2.16)}\right)\$1$$
$$= 1.86 \times \$1 = \$1.86$$

In this case the markup over variable cost is 86%.

c.   From the above two examples, note that in the case where customers are more sensitive to price (i.e., unit sales drop by 10% rather than by 8%), the price elasticity of demand is greater and the price and the markup are lower. This is consistent with how many products are actually priced. For example, markups on luxury items are generally higher than on mass-market merchandise because consumers of luxury items are less sensitive to price than are other consumers.

d.   The computed profit-maximizing price should be used with caution since it assumes that the price elasticity of demand is constant. It should be interpreted as a signal of the direction the price should move in rather than as a precisely accurate estimate of the price at which profits are maximized.

D.   The absorption approach attempts to set a price without taking into account consumer demand. In this approach, a product's absorption costing unit product cost is used as the cost base. Selling, general, and administrative (SG&A) expenses are not included in the cost base, but rather are provided for through the markup.

1.   For example, suppose a product's unit product cost is $50 and the markup is 40%:

Unit product cost $50
Markup to cover SG&A expenses,
  and desired profit—40% 20
Target selling price $70

2.   The markup percentage may simply be a thumb-rule the company uses or it may be computed using the following formula:

$$\text{Markup \% on absorption cost} = \frac{\left(\text{Required ROI} \times \text{Investment}\right) + \text{SG\&A expenses}}{\text{Unit sales} \times \text{Unit product cost}}$$

For example, suppose the following: the company's required return on investment is 15%; the company has $100,000 invested in the product; selling, general, and administrative expenses associated with the product are $25,000; anticipated unit sales are 10,000 units; and the unit product cost is $20. Then the markup would be computed as follows:

$$\text{Markup \% on absorption cost} = \frac{(0.15 \times \$100,000) + \$25,000}{10,000 \times \$20} = 20\%$$

3.   However, *the target ROI will be attained only if the anticipated unit sales volume is attained.* There is absolutely no guarantee that the company will earn its desired profit or even break-even simply because it uses these formulas.

E.   Some companies use target costing for new products.

1.   Under the target costing approach, managers estimate how much the new product can be sold for and then deduct the desired profit per unit to arrive at the target cost figure. The formula is:

$$\frac{\text{Target}}{\text{cost}} = \frac{\text{Anticipated}}{\text{selling price}} - \frac{\text{Desired}}{\text{profit}}$$

The product development team is given the responsibility to produce and market the product for no more than this target cost.

2.   The target costing approach is radically different from the traditional cost-plus approach in which the product is first designed, then costs are determined, and then finally the price is computed with a markup based on desired profits. Unfortunately, the traditional cost-plus approach may result in prices that customers are not willing to pay.

F.   Some organizations—particularly in service industries—use a variation on cost-plus pricing called time and material pricing. Under this method two pricing rates are established—one based on labor time and a second one based on direct material used. The time component is typically expressed as a labor rate per hour. The material component is determined by adding a material loading charge, usually expressed as a percentage, to the invoice cost of the materials used on the job.

REVIEW AND SELF TEST
Questions and Exercises

True or False

Enter a T or an F in the blank to indicate whether the statement is true or false.

____ 1. The price elasticity of demand measures how much costs increase as a consequence of lowering a product's price and thereby increasing the number of units sold.

____ 2. A given percentage price increase will result in a larger percentage decrease in the quantity sold if the price elasticity of demand for a product is -2.00 rather than -1.50.

____ 3. The more elastic the demand for a product, the higher the markup over variable cost should be.

____ 4. Since the profit-maximizing price does not include any allowance for fixed costs, the price may have to be increased to ensure that the fixed costs are covered.

____ 5. If a company has a 20% desired rate of return on investment, then it should add a 20% markup to its products under the absorption costing approach.

____ 6. Both the markup and the cost base under absorption costing depend on the anticipated unit sales. (Assume that all units produced are sold.)

____ 7. The absorption costing approach may not maximize profits, but at least it ensures that the company will not lose any money on a product and will earn its required rate of return.

____ 8. Under target costing, the selling price is first estimated and then a target for the product's cost is established.

____ 9. If a manager uses time and material pricing properly, he or she can be assured that the company will meet its profit target.

Multiple Choice

Choose the best answer or response by placing the identifying letter in the space provided.

____ 1. Every 5% decrease in price leads to a 7% increase in units sold for a particular product. The product's price elasticity of demand is: a) -1.60; b) 1.60; c) -1.32; d) 1.32.

____ 2. What is the profit-maximizing price for a product whose price elasticity of demand is -2.30 and whose unit variable cost is $10? a) $23.00; b) $17.69; c) $13.00; d) $33.00.

____ 3. Lerner, Inc. has provided the following data for one of its products:

Direct materials	$8
Direct labor	7
Variable manufacturing overhead	2
Variable SG&A expenses	3

The company produces and sells 15,000 units of this product each year. Fixed manufacturing overhead cost totals $15,000 per year and fixed SG&A expenses total $30,000 per year. If the company uses the absorption approach to pricing and desires a 50% markup, the target selling price per unit would be: a) $34.50; b) $31.50; c) $27.00; d) $23.00.

____ 4. Justin Corp. estimates that an investment of $800,000 would be needed to produce and sell 20,000 units of a new product each year. At this level of activity, the unit product cost would be $100. Selling, general, and administrative expenses would total $500,000 per year. If a 25% return on investment is desired, then the markup for the new product under the absorption costing approach would be: a) 35%; b) 25%; c) 62.5%; d) 100%.

____ 5. Vintage RR, Inc. is considering a new line of model railroad engines. To compete effectively, the engines would be priced at $45. The company expects to be able to sell 2,000 engines a year at this price. The company requires a return on investment of 20%. The new product line would require an investment of $150,000. The target cost per engine would be: a) $30; b) $45; c) $15; d) $60.

___ 6. Larry's Downtown Motors uses time and material pricing in its service shop. The shop charges $35 per hour for repair time and uses a material loading charge of 55% of invoice cost. An electrical repair required two hours of repair time and $40 of materials. The total charge for the repair would be: a) $70; b) $132; c) $92; d) $75.

Exercises

A-1. Karling Furniture recently raised the selling price of its colonial desk from $495 to $529. As a consequence, unit sales fell from 300 units to 270 units per period.

a. Estimate the price elasticity of demand of the colonial desk.

% change in price = $\dfrac{\overline{\quad\quad} - \overline{\quad\quad}}{\overline{\quad\quad}}$ = _____

% change in quantity sold = $\dfrac{\overline{\quad\quad} - \overline{\quad\quad}}{\overline{\quad\quad}}$ = _____

$$\varepsilon_d = \frac{\ln(1+\%\ \text{change in quantity sold})}{\ln(1+\%\ \text{change in price})} = \frac{\ln(1+\underline{\quad})}{\ln(1+\underline{\quad})} = \frac{\ln(\underline{\quad})}{\ln(\underline{\quad})} = \frac{\overline{\quad\quad}}{\underline{\quad\quad}} = \underline{\quad}$$

b. If the variable cost of producing and selling the desk is $280, what effect did raising the price of the desk have on the company's net operating income?

c. Estimate the profit-maximizing price for the desk.

$$\text{Profit-maximizing price} = \left(\frac{\varepsilon_d}{1+\varepsilon_d}\right)\ \frac{\text{Variable cost}}{\text{per unit}}$$

$$= \left(\frac{\overline{\quad\quad}}{1+(\underline{\quad})}\right)\underline{\quad\quad} = \underline{\quad\quad} \times \underline{\quad\quad} = \underline{\quad\quad}$$

Pricing Appendix

A-2.   Costs relating to a product made by Mackey Company are given below:

Direct materials $10
Direct labor 12
Variable manufacturing overhead 1
Fixed manufacturing overhead ($210,000 total) 7
Variable SG&A expenses 2
Fixed SG&A expenses ($90,000 total) 3

Assume that the company uses the absorption approach to cost-plus pricing and a 50% markup. Compute the target selling price for the above product.

_____ $ _____
_____   _____
_____   _____
_____   _____

Unit product cost   _____

Markup—50%   _____

Target selling price $_____

A-3.   Speckart Company's required return on investment is 25%. An investment of $800,000 will be needed to produce and market 30,000 units of a particular product each year. The company's cost accountant estimates that the unit product cost will be $50 at this level of activity, and that SG&A expenses will total $400,000 per year. Compute the markup percentage for the product, assuming that the company uses the absorption approach to pricing.

$$\text{Markup \% on absorption cost} = \frac{\left(\text{Required ROI} \times \text{Investment}\right) + \text{SG\&A expenses}}{\text{Unit sales} \times \text{Unit product cost}}$$

$$\text{Markup \% on absorption cost} = \frac{(\underline{\quad} \times \underline{\qquad}) + \underline{\qquad}}{\underline{\qquad} \times \underline{\quad}} = \frac{\underline{\qquad}}{\underline{\qquad}} = \underline{\quad}\%$$

Answers to Questions and Exercises

True or False

Multiple Choice

1. F The price elasticity of demand has nothing to do with cost.

2. T The larger the absolute value of the price elasticity of demand, the larger the percentage change in units sold for a given percentage change in price.

3. F The opposite is true. The more elastic the demand for a product, the lower the markup over variable cost should be. Elastic demand indicates that customers are very sensitive to price and even a small increase in price will have a large impact on the number of units sold.

4. F If the formula for the profit-maximizing price really provides the price that maximizes the company's profit, increasing the price would result in a decline in the company's profit. If fixed costs are not covered at the profit-maximizing price, the product should be dropped. Raising its price won't help.

5. F The markup is determined in a more complicated manner than simply marking up cost by the desired ROI.

6. T Unit sales appears in the denominator of the formula for the markup. The cost base also depends on the unit sales since the unit product cost under absorption costing is an average cost that depends on the number of units produced.

7. F There is no assurance that the company will break even using the absorption costing approach. If customers do not buy as many units as anticipated, the company may lose money.

8. T Target costing is used to establish allowable costs, not selling prices.

9. F Business is not this simple. Like the absorption costing approach, the target profit will be attained only if the anticipated unit sales actually happen. The sales may not materialize if the company prices itself out of the market.

1. c
$$\varepsilon_d = \frac{\ln(1+(+0.07))}{\ln(1+(-0.05))} = \frac{\ln(1.07)}{\ln(0.95)} = \frac{0.06766}{-0.05129} = -1.32$$

2. b
$$\text{Profit-maximizing price} = \left(\frac{-2.30}{1+(-2.30)}\right)\$10$$
$$= 1.769 \times \$10$$
$$= \$17.69$$

3. c

Direct materials	$ 8
Direct labor	7
Variable manufacturing overhead	2
Fixed manufacturing overhead ($15,000 ÷ 15,000 units)	1
Unit product cost	18
Markup—50%	9
Target selling price	$27

4. a
$$\text{Markup \% on absorption cost} = \frac{(0.25 \times \$800,000)+\$500,000}{20,000 \times \$100}$$
$$= 35\%$$

5. a

Projected sales ($45 × 2,000)	$90,000
Less desired profit (20% × $150,000)	30,000
Target cost for 2,000 units	$60,000

$$\text{Target cost} = \$60,000 \div 2,000 \text{ units}$$
$$= \$30 \text{ per unit}$$

6. b

Labor time (2 hours × $35)	$ 70
Parts used:	
Invoice cost	40
Material loading charge (55%).	22
Total price of the job	$132

Pricing Appendix

Exercises

A-1. a.

$$\% \text{ change in price} = \frac{\$529 - \$495}{\$495} = +6.87\%$$

$$\% \text{ change in quantity sold} = \frac{270 - 300}{300} = -10.00\%$$

$$\varepsilon_d = \frac{\ln(1 + \% \text{ change in quantity sold})}{\ln(1 + \% \text{ change in price})} = \frac{\ln(1 + (-0.1000))}{\ln(1 + (+0.0687))} = \frac{\ln(0.9000)}{\ln(1.0687)} = \frac{-0.10536}{0.06644} = -1.59$$

b. The impact of the increase in price on net operating income can be computed as follows:

	Selling Price of $495	Selling Price of $529
Unit sales	300	270
Sales	$148,500	$142,830
Variable expenses	84,000	75,600
Contribution margin	$ 64,500	$ 67,230

    Assuming that the change in price and quantity sold had no effect on fixed costs, the result of increasing the price was an increase in net operating income of $2,730 ($67,230 − $64,500).

c. Profit-maximizing price $= \left(\dfrac{\varepsilon_d}{1 + \varepsilon_d}\right) \dfrac{\text{Variable cost}}{\text{per unit}} = \left(\dfrac{-1.59}{1 + (-1.59)}\right) \$280 = 2.70 \times \$280 = \$756$

Since this price is a lot higher than the price that is currently being charged, it would be prudent to raise the price slowly, checking to make sure that profits really do increase after each increase in price.

A-2.

Direct materials	$10
Direct labor	12
Variable manufacturing overhead	1
Fixed manufacturing overhead	7
Unit product cost	$30
Markup—50%	15
Target selling price	$45

A-3. $\text{Markup \% on absorption cost} = \dfrac{(0.25 \times \$800,000) + \$400,000}{30,000 \times \$50} = \dfrac{\$600,000}{\$1,500,000} = 40\%$

248

Appendix B

Cost of Quality

Chapter Study Suggestions

The four types of quality costs are listed in Exhibit B-1, along with a number of examples. This is the key exhibit in the chapter. The four types of quality costs are used to structure a quality cost report as illustrated in Exhibit B-3.

CHAPTER HIGHLIGHTS

A. The term quality is used in many ways. It can mean a luxurious product with many features or it can mean a product that is free of defects. In this chapter, we use quality in the latter sense. *Quality of conformance* is the degree to which a product or service meets its design specifications and is free of defects or other problems that might affect appearance or performance.

B. Defects (i.e., poor quality of conformance) rsult in costs that can be classified as prevention costs, appraisal costs, internal failure costs, and external failure costs.

1. Internal failure costs and external failure costs result from defects in products.

a. *Internal failure costs* result from correcting defects in products before they are shipped to customers. Internal failure costs include scrap, reworking of defective units, and downtime.

b. *External failure costs* result when a defective product is delivered to a customer. These costs include warranty repairs, exchanges, returns, and loss of future sales. These are the least desirable of all quality costs. A dissatisfied customer will not buy from the company in the future and is likely to tell others of his or her dissatisfaction. If there are defects, it is generally better to identify them internally than to sell dfective units to customers.

2. Prevention costs and appraisal costs are incurred to prevent defects and reduce the likelihood of external failures.

a. *Prevention costs* are incurred to reduce or eliminate defects. Prevention is often simple and inexpensive. For example, defects can be prevented by a simple metal shield that prevents drilling a hole in the wrong place. Prevention costs include the costs of quality engineering and quality improvement projects.

b. *Appraisal costs* are incurred to identify defective products before the products are shipped to customers. These costs include wages of inspection workers and the costs of testing equipment.

C. In most companies, the total cost of quality (the sum of prevention costs, appraisal costs, internal failure costs, and external failure costs) decreases as the quality of conformance increases —at least until very low levels of defect rates occur. (A higher quality of conformance means a lower defect rate.) Exhibit B-2 illustrates this relation between total cost of quality and defect rates.

1. Reducing the defect rate (e.g., defects per million parts) involves spending more on prevention and appraisal. However, this additional spending is usually more than offset by reductions in the costs of internal and external failures caused by defects.

2. Most companies would benefit from putting more effort into prevention. This reduces the need for appraisal and decreases the incidence of internal and external failures.

D. Quality costs are summarized for management on a *quality cost report* such as in Exhibit B-3.

1. The report classifies the costs of quality into the four categories discussed above.

2. The report should summarize costs associated with defective products and services throughout the organization—all the way from research and development through customer service. The report should not be limited to just manufacturing costs.

3. Such a report helps managers see the financial significance of defects and it aids managers in diagnosing whether their quality costs are poorly distributed (e.g., too much external failure cost relative to prevention cost).

REVIEW AND SELF TEST
Questions and Exercises

True or False

Enter a T or an F in the blank to indicate whether the statement is true or false.

___ 1. A product containing defects has a poor quality of conformance.

___ 2. The best quality systems are those that put their emphasis on appraisal costs

___ 3. It is usually better to incur internal failure costs than to incur external failure costs.

___ 4. Quality cost reports focus on quality costs associated with just the manufacturing process.

Multiple Choice

Choose the best answer or response by placing the identifying letter in the space provided.

___ 1. The cost of quality training is an example of a(n): a) prevention cost; b) appraisal cost; c) internal failure cost; d) external failure cost.

___ 2. The cost of warranty repairs is an example of a(n): a) prevention cost; b) appraisal cost; c) internal failure cost; d) external failure cost.

___ 3. The cost of rework labor is an example of a(n): a) prevention cost; b) appraisal cost; c) internal failure cost; d) external failure cost.

___ 4. The cost of supplies used in testing and inspection is an example of a(n): a) prevention cost; b) appraisal cost; c) internal failure cost; d) external failure cost.

___ 5. The cost of lost sales due to a reputation for poor quality is an example of a(n): a) prevention cost; b) appraisal cost; c) internal failure cost; d) external failure cost.

Exercise

B-1.   The management of Jehrol Fantasy Products would like for you to compile a quality cost report for the company using the following data.

Net cost of scrap	$90,000
Disposal of defective products	$17,000
Maintenance of test equipment	$61,000
Rework labor and overhead	$69,000
Depreciation of test equipment	$28,000
Systems development	$40,000
Quality training	$82,000
Warranty repairs and replacements	$89,000
Liability arising from defective products	$61,000

The company's total sales for the year was $10,000,000.
Prepare the company's quality cost of report using the form below:

JEHROL FANTASY PRODUCTS
Quality Cost Report

	Amount	Percent of Sales
Prevention costs:		
....	$	
....		
Total		
Appraisal costs:		
....		
....		
Total		
Internal failure costs:		
....		
....		
....		
Total		
External failure costs:		
....		
....		
Total		
Total quality cost	$	

Answers to Questions and Exercises

True or False

1. T Quality of conformance indicates how well a product meets its design specifications and is free of defects and other problems.

2. F The best quality systems are those that put their emphasis on prevention costs.

3. T Internal failure costs keep defective products from being shipped to customers, which can have a devastating effect on the company's reputation.

4. F Quality cost reports should focus on all quality costs throughout an organization from research and development through customer service.

Multiple Choice

1. a See Exhibit B-1.

2. d See Exhibit B-1.

3. c See Exhibit B-1.

4. b See Exhibit B-1.

5. d See Exhibit B-1.

Exercise

B-1.

JEHROL FANTASY PRODUCTS
Quality Cost Report

	Amount	Percent of Sales
Prevention costs:		
Systems development	$ 40,000	0.40%
Quality training	82,000	0.82
Total	122,000	1.22
Appraisal costs:		
Depreciation of test equipment	28,000	0.28
Maintenance of test equipment	61,000	0.61
Total	89,000	0.89
Internal failure costs:		
Rework labor and overhead	69,000	0.69
Net cost of scrap	90,000	0.90
Disposal of defective products	17,000	0.17
Total	176,000	1.76
External failure costs:		
Warranty repairs and replacements	89,000	0.89
Liability arising from defective products	61,000	0.61
Total	150,000	1.50
Total quality cost	$537,000	5.37%